WORKS BY DAVID L. COOPER

MESSIANIC SERIES

The God of Israel
Messiah: His Nature and Person
Messiah: His Redemptive Career
Messiah: His First Coming Scheduled
Messiah: His Historical Appearance
Messiah: His Glorious Appearance Imminent
Messiah: His Final Call to Israel

OTHER BOOKS

Future Events Revealed, according to Matthew, Chapters 24 and 25
Israel's Return to God
Man: His Creation, Fall, Redemption, and Glorification
Preparing for the World-wide Revival
Prophetic Fulfillments in Palestine Today
The Eternal God Revealing Himself to Suffering Israel and to Lost
    Humanity
The 70 Weeks of Daniel
The Shepherd of Israel Seeking His Own
The World's Greatest Library Graphically Illustrated
What Men Must Believe, or God's Gracious Provision for Man
When Gog's Armies Meet the Almighty
When Will Wars Cease?
Why God's Interest is in the Jew

BOOKLETS

Antichrist and the World-wide Revival
God's Torchbearers
Grand March of Empire
Image Vision of Daniel Two
Invading Forces of Russia and of the Antichrist Overthrown in Palestine
Is the Fig Tree Cursed Forever?
Sowing and Reaping a Bumper Crop
They that Sow in Tears
Unfolding of the Ages
Will the Church Go Through the Tribulation? According to Matthew,
    Chapter 24
Will the Church Go Through the Tribulation? According to Luke, Chap-
    ter 21

And other booklets and tracts

לְכוּ־נָא וְנִוָּכְחָה יאמַר יְהוָה Isa. 1:18

"Come now, and let us reason together, saith Jehovah"

THE SHEPHERD OF ISRAEL SEEKING HIS OWN

By

DAVID L. COOPER, Th.M., Ph.D., Litt.D.

Founder and President, Biblical Research Society
Editor, Biblical Research Monthly
Bible Teacher

BIBLICAL RESEARCH SOCIETY
(A California Corporation)
4005 Verdugo Road, Los Angeles 65, California

Copyrighted 1962

BY

DAVID L. COOPER

_The Scripture quotations in this volume are taken from the
American Standard Version, published 1901_

Library of Congress, Catalogue Card Number 62-15105

Printed in the United States of America

To the memory of

FLORENCE LITA COOPER,

the faithful and loyal wife of the author
and a lover of Israel,
is this volume
affectionately
dedicated

Preface

IN 1928 I published my volume *The Eternal God Revealing Himself to Suffering Israel and to Lost Humanity.* In it I present evidence concerning the Eternal God as seen in nature, as seen in the Old Testament, and as seen in the New Testament. On account of limited space, the discussions are very brief.

In 1930 I was providentially led to form the Biblical Research Society with a two-fold purpose in view: first, to break down anti-Semitism; and second, to broadcast facts and truths concerning God and Messiah to Israel, the Chosen People; for the message of redemption is "to the Jew first and also to the Greek" (Rom. 1:16).

Since then I have done much research and have written my Messianic Series of seven volumes, namely:

> *The God of Israel*
> *Messiah: His Nature and Person*
> *Messiah: His Redemptive Career*
> *Messiah: His First Coming Scheduled*
> *Messiah: His Historical Appearance*
> *Messiah: His Glorious Appearance Imminent*
> *Messiah: His Final Call to Israel*

This Series is a written report of some of my discoveries in my quest for truth and facts on the subjects investigated; for I wish to make available to the public my findings, that others may be profited and blessed by these truths as I have been. In these books I expand the various cardinal doctrines of the subjects discussed in my original volume. They are primarily for the student class and leaders.

The abridged editions of the Series are designed for the great middle classes of the people.

In the present volume, *The Shepherd of Israel Seeking His Own,* I follow the general pattern of the development of thought found in *The Eternal God Revealing Himself to Suffering Israel and to Lost Humanity.* To expedite matters, I use Chapters I and II of this original volume as Chapters I and II of the present volume, without any change of material. In Chapters III to XI, I use certain sections of the Chapters of the original work. Chapter XII is entirely new material.

In my earlier writings I refer to Israel as a nation, as in modern usage, in the feminine gender, *she* and *her*. In my later writings I follow the Biblical terminology and use the masculine pronouns, *he, his,* and *him,* in referring to Israel.

As a rule, in referring to dates, I use the Anno Hominis chronology (in the year of man) instead of the popular Ussher dates. The entire Anno Hominis system is fully discussed and presented in my volume, *Messiah: His First Coming Scheduled.*

In all fields of research every scientifically-minded truth lover, being unselfish, is eager to tell others about the discoveries he has made in order that they, too, may enjoy and reap the benefits made possible by his labors. This principle always has the pre-eminence in the life and labor of those engaged in the spiritual realm. They realize that within this sphere these materials, with which they deal, are of eternal value. For over fifty years I have diligently searched the Scriptures, especially in their original languages, to ascertain what God has revealed to man. I lay claim for myself that the Lord, only in answer to believing prayer and as a reward for hard study, has shown me many things in the Word of which I had never heard, nor read. Whenever I experience the joy of some new discovery, it is my delight to pass the same on to others—especially to the Hebrews, God's Chosen People.

God chose the Jewish people through whom He made His revelation to man. Israel, therefore, was God's channel of blessing to the world. Whatever truth the Christians have, God first channeled it to them through the Chosen People. We Christians are therefore, humanly speaking, indebted to the Jews for all spiritual and scriptural truth that we have. The only way we can pay our debt to Israel is by giving back to them the Scriptures which they gave to us—the Old and the New Testaments—and the proper interpretation of the Scriptures. The Biblical Research Society is endeavoring by the grace of God to pay its indebtedness, especially by means of the Messianic Series, which the Society is sending free (without any obligation) to those Hebrews who will make their wants known.

David L. Cooper.

Los Angeles, California
April 30, 1962

Table of Contents

THE EXISTENCE OF GOD

SINCE man is "incurably religious," the evidence of which is seen in the fact that there are "gods many and lords many" —heathen gods—a statement of which is especially true of the Hebrew people, for they are a people with a "genius for religion," and since every shade of idea, ranging from atheism to the devout, sincere, orthodox position is found among them, it seems most appropriate to begin the study of the subject of Israel's God with _____ f His existence and of His

[A torn piece of paper partially obscures the text. Fragments of another page are visible:]

pendence, his ov
sive, silent woman
o what his father
om had been the
f five children, his
him.
netimes how, or
allen in love with
ourse, was simple
her in church one
e'd spent a week-
m the university.
urchgoer, strictly
is friend's family
nly good manners
nd that was when
—in a blue dress
s and shoes, look-
e was the prettiest
and he had kept
uring the sermon.
blue in the third
friend.

beyond and abo

s GROUPS

ic

y few people entertain any
evidence of design, which
nce as its "trade-mark," is
or and seeker after facts,
ess of this statement is
test-tube, in the biological
pe, and in the astronom-
troscope.
ce in the facts that the
etable kingdom, out of
s dependent for its con-
is dependent upon both
hat the human kingdom
ree for its being. In
design is seen to run
ed as finding its goal
nich points infinitely far
ultimate and final goal. On the

one hand, the student who studies the world about him at close range finds that in every organism—whether it be the uni-cellular amoeba or the most highly developed organism of man, every organ of whose anatomy is highly specialized and co-ordinated with its fellow-members to the *nth* (the last) degree to function for the benefit of the entire organism—design and purpose are the dominating factors. On the other hand, in studying the universe at distant range by means of modern astronomical instruments, the higher branches of mathematical science, and astronomical physics, one learns that it is an immense chronometer, by which every watch and clock which control modern business and social life are regulated. In every watch and clock there are numbers of wheels of different sizes and weights, some running in one direction while others run in the opposite, each running at a different rate of speed; but at the same time they are so formed, adjusted and placed that each contributes its part to the one common purpose, namely, that of keeping the correct time. No man in a rational, serious mood would for a moment deny intelligent design and purpose in the manufacturing of the watch and claim that the materials which enter into its construction came into existence, assumed their present form, and took their position in the mechanism by chance or evolutionary processes. Should one in a serious moment argue thus, no one would take him seriously but would have sufficient reason to doubt his sanity.

Since the *Universe,* consisting of our solar system of planets and satellites, together with the innumerable and inconceivably great solar systems, flung out into illimitable space, which move in their appointed orbits of different sizes and at different rates of speed and in innumerable ways ("wheels within wheels"), according to inviolable laws, forms one great chronometer, likewise no man in a serious, rational mood will deny the existence of a SUPREME INTELLIGENCE, Who has created and Who governs this great Universal Chronometer.*

The recent astronomical discoveries have greatly enriched and enlarged man's conception of the vastness of the universe, so that he no longer speaks of distances in the great fields of universal space in terms of miles, as formerly; but now he speaks of these vast distances in terms of "light years." This enlarged conception of the material universe has likewise enlarged and enriched his

---

* According to the latest scientific research concerning the great pyramid at Gizeh, its builders were far advanced in the knowledge of the physical sciences and astronomy, since many of the fundamental and basic principles of the same, which have only in comparatively recent years been discovered by modern science, took on permanent form in stone in that structure.

conception of the Creator of the same, since the Creator and Controller is vastly greater than that which is created. Hence in another figure, one may think of the universe as one great Declaration, written in emblazoned letters, *"GOD IS!"* Psa. 19:1, 2: "The heavens are recounting the glory of God, and the expanse is making known the work of His hands" (Author's Tr.).

B. *Freethinking*

Within Judaism there is quite a growing class of people who, intellectually speaking, have cut loose their moorings from their ancestral faith, repudiating the idea of a personal God from Whom they draw their very existence and to Whom they owe allegiance and responsibility, and who conscientiously believe in the autonomy of the individual, and being thoroughly convinced that the human intellect is sufficient of itself to solve all the problems of existence. Thus in their thinking they become "a law unto themselves," possessing latent powers upon which they can draw to meet every emergency.

In reply to this position it is sufficient to call attention to the fact that this boasted freedom is purely a creation of the pride of man, there being no objective reality corresponding to this subjective creation. This fact is apparent to everyone who thinks, being demonstrated by the fact that the freethinker is limited, notwithstanding his daring boastfulness, in the same way in which all men are limited. Notwithstanding the fact that many barriers which hitherto have been considered insurmountable have been overcome by the many discoveries of modern inventive genius, these barriers really have not been removed, but have been pushed a little farther back, and still say to man, "Thus far and no farther shalt thou go." Furthermore, it is a fact known to all that freethinkers, who have made their boast that they possess all of the powers of the universe within their own souls, and that they can live a certain number of years, which number is often placed at from three to four times the age which is now recognized as the limit of man's life, very frequently at the time of their boasting are overcome by the ills of life, as are others who make no such claims, and are dashed into eternity. The present age is highly pragmatic. demanding the clear, scientific demonstration of a theory before accepting the same as true. Hence since the free-thinker has thus far given no evidence of "the latent powers within," but is subject to the accidents of life, a thinking public will never accept his unproved theories.

C. *Agnostic*

Again, an attitude which characterizes another group within the pale of Judaism may be called "Agnostic" which simply means *one who does not know.* Historically, Herbert Spencer was the one who coined this word from the material supplied by the Greek word meaning "know," prefixed by the negative particle, the combination of which words means "not know." Since his day the number taking this attitude has grown until at present a not inconsiderable number has assumed the same.

As a fundamental theory in an ideal system of philosophy it may satisfy a certain type of mind, but in a practical world in which men live it is utterly unable to meet the stress and strain of life as it is, and to satisfy the inquiring mind of an honest seeker after truth. Again, the agnostic cannot live a life in a practical world consistently with his philosophy, for the moment he attempts to put into practice his philosophy, he is automatically by the same bound hand and foot, being unable to enter into any of the affairs of life. Hence agnosticism, as an ideal philosophy divorced from practical life, may satisfy those who are super-sensitive and overly cautious in avoiding the errors of an over-confident, dogmatic, materialistic philosophy; but it can never relieve one of the moral and spiritual responsibility which is resting upon him, since he is a sentient, intelligent being in a real world.

II. Religious Groups
A. *Rationalistic*

Rationalism, unfortunately, has invaded Judaism. The rationalist, concerning whom this section deals, is, as the term implies, one who is following human reason, or who believes that he is following reason. He is, figuratively speaking, worshipping at the shrine of modern scholarship.*

---

*The reader is not to infer that the author is opposed to learning and scholarship, because he delights in the acquisition of knowledge: *principles, truths,* and *facts.* For many years he has practically devoted his entire time

The latest pronouncements of the scientific world are for him final on all matters. Every statement of belief in all spheres of human thought must be stamped with the seal of the approval of "scholarship" before it is considered worthy of his acceptance. If scholarship sends forth its dictum that God is an impersonal, unknowable substance, to this tenet he willingly subscribes. If, on the other hand, it explains the world purely along materialistic lines, then that tenet becomes his dogma.

By such as are under the bondage of rationalism and tyrannical "scholarship" let it be noted that the voices of rationalism and scholarship are "legion," for they are many. The proof of the above statement is easily found by a rapid survey of the history of philosophy, which study will convince the unbiased mind that no two philosophers agree in general; but what one affirms the other denies, either in part or in toto. Furthermore, the theories and explanations of the scientific world as set forth in the standard text-books and periodicals of today contradict and reject the theories and explanations, in many instances, of the books and publications of a decade ago. The scientific world changes so very

---

to his search for knowledge and education. The thing which he condemns in modern scholarship is its rabid dogmatism, speculation, and ostracism of all who do not subscribe to its theories and speculation. Furthermore, after having studied the situation from various angles, he is thoroughly convinced that there is no conflict between real scholarship and the Bible. The latter, having been subjected to the most terrific attacks by enemies who concentrated all of their intellectual powers against it for its destruction, survives today and will continue to survive in the future. The work of faithful, scholarly archaeologists is constantly confirming it.

The rationalistic criticism against the Scriptures, especially the Old Testament, is, as one noted critic well said, "nine-tenths purely subjective."

Frequently the statement is made that all scholars are agreed on certain propositions. Especially are such statements the current coin in circles where the Bible is looked upon as purely a human book.

This statement denies scholarship to all of those who believe that the Bible is inspired of God. When the facts are known, it is evident that there is a very large group of men who, in native ability, keen discriminating and analytical powers, and scholastic attainments, equal any of the scholars who hold to the rationalist position.

In the same circles the believing scholars are often spoken of as "traditionalists." If this term is applied to one because he believes those narratives and events which have been established by historical testimony and archaeology, to be a traditionalist is the proper thing. If, however, it is used to mean those who blindly hold to certain positions handed down from former generations without any investigations, it is improper and unethical to apply it to the large group of men referred to in the last paragraph. They have "by their works" proved that they refuse to accept as true things formerly believed and that they are diligent seekers after facts.

rapidly that the one who was then thoroughly familiar with scientific thought but who since then has been unable to pursue his studies is almost a total stranger in that field.

From these facts it is very clear that one cannot pin his faith in religious matters to the dicta of scholarship.

The cumulative experience of the race should teach one that, although the human mind is wonderful and has accomplished amazing things, it is finite and there are boundaries beyond which lie innumerable things which it can never comprehend.*   This statement being true, the finite mind can never fathom the problem connected with the existence of God, Who is infinite.   Hence rationalism is a very insecure foundation upon which one may build for the future life.

B. *Orthodox*

The word *orthodox* is of Greek origin and means literally "thinking straight."   When applied to the Jew it refers to that great mass of Hebrews who believes in the God of Israel and in the Tenach as His revelation.   Likewise, the orthodox Jew confidently believes in the Talmud as an authoritative revelation of God which inherently was contained in the statutes, ordinances, and commandments referred to in Exodus 24:12.   A further characteristic which especially distinguishes him is that he holds very tenaciously to the customs and manners which have been handed down to him through the centuries.

The cardinal doctrines around which all things religious center, for him, is Israel's Great Confession, "Hear, O Israel, the Lord our God is One."   His God is the God Who made the heavens and the earth, Who chose the Hebrew people to be a people for His own possession, having called Abraham, the great ancestor of the race, and his descendants, to be a channel of blessing to the entire world.   He, furthermore, believes that eventually his God will regather the nation and restore it to its own land and send the Messiah, Who shall reign from sea to sea, subjecting

---

* As examples of such things note the following expressions: the soul, spirit, immortality, life, the processes of digestion and assimilation of foods in their sustaining life of the organism, electricity, and epistemology.   With these expressions philosophers and scholars have grappled throughout the centuries and at present they know practically nothing more than when they began the study of the same.

the Gentile nations unto Israel. In all of these fundamental tenets he is correct, generally speaking. As to his understanding of the Great Confession the reader will find a full discussion of it in Chapter IV of this book. Since the limits of this work prohibit an extensive investigation of the proofs of the existence of God, the reader is referred to any standard text-book on evidences for the many and indisputable proofs of a Supreme Being.

According to the testimony of the Old Testament, man had, from the beginning of the race, a knowledge of the true God. "The heavens declare the glory of God and the firmament showeth his handiwork" (Ps. 19:1). Although he had this knowledge, which God revealed to him, he, not glorifying God and not being thankful, refused to retain God in his knowledge. Therefore, God gave him up to a reprobate mind to practice all ungodliness and unrighteousness.

18 For the wrath of God is revealed from heaven against all ungodliness and unrighteousness of men, who hinder the truth in unrighteousness; 19 because that which is known of God is manifest in them; for God manifested it unto them. 20 For the invisible things of him since the creation of the world are clearly seen, being perceived through the things that are made, *even* his everlasting power and divinity; that they may be without excuse: 21 because that, knowing God, they glorified him not as God, neither gave thanks; but became vain in their reasonings, and their senseless heart was darkened. 22 Professing themselves to be wise, they became fools, 23 and changed the glory of the incorruptible God for the likeness of an image of corruptible man, and of birds, and four-footed beasts, and creeping things. 24 Wherefore God gave them up in the lusts of their hearts unto uncleanness, that their bodies should be dishonored among themselves: 25 for that they exchanged the truth of God for a lie, and worshipped and served the creature rather than the Creator, who is blessed for ever. Amen. 26 For this cause God gave them up unto vile passions: for their women changed the natural use into that which is against nature: 27 and likewise also the men, leaving the natural use of the woman, burned in their lust one toward another, men with men working unseemliness, and receiving in themselves that recompense of their error which was due. 28 And even as they refused to have God in *their* knowledge, God gave them up unto a reprobate mind, to do those things which are not fitting; 29 being filled with all unrighteousness, wickedness, covetousness, maliciousness; full of envy, murder, strife, deceit, malignity; whisperers, 30 backbiters, hateful to God, insolent, haughty, boastful, inventors of evil things, disobedient to parents, 31 without understanding, covenant-breakers, without natural affection, unmerciful: 32 who, knowing the ordinance of God, that they that practice such things are worthy of death, not only do the same, but also consent with them that practice them (Rom. 1:18-32).

CHAPTER II

THE REVELATION OF GOD

SINCE the world, as seen in Chapter I, gives abundant evidence of the existence of a Supreme Being, Who has stamped His handiwork with the unmistakable trade-mark of teleology, which fact proves conclusively that the present condition of the world is not an end within itself but, like a prophetic utterance, points forward to a higher and a more glorious existence in the future, and since His providences in this life set forth clearly His beneficent character and love for His creatures, it is most reasonable to suppose that He has spoken to them. The Bible claims to be this Word which He, in His love, has revealed for the good of humanity.

Various attitudes are taken by different groups of people toward this collection of sacred literature.

I. VARIOUS ATTITUDES TOWARD THE BIBLE

A. *Rationalistic**

There are those among the Hebrew people as well as among the Gentiles who look upon the Bible as of human origin and treat it accordingly. To them the religion of Israel is but one of the great religions of the human race, and the Bible is to be classed along with the "sacred books" of the heathen nations. This group of men conscientiously believes that the writers of the Hebrew Bible were inspired only as poets of other nations lay

---

* The fundamental principle of rationalism is a predisposition and hostility toward all Divine interposition in the affairs of men. Hence for it a miracle is impossible. Since the miraculous element stands out most conspicuously throughout the historical books, they are by rationalistic scholars considered only as fallible works of men from which all miracles must be expunged as legends and fictitious history. Therefore they do not hesitate to use the "pen knife" to cut out all of this so-called unreliable legendary history. The process goes on *ad liberatum.*

To approach the record with a predisposition against miracles is most unscientific and unscholarly. To be scientific one must take the data which are supplied and investigate the same thoroughly. Many things today are being done which a century ago men would have pronounced absolutely impossible. Hence one is acting unwisely and unscientifically in approaching any subject with a decided predisposition, either for or against it. A passion for facts should be the governing principle. Historical facts are established

claim to inspiration,* namely, Homer, Virgil, Dante, Milton, Shakespeare, et al. This inspiration is nothing more than the resultant of an inherited mental state and bias toward things religious, stimulated by environment, which at times lifted the writers to sublime heights. To them, since the Bible is purely a human book, it, like all other works of men, contains mistakes and errors which must be corrected by research and comparison with the evidence from the monuments of antiquity and made to tell a truthful story concerning the past.

In this connection let the reader note the fact that many things mentioned in the Scriptures which were called in question by the rationalistic critics prior to the modern discoveries in oriental lands have been proved to be correct, and the critics have had

---

by historical testimony. Logic and philosophy, though seemingly flawless, can never overthrow a fact that is established by genuine historical testimony.

The seemingly impossible does occur. If men who have learned many of the "laws of nature" can so manipulate, combine, and utilize them as to bring about results which Nature unaided cannot accomplish, is it incredible that the Eternal God, the Creator of the Universe, Who subjected the material creation to certain laws, can manipulate, combine, and utilize these, His laws, and bring about results which are unknown to men? As an example of man's combining and utilizing the laws of nature and producing results which Nature alone could not accomplish, note the "heavier-than-air machines" which are commonplace with us today. The God Who created this world can intervene whenever in His good will and pleasure He chooses. Hence a "miracle" is possible. What is a miracle? A miracle is an act of God which ordinarily He performs in a hidden and veiled manner (Isa. 45:15), but which, for some moral or spiritual purpose, He performs in an open and manifest way. When *competent* witnesses testify that God has intervened, the fact must be accepted as true. (See Chapter XI for a competent witness.)

* Considering the Hebrew Scriptures as works of men, the "critics" approach them as they do any ordinary document.

Allow the author to assert that the science of literary criticism has rendered an invaluable service to humanity, especially in its detecting fraudulent and fictitious documents, which have been used in the past by unscrupulous men for the purpose of promoting their own designs and purposes. But this noble science of literary criticism has been prostituted and, in an illegitimate and illogical manner, made to serve the purposes of rationalism. With the tools of literary criticism rationalists have approached the Tenach and have dissected it, especially the historical portions, and have apportioned it to various writers who lived in the period of time beginning with the ninth century to the Maccabean period. Biblical criticism began with the dissection of the Torah. At the present time that theory which holds the field is what is known as the Documentary Theory. According to this hypothesis, Moses did not write the Torah, but there were two historians who lived some time during the seventh or eight centuries before the common era and who wrote histories from the creation of the world to their day. They are known as J and E. About the time of Josiah, who reigned about 622 before the common era, some priest, who wanted to

to retreat from their position of attack. It is a fact, well known to all who are familiar with the science of Biblical criticism, that in every instance where an attack has been made upon the historicity and genuineness of a certain portion of the text or of the data contained therein, the evidence brought to light by archæological research has not in one instance discredited the Biblical record, but rather has proved and confirmed the same. If the Scriptures were of human origin, as is claimed by the rationalists, archæological data would not confirm them. Therefore since archæology establishes their truthfulness, they cannot be classed with ordinary writings of uninspired men.

---

exalt the sanctuary at Jerusalem, fabricated a code of laws in such an ingenius manner that he was successful in convincing the king and the people that it was an ancient code which had been delivered by Moses. This was the Deuteronomic Code. Later a school of prophets, following the lines of Ezekiel, drafted what is known as the Priestly Code. Finally, in the post-exilic days and probably in the days of Ezra there were "redactors" or editors who combined these various documents, editing and cementing them together with their own comments. Thus came into existence the Torah as it now stands. This theory has been carried to a most minute and detailed analysis by some so that it is claimed that there were several other documents used in the composition of the Torah.

The critics are very confident that with their critical apparatus they are able to dissect the Torah (and also the entire Tenach) into the exact original documents and to tell who wrote each sentence and word. Hence they speak most confidently of the "assured results" of criticism.

Since this age is highly scientific and pragmatic, the author would like to restate the challenge which has been proposed to the critics, but which, so far as he knows, has never been accepted. The challenge is this: let a committee of ordinary practical business men select, say, four different lengthy compositions on a certain subject written by different men who have a different outlook and whose education differs. Let them turn over two of these documents to some writer who will take them and weave them into a single document. In accomplishing this task the "redactor" is to make such changes and alterations as will serve his purpose: rejecting certain words, phrases, clauses, sentences, and paragraphs; adding such material as he wishes; and making such editorial revisions as are necessary. This work being done, let another "redactor" take this new composite document and another one of the originals and "edit" them, and from them produce another single document. Likewise, let a third take this second composite document and weave it together with the fourth original one. Then let the four original and the first two composite documents be put in a vault by this committee for safekeeping.

Then let the committee turn over exact copies of the final composite document into the hands of critics (experts) who possess special literary and analytical powers in order that they may restore each of the original documents and also each resultant new document. When the work has been finished let each critic submit his work to this committee who will in turn compare the "assured results" with the original documents.

If they are unable, with their critical apparatus, to dissect and to analyze such a modern document, apportioning to each writer his very words, no one

B. *Believers in* עֲשֶׂרֶת הַדְּבָרוֹת *The Ten Words Only*

Another attitude taken toward the Scriptures by certain Hebrews is that only the "Ten Words" are the words of God, but that the rest of the Scriptures is the writing of the wise men of Israel. It is difficult to see how one may maintain this position, since the same record which states that God spoke orally the Ten Words at Sinai also claims that He spoke the rest of the Torah. If the numerous statements throughout the Tenach which say that the "word of the Lord" came to such and such a prophet are not true, since one is dependent upon the record which is preserved to him for his knowledge of what actually occurred, it is impossible to affirm that God spoke the "Ten Words." But the same record which states that God spoke these, also says He spoke the rest of it. One must accept all or reject all.

C. *Believers in "The Ten Words" and "Book of the Covenant"*

There is another group of people who conscientiously believe that the Lord spoke the "Ten Words" and "The Book of the Covenant" (Ex. 21:1-24:8). What has just been said in the last paragraph is applicable with the same force to the position held by this group.

D. *Believers in the Torah or the Five Books of Moses*

A still larger group believes confidently that God spoke the Torah, the Five Books of Moses, but did not inspire in the same degree the writings of the prophets and the Psalms. Hence the

can have confidence in their ability to dissect the Torah, which was completed, according to the critical theory, in the period between the Exile and the Maccabean period, and to restore the supposed original documents. If they cannot accurately dissect the Torah, neither can they any portion of the Tenach.

To ask the critic, by the test given above, to demonstrate his ability to restore original documents is no unreasonable request, for scholarship has been subjected to such an acid test, at least, once before. In order to prove that George Rawlinson had the proper clew to the deciphering of the cuneiform writing, the trustees of the British Museum gave lithographic copies of a long historical inscription (Tiglath-pileser I, ca. 1120-1100 B. C.) to four men who worked independently. When they had finished the work, the translations were submitted for comparison. To the unbounded joy of scholars these translations agreed substantially from beginning to end. Thus scholars demonstrated their ability to decipher the cuneiform inscriptions. Not until the literary critics are able to demonstrate by such a practical test their ability to restore original documents, is it reasonable for them to ask intelligent, thinking people to accept the "assured results" of Biblical criticism.

former are studied most minutely and are considered as authoritative and binding, whereas the latter are read largely as religious literature. The Five Books give overwhelming evidence that they are "The Word of God" in a special and unique sense, being the very thoughts and words which God gave to His servant Moses to deliver to His people. In this connection, for the purpose of strengthening faith in the inspiration of the Five Books of Moses, it is well to call attention to a few outstanding characteristics of these books, which differentiate them from the writings of uninspired men.

A comparison of the cosmogonies of the ancient oriental nations with that set forth in Genesis shows clearly that the Genesis account stands in a class by itself. All of these ancient cosmogonies are characterized by polytheism, jealousy, hatred, and wars among the gods. Likewise, a confusion of thought and a general vagueness permeate them. In the Genesis account of creation, however, a pure monotheism shines forth in splendor and glory. Furthermore, the low moral tone of the other accounts is entirely absent from the Genesis record. In them there appears no well-defined progressive action, whereas in the Mosaic account appears the stately, forward march of the Eternal God in the unfolding of His great plan and purpose in the creation of the heavens and the earth, and of the restoration to order and beauty of the destroyed earth in anticipation of the creation of man.

There is a very close parallel between the Biblical account of bringing order out of chaos in Gen. 1 and the facts and data discovered by intelligent thoughtful scientists.* Concerning the

---

* Many scientists endeavor to throw doubt on the Mosaic account of creation by affirming that the Bible asserts that the world in round numbers is about 6000 years old, whereas they believe they have absolute evidence that it has been in existence for hundreds of thousands of years. One of the reasons for such conclusions is based upon speculations concerning the various strata of the earth's surface. These speculations date back to the adoption of the "onion coat" theory of the earth first propounded by Werner. The current theories used in explaining the long "geological and prehistorical periods" or epochs are but modifications and adaptations of this long exploded "onion coat" theory. To prove it resort is had to the supposed evidence furnished by such places as the Grand Canyon of the Colorado and the Niagara Falls and Gorge. Scientists today know the yearly rate at which these rivers are cutting their way through the strata of rocks. They measure the depths of these gorges and the recession of the Falls and make their simple calculation by division. By so doing they assume that the same causes and conditions have existed from the

onward progressive development of the Mosaic account, Prof. Dana remarks: "The record in the Bible is therefore profoundly philosophical in the sense of creation which it presents. It is both true and divine. It is a declaration of authorship, both of creation and the Bible on the first page of the sacred volume" (Manual of Geology, p. 745). In the Biblio. Sacra, Jan., 1856, Prof. Dana states: "The first thought that strikes a scientific reader (of Genesis) is the evidence of divinity, not merely in the first verse of the record and the successive fiats, but in the whole order of creation. There is so much that the most recent readings of science have for the first time explained, that the idea of man as the author becomes utterly incomprehensible. By proving the record true, scientists pronounce it divine; for who could have correctly narrated the secrets of eternity but God Himself?"

A third characteristic which differentiates the Torah from the works of men is its high and holy system of ethics. An honest comparison of the ethical code of Moses with that found in the law of Hammurabi* proves conclusively that the author of the former was inspired by the Spirit of the Eternal, Holy God.

---

beginning. But it is a well-known fact that according to the generally accepted theories concerning the glacial periods the same conditions have not prevailed upon the earth all along. This fact being true, conditions have varied, hence any estimates based upon such calculations are fallacious and unreliable.

Resort is, likewise, had to the evidence furnished by the anthropologists. Assuming what is only a theory and cannot be proved, that there are skulls and human remains that date back thousands of years, one does not have to surrender his faith in the Bible as the Word of God. In Gen. 1:2 is a record of the destruction of the earth which originally was created in a perfect condition (Isa. 45:18). In Gen. 1:28 God told Adam to "be fruitful, and multiply, and replenish the earth." The word translated "replenish" is the same as used in Gen. 9:1 where God told Noah to replenish the earth. So far as our knowledge is concerned there may have been a pre-Adamic race upon the earth before the catastrophe of Gen. 1:2. If this theory (the author simply states the theory, but frankly admits that he does not know) is true, these ancient skeletons may be of the pre-Adamic race.

* The similarities and verbal agreements between the Mosaic code and that of Hammurabi are so very pronounced and striking that most critics reach the conclusion that Moses borrowed many things from Hammurabi when he made his code; or worked over the former code, expunging from it all undesirable matter and altering the text to serve his purpose. That there is a very close and vital connection between the codes is beyond dispute. It is certain that Hammurabi did not borrow from Moses for the former lived, in round numbers, 400 years prior to the latter. Did Moses borrow from Hammurabi? To this question most critics answer in the affirmative; but the author begs to differ from them on this point,

Again the scientific world has discovered the fact that the "Law of the Octave" is the fundamental principle underlying the physical world, the evidence of which is seen in the fact that it obtains in the fields of chemistry, music, color, snow flakes, etc. The same law, likewise, obtains in the Bible. In the first place, it is clearly seen that in the Hebrew text of Gen. 1:1 the number of words and also the number of letters are *seven* and *twenty-eight*. Hence two applications of THE LAW OF THE OCTAVE here are seen in the numbers seven and twenty-eight, the latter being a multiple of the former. This basic rule finds thousands of applications throughout the entire body of Scripture, which fact proclaims to the world, with no uncertain sound, that the Creator of

---

since the Mosaic writings give positive evidence of having been written by a man inspired by God Himself.

How, then, can these similarities be accounted for scientifically? Gen. 26:5 supplies what, to the author, seems to be the solution to the problem: "Because that Abraham obeyed my voice, and kept my charge, my commandments, my statutes, and my laws." From this passage it is absolutely certain that in the days of Abraham there were "commandments, statutes, and laws" which were in force and which God Himself had given. This passage becomes very luminous in the light of the facts presented in Gen. 14 from which one learns that Melchizedek was king of Salem and priest of God Most High. Evidently there was some kind of a "system of worship" or ritual over which he presided, since he was "priest of God Most High." Being king of Salem (Jerusalem), he ruled a kingdom in which laws were enforced. These laws and the ritualistic service were of divine origin.

Confirmatory evidence supporting the proposition that God gave a revelation which antedates the Mosaic is found in the fact that there were prophets outside the borders of Israel. As an example of one, note the prophecies of Balaam who was a Syrian and who endeavored to curse Israel (Num. 22-25). By some scholars it is asserted that many of the Messianic prophecies found in Egypt, which antedate the days of Moses by centuries and in which the names of the gods of Egypt appear, read like prophecies of the Tenach if the names of these heathen deities are expunged and the Name of the God of Israel inserted. These facts point very definitely to the conclusion that there were true prophets of God who lived and spoke messages of God prior to the days of Moses. These messages from God, however, were corrupted by men after they refused to retain God in their knowledge. The original meaning, however, still was conveyed, though veiled greatly, when read in the light of the pure unadulterated Word of God as it appears in the Tenach.

Instead of Moses' borrowing from Hammurabi, one would conclude that the similarities between the Hammurabi code and that of the revelation of God, as found in the Torah, may more scientifically be explained upon the basis that Hammurabi borrowed from these primitive revelations of God.

It is quite likely that the tradition preserved among the Hebrews that God offered His law first to all nations and, when they refused it, He

the World, Who, speaking in a figure, placed the watermark of the Law of the Octave both in the material world and upon the Scriptures is the Creator of the Universe and the Author of the Scriptures.*

The question arises at this point, How was it that the Author of Gen. 1 anticipated modern science by hundreds of years? The only plausible answer is that he received this knowledge by the inspiration of God through the Holy Spirit.

Once again, the inspiration of the Torah is seen in the accurate statement concerning the propagation of the species in the vegetable kingdom in the expression "bearing fruit after their kind." This statement, much overlooked by scientists, in the light of modern research appears sublime. Its significance was never realized fully by real scientists until in recent years. This statement is a Biblical way of expressing Mendel's law which was discovered by Gregor J. Mendel in the latter half of the nineteenth century. The results of his experiments were unknown to the scientific world until his work was discovered in 1900. Since then innumerable experiments have been made by painstaking investigators who have demonstrated the scientific accuracy of what is now known as "the law of alternative inheritance," or Mendel's law. The discovery of this law revolutionized scientific thinking. Bateson's definition of it is as follows: "The essence of the Mendelian principle is very easily expressed. It is, first, in great measure the properties of organisms are due to the presence of distinct detachable elements separately transmitted in heredity, and secondly, that *the parent cannot pass on to the offspring an element, and consequently the corresponding property, which it does not itself possess.*" Mendel simply proved the scientific accuracy of the Biblical expression.

gave it to Israel who accepted it, is to be traced historically to this primitive revelation.

Since God is the Author both of the primitive revelation, from which, doubtless, Hammurabi borrowed the highest and best elements of his code, and since He is the Author of the Mosaic Code, it is easy to account for the similarities of the heathen code with that of the divine Mosaic Code.

*In no other writings, either ancient or modern, does this phenomenon occur. This statement being a proven fact, the law of the octave which is stamped both upon the book of nature and the book of revelation proves without a doubt to the candid, careful investigator for truth that the Bible is the Word of the Living God Who created the heavens and the earth, and in Whom man lives and moves and has his being.

Another illustration of the scientific accuracy of the Torah is seen in the statement that the stars are innumerable. The Greek philosophers in the palmy days of Grecian history when human culture and education reached the highest points claimed that there were about 1028 stars. Modern science has demonstrated the accuracy of the Biblical account. The only way to account for the exact knowledge set forth in the Biblical record is to accept the only reasonable hypothesis, namely, that the Eternal God revealed these facts, then unknown to the world, to His servant Moses who wrote accurately what God revealed to him.

Hundreds of years prior to this time God, in promising a glorious posterity to Abraham, used the number of the stars as a comparison. How did the writer know that the stars were so very numerous, since the wisdom of the world limited their number to ten hundred and twenty-eight? As stated above, the only satisfactory answer is found in the thought that God's Spirit inspired the writer. Again, the Divine Source of knowledge which the writer of the Torah possessed is seen in the fact that the sanitary laws embodied in the Torah anticipated modern discoveries. Furthermore, a comparison of the code of Moses with the laws of Hammurabi of Babylon, who was a contemporary of Abraham (he being the "Amrafel" or *Amraphel,* of Gen. 14: 1) shows the superiority of the Mosaic code to that of Hammurabi. The scintillations of Divine light flashing forth in these scientific statements and anticipating science by hundreds of years prove conclusively the Divine inspiration of the author.

II. TESTIMONY OF THE TORAH TO THE PROPHETS AND WRITINGS

When one admits the Divine origin of the Five Books of Moses, he is logically bound to accept the Divine origin and authority both of the Prophets and the Psalms, for Moses in two passages, assumed unmistakably that God would raise up prophets for them who would deliver His Word to them.

A. *Exposition of Deuteronomy 13:1-5*

In Deut. 13:1-5 Moses gave Israel the negative test whereby she could ascertain whether a man who claimed to be a prophet of God with a message of God to them was a prophet of God or not. He says, "If there arise in the midst of thee a prophet

. . . and he give thee a sign or a wonder, and the sign or wonder come to pass, whereof he spake unto thee, saying, 'Let us go after other gods' . . . thou shalt not hearken unto the words of that prophet . . . and that prophet . . . shall be put to death."

The expression, "If there arise," etc., assumes the possibility of the appearance of prophets in their midst. The test by which they were to determine whether a prophet was true or false was this, "and he give thee a sign . . . and the sign come to pass . . . saying, 'Let us go after other gods.' " The giving of this test assumed unmistakably that there would arise true prophets who would bring a message to them from God. The credentials which a prophet was to bring, said Moses, were that he should give a sign or wonder which was to come to pass. Of course, if the sign or wonder which he gave did not come to pass, it was self-evident that he was not sent from God; but if the sign or wonder did come to pass that fact was not in and of itself a sure guarantee that God had sent him, for there is a world of evil spirits which at various times worked through false prophets as they did through the magicians who opposed Moses when he went to deliver Israel from Egyptian bondage. These magicians possessed supernatural power which was from Satan, the adversary of God. If the sign or wonder came to pass the final test of the prophet was to be found in the character of his message, namely, if he said, "Let us go after other gods," that message was positive proof that the supernatural power which he manifested in giving the sign or wonder that came to pass was not from God but from the evil one. This test also assumed that if the message which the prophet brought was, "Let us go after the Lord," then this message was to be the final proof that God had sent the prophet.

B. *Exposition of Deuteronomy 18:20-22*

Again, in Deut. 18:20-22 God supplemented the original test in the following words, "But the prophet, that shall speak a word presumptuously in my name, which I have not commanded him to speak, or that shall speak in the name of other gods, that same prophet shall die." This passage unmistakably assumes the appearance in Israel both of true and of false prophets. The identification of the true prophet is that he should speak in the Name of the Lord what the Lord commanded him to speak. Upon the appearance of a prophet speaking in the Name of the Lord, should Israel say in her heart, "How shall we know the word which the Lord hath not spoken?" the absolute test of the prophet is found in the following words: "When a prophet speaketh in the name of the Lord, if the thing follow not, nor come to pass, that is the thing which the Lord hath not spoken: the prophet hath spoken it presumptuously, thou shalt not be afraid of him." Hence the final test of a prophet and his message was found in his speaking in the Name of the Lord, and in the fulfillment of the prediction. This same passage also assumes that two types of false prophets would appear: first, the one who speaks in the Name of God that which God had not commanded; secondly, the prophet who would speak in the name of other gods. According to this verse, if a prophet spoke in the Name of God presumptuously, or if he spoke a message in the name of the heathen gods, God positively says, "that same prophet shall die." The context shows that He is not talking about a natural death, for such would be no sign whereby Israel might know whether the message was true or false, when delivered by a prophet speaking presumptuously in the Name of God. Hence the death here coming to either type of false prophet is a judgment which God would send upon false prophets, whereby Israel would know conclusively that they were false. Such a prophet arose in the days of Jeremiah (Jer. 28:1-17) in the person of Hananiah, who spoke a message presumptuously in the Name of God and who died in the seventh month of the same year, which death was the judgment of God sent upon him, and which was God's method of showing Israel that Hananiah was a false prophet.

At different times in Israel's history God raised up prophets who, according to His promise in these passages from Deuteronomy, gave a sign in the Name of God which came to pass. The fact that they spoke in the Name of Israel's God and that the sign came to pass was God's absolute guarantee that these prophets were speaking His word just as Moses had, and that their words were as authoritative and binding upon Israel as those which

he had given through Moses. Israel in the prophetic days was
very cautious to ascertain what message was from God and what
was not. When such men as Isaiah, Jeremiah, Ezekiel, et al.,
appeared upon the scene and gave the Divine credentials of their
Divine calling, their words were accepted and preserved until
this day, as one finds them in the Prophets and Psalms. Hence
these writings are the Word of the Living God and are to be
received at their face value and acted upon even in the same way
as the Five Books of Moses are to be accepted.

Corroborative proof sustaining the conclusion just arrived at is
found in the fact that there is a unity of thought, plan and purpose
which runs through the Law, Prophets, and Psalms. These thirty-
nine books are, according to the scholarship of the world, accredited
to about twenty-odd authors, who wrote at different times in a
period of approximately one thousand years—from Moses to
Malachi. It is but natural that discrepancies and contradictions
should appear in the works of men who lived during such a long
period. Is it possible now for anyone to gather thirty-nine other
books from Hebrew writers who have lived at various times during
a period of a thousand years and find them displaying perfect
unity, plan and purpose flowing through them without any contradiction? To this question the universal answer is "No!" Furthermore, in no literature covering any like period of time can
such unity be found. Therefore this collection of thirty-nine
books stands in a class by itself, since it is free from discrepancies
and displays perfect unity.

This unity cannot be explained reasonably upon any basis other
than that the Spirit of the Living God spoke in and through their
authors, consecrated men of God. The conclusion arrived at is
not of modern origin, but was the faith of the Hebrew race
in the centuries prior to the beginning of the common era. In
the first century of this era, Josephus, the noted Jewish historian,
in his letter against Apion, contrasted the sacred books of the
Hebrews with those of the Greeks and claimed that the Hebrew
Scriptures were justly considered by them as the Word of God.
Following is his statement: "For we have not an innumerable
multitude of books among us, disagreeing from and contradicting
one another (as the Greeks have), but only twenty-two books,

which contain the records of all the past times; which are justly believed to be divine; and of them five belong to Moses, which contain his laws and the traditions of the origin of mankind till his death. This interval of time was little short of three thousand years; but as to the time from the death of Moses till the reign of Artaxerxes, king of Persia, who reigned after Xerxes, the prophets, who were after Moses, wrote down what was done in their times in thirteen books. The remaining four books contain hymns to God, and precepts for the conduct of human life. It is true, our history hath been written since Artaxerxes very particularly, but hath not been esteemed of the like authority with the former by our forefathers, because there hath not been an exact succession of prophets since that time; and how firmly we have given credit to these books of our own nation is evident by what we do; for during so many ages as have already passed, no one has been so bold as either to add anything to them, to take anything from them, or to make any change in them; but it is become natural to all Jews immediately, and from their very birth, to esteem these books to contain Divine doctrines, and to persist in them, and, if occasion be, willingly to die for them."*

The Jews, according to Josephus, had sufficient and positive evidence which led them to the conclusion that the Tenach was the very Word of God; therefore, they were, "if occasion be, willing to die for them." They had no more sufficient proof than the present generation has. One of the infallible proofs that the thirty-nine books, commonly called the "Old Testament," are the Very Word of God is the fact that numerous prophecies which were spoken by the prophets of Israel during a period of a thousand years antedating the fifth century before the common era, and which deal with cities, countries, nations and their condition and destinies during this common era, were fulfilled even in the

---

* Josephus claimed inspiration for only twenty-two sacred books whereas the Tenach as it has been preserved to the present day contains thirty-nine. When the facts are known it will become apparent that the twenty-two books mentioned by Josephus are those which are counted as thirty-nine in modern times. The difference in the count is seen in the fact that Josephus counted the two books of Samuel as one, whereas now they are counted as two; the same count obtained with reference to Kings and Chronicles. Josephus counted the twelve Minor Prophets as one book, whereas they in modern times are counted twelve. These different viewpoints account for the difference in numbers.

most minute and detailed manner. These predictions cannot be explained upon the basis that their authors were shrewd, far-sighted politicians who, seeing the trend of events of their day, arrived at the conclusions expressed in the prophecies. It is unthinkable to suppose that anyone, regardless of his shrewdness, insight and comprehension, could penetrate the veil separating him from the future and could accurately detail in the most specific and minute manner the condition of nations and peoples five hundred years in the future. It might be conceded possible but at the same time most highly improbable that some statesman might have sufficient mental grasp to depict in a vague, indefinite and general way the condition of his country even a century or two later; but no rational man will concede that even the most brilliant statesman who has ever lived had sufficient intelligence and insight into human affairs which would enable him to give a clear, accurate and minute outline of the history and fortunes of his nation five hundred to a thousand years later.

The prophets of Israel, on the other hand, with boldness foretold accurately what fortunes and calamities during the common era would come to the nations which surrounded Israel and their lands. Furthermore, they painted most accurately pictures of the desolations which have obtained in many of these countries during this era and which continue to the present day. The only rational explanation of their ability to portray the future as they did is that THEY SPOKE THE MESSAGES* WHICH GOD GAVE

---

* To those who feel that the Bible is purely of human origin and full of mistakes and errors, the author would like to call attention to the fact that the old challenge which has many times been proposed to skeptics, infidels, and atheists has never been accepted. The challenge is this: Let those who discredit the Bible as the Word of God produce a volume like it which will stand the severe test of centuries, as the Bible has done. Let them select men from the various callings of life (but if they choose, let them appoint the most highly-educated university professors—experts in their fields—and scientists) who can produce a number of volumes which, when taken together, harmonize and constitute a unity. It will be necessary for them to begin their work where the Bible begins, namely, with the creation of the world. Let them, therefore, write a history of the world from its creation to the present time since the Biblical historians wrote an account of the world from creation to their own times. Let them also look out into the future and outline accurately the specific courses of the various nations, delineating the vicissitudes and changes of nations, peoples, and cities.

Since rapid progress has been made in the sciences of psychology and sociology. let experts in these fields be employed who will be able to analyze

THEM; therefore their messages were not theirs in the sense that they composed them, but were the very messages of God.

Should any reader entertain doubts concerning the inspiration of the Sacred Writings of these men of God, he is urgently requested to procure a copy of "The Wonders of Prophecy, or What Are We to Believe?" by John Urquhart. Read this volume with one purpose in view, dear friend, namely, to see facts and truths and to act accordingly.

III. THE HOPELESS CONDITION OF THE ATHEISTS AND SKEPTICS

Thomas Paine, who rejected all religion, and whose last utterances were in anguish of a soul in despair, cried out, "My God, my God, why hast Thou forsaken me?" "I would give worlds, if I had them, if THE AGE OF REASON had never been published. Oh, Lord, help me! . . . Help me! Stay with me! It is hell to be left alone!"

Edward Gibbon, the noted infidel and author, upon his death-bed said, "All is now lost; finally, irrecoverably lost. All is dark and doubtful."

Thomas Hobbes, the atheist and philosopher, as he was drawing near death, said, "I am about to take a leap in the dark," and his last audible words were, "I shall be glad to find a hole to creep out of the world at."

The last words of the atheist Mirabeau: "My sufferings are intolerable; I have within me a hundred years of life but not a moment's courage. Give me more laudanum that I may not think of eternity."

---

human nature and reveal to man his innermost being; and let them formulate a system of ethics, morals, and politics which will appeal to the common consciousness of the race.

When the work has been completed, it will be tested by conscientious truthseekers who will examine it microscopically to ascertain if it is correct, scientifically, archæologically, chronologically, geographically, and topographically. Let it be tested not only in the school of every-day life but also by experts in the various fields of human knowledge and endeavor. If, when thus tested, it is found that it has given a truthful and accurate account which accords with all of the data of archæology; that all of its statements are historically accurate; that all geographical allusions are correct; that all topographical references accord with the known facts; and that the ethics and principles of government have reached the acme of perfection; then, and only then, can the unbeliever logically ask the world to discard the Bible and to accept his dogmas. Until such a work is produced the sane, scientific truthseeker will hold on to the Bible as the Word of God.

Voltaire's dying words were, "I am abandoned by God and man! I shall go to hell! . . ."

Of Sir Francis Newport it is reported that in reply to an infidel companion he said: "That there is a God, I know, because I continually feel the effects of His wrath; that there is a hell I am equally certain, having received an earnest of my inheritance there already in my breast; that there is a natural conscience I now feel with horror and amazement, being continually upbraided by it with my impieties, and all my iniquities, and all my sins brought to my remembrance. Why God has marked me out for an example of His vengeance, rather than you, or any one of my acquaintance, I presume is because I have been more religiously educated, and have done greater despite to the Spirit of grace. O that I was to lie upon the fire that never is quenched a thousand years, to purchase the favor of God, and be reunited to Him again! But it is a fruitless wish. Millions and millions of years will bring me no nearer to the end of my torments than one poor hour. O, eternity, eternity! Who can discover the abyss of eternity? Who can paraphrase upon these words, *forever and ever?*" Lest his friends should think him insane, he said: "You imagine me melancholy, or distracted. I wish I were either; but it is part of my judgment that I am not. No; my apprehension of persons and things is more quick and vigorous than it was when I was in perfect health; and it is my curse, because I am thereby more sensible of the condition I am fallen into. Would you be informed why I am become a skeleton in three or four days? See now then. I have despised my Maker, and denied my Redeemer. I have joined myself to the atheist and profane, and continued this course under many convictions, till my iniquity was ripe for vengeance, and the just judgment of God overtook me when my security was the greatest, and the checks of my conscience were the least." As his mental distress and bodily disease were hurrying him into eternity, he was asked if he would have prayer offered in his behalf; he turned his face, and exclaimed: "Tigers and monsters! are ye also become devils to torment me? Would ye give me prospect of heaven to make my hell more intolerable?" Then with a failing voice he cried, "Oh, the insufferable pangs of hell!" and expired.

IV. THE BLESSED CONDITION OF THE RIGHTEOUS

The death of the true servant of God is entirely different. "Let me die the death of the righteous, and let my last end be like his!" Num. 23:10. "Precious in the sight of the Lord is the death of His saints." Psa. 116:15. "As I live, saith the Lord God, I have no pleasure in the death of the wicked; but that the wicked turn from his way and live: turn ye, turn ye from your evil ways; for why will ye die, . . ." Ezek. 33:11.

CONCLUSION

If, according to the quotations from men given above, skeptics, infidels, and atheists* in approaching death realize their mistake in denying the existence of God or the inspiration of the Bible, and in refusing to accept His Salvation, there evidently is a reason for their changing their views and making the sad confessions as they launch out into the future to meet a God into Whose face they have flung defiance during life. The cause which leads them thus to confess is the fact that they, as their spirit begins to leave the body, see the stern realities of the life beyond the grave and realize that they must face the True and Living God, having spurned His offers of mercy. These statements being true, it is now proper to turn to an investigation of the message contained in the Tenach.

---

* Often, instead of reading the Bible itself with an open mind, skeptics procure works teaching infidelity and skepticism. A certain infidel boasted of his unbelief. Upon being asked what books he read he referred to the works of Ingersoll, Paine, et al. When questioned closely if he had ever read the Bible one time he finally admitted that he never had. The health of the body depends upon the nature of the food which is eaten; the health of the heart and soul, likewise, depends upon the intellectual and spiritual food upon which one feasts.

Speaking in a figure one may say that truth is modest and will never force herself upon him who does not seek her association. The Scriptures are so constructed that those who are hunting for difficulties will find many seeming contradictions; but the truthseeker will make a thorough, sympathetic investigation of the facts and endeavor to find harmony. According to the best legal authorities, testimony which, especially in minor details seems to be contradictory but in the outstanding features agrees in general is considered the very best of evidence. Hence the seeming difficulties to which atheists and infidels have pointed as proof against the Divine origin of the Scriptures, when studied honestly and conscientiously with a desire to know the truth, vanish into oblivion.

A few illustrations will suffice to show how these seeming difficulties vanish. The miracle of the prolonged day in the days of Joshua (Josh. 10) has been to some a stumbling block. Various explanations have been given of this record. The existence of a Supreme Omnipotent God being granted, no one should have any difficulty with this miracle. According to the record the day was prolonged in order that Joshua might complete the victory. At his command the sun and moon stood still. Did these heavenly bodies really stand still or did the earth cease rotating on its axis? Or did the Almighty by miraculous intervention intensify refraction and reflection so that those bodies appeared to stand still (the language of appearance)? People today who believe in the rotundity of the earth still speak of the rising and the setting of the sun. This usage is the language of appearance. It will never be settled scientifically as to which of these methods was used. The great fact established by historical testimony is that there was miraculous intervention which prolonged that day. A faint echo of this miracle is heard in the Greek world in the fable of Phaethon, who was driving the chariot of the Sun and threw everything into disorder, thus causing one day wholly unlike all before and after it. Likewise, another faint echo is heard in the Chinese record: "Some traces of this miracle are discovered in the Chinese records, as well as in the disfigured account of Statius and Ovid."

Another seeming flat contradiction disappears in the light of the knowledge of the Hebrew text. In II Kgs. 8:17 it is stated that Joram, king of Judah, reigned eight years in Jerusalem, dying forty years old. In verse 26 the statement is made that his son, Ahaziah, was twenty-two years old, ascended the throne and reigned one year. In II Chron. 22:2 the statement is made that Ahaziah was forty-two years old when he began to reign and reigned one year. Thus the records appear in the English translation. There is a seeming contradiction. The father is forty years old when he dies; the son is forty-two when he dies and reigns only one year. No son can be older than his father. This seeming difficulty vanishes when one realizes the fact that the Hebrew expression translated "when he began to reign" also is grammatically translated "in his kingdom" or "in his reign." Since the son could not be two years older than the father and since the Hebrew expression has two meanings, that significance must be chosen in the Chronicles passage which will accord with the facts. When it is seen that Ahaziah was the son of Athaliah, who was the daughter of Jezebel of the house of Omri, of the Northern Kingdom, and when the years are counted from the usurpation of the throne of Omri to the death of Joram and it is seen that there were exactly forty-two years, the only conclusion to be drawn is that the writer of Chronicles was speaking of the length of the dynasty instead of the age of Ahaziah when he mounted the throne.

Another seeming contradiction of the same character has been pointed out by infidels. In I Kgs. 16:5-8 is the record of the death of Baasha of Israel in the twenty-sixth year of the reign of Asa, king of Judah. In the thirty-sixth year of Asa—ten years after Baasha's death—the latter is said to have warred against Judah (II Chron. 16:1). There seems to be an undoubted contradiction. The same Hebrew expression is used here which was used in the other Chronicles passage and should be translated "in his kingdom." A count of the years from the disruption of the kingdom—the beginning of the kingdom of Judah—to the time of this war is thirty-six years. Hence this expression should be translated "in the thirty-sixth year of his reign," that is, the reign of the dynasty to which he belonged.

Many seeming contradictions could be mentioned but these suffice to show that a careful study of the facts will remove the supposed contradiction.

CHAPTER III

THE PLURALITY OF GOD

UPON opening the Bible one is immediately confronted in the Hebrew text (Gen. 1:1) with the word "God" in the plural number; hence it is proper to begin this study with:

THE PLURALITY OF THE DIVINE PERSONALITIES

I. SIGNIFICANCE OF THE PLURAL NOUN אֱלֹהִים

In the first statement of the Tenach (Old Testament) בְּרֵאשִׁית בָּרָא אֱלֹהִים אֵת הַשָּׁמַיִם וְאֵת הָאָרֶץ: "In the beginning God created the heavens and the earth," the word which is translated "God" is אֱלֹהִים, and is in the plural number, as is well known to all Hebrew scholars. All Hebrew nouns ending with ים– are masculine and are in the plural number. As an example note the word כְּרֻבִים, which means more than one, the singular being כְּרוּב, cherub (see Psa. 18:10 (11)). Another illustration is שְׂרָפִים, which is the plural of שָׂרָף.

For conclusive proof that אֱלֹהִים is in the plural number, and means more than one, look, dear reader, at the First Commandment found in Exodus 20:3. לֹא־יִהְיֶה לְךָ אֱלֹהִים אֲחֵרִים עַל־פָּנָי: "Not shall there be to you other gods before me" (Author's literal Tr.). The word אֱלֹהִים here is correctly translated "gods," meaning many gods, and is modified by אֲחֵרִים which means "strange" or "other" and is likewise in the plural number. Another instance may be cited which is found in Deut. 13:2(3). נֵלְכָה אַחֲרֵי אֱלֹהִים אֲחֵרִים אֲשֶׁר לֹא־יְדַעְתָּם וְנָעָבְדֵם: saying, "Let us go after other gods, which thou hast not known, and let us serve them." Here the words translated "other gods" are the same as occurred in the First Commandment (see Ex. 18:11 and Judg. 10:13). All translators, both Jewish and Gentile, correctly translate אֱלֹהִים "gods" in these and in all other passages where it refers to idols. Hundreds of instances could be adduced, but these are sufficient to make the point clear.

If, when this word refers to heathen gods, it is to be translated grammatically and correctly in the plural number, why should

26

the grammar be ignored and the word be translated as if it were a singular noun when it refers to Israel's God, since the facts are that it is a plural noun and means more than one?*

II. SIGNIFICANCE OF PLURAL VERBS USED WITH אֱלֹהִים

In addition to the proof which is furnished by the plural noun אֱלֹהִים, the use of the verb in the plural number, used in connection with אֱלֹהִים, indicates that there is a plurality of Divine Personalities.† In Gen. 20 there is recorded a conversation which took place between Abimelech and Abraham, in which conversation Abraham (v. 13) said: וַיְהִי כַּאֲשֶׁר הִתְעוּ אֹתִי אֱלֹהִים מִבֵּית אָבִי . "And it came to pass, when God caused me to wander from my father's house." The word הִתְעוּ is in the plural number and has as its subject אֱלֹהִים. From the use of this plural verb the one legitimate inference that may be drawn is that Abraham recognized that there is a plurality of Divine Personalities. Again,

---

*The writer is aware of the argument that the plural noun אלהים is the plural of "excellency, majesty." He admits, frankly, that in the Semitic world such usage was common when subjects addressed their king or at times spoke concerning him; but in the passages examined in this section, and in numerous other passages, there is nothing in the context of any of them which warrants a departure from the strict grammatical interpretation of the words and the substitution of an interpretation invented to support a theological bias.

Proof for "the plural of Majesty" is sought for in such passages as Judg. 11:24: "Wilt not thou possess that which כמוש (Chemosh) thy God giveth thee to possess?" כמוש is in the singular number and is the name of the God of Moab, and in apposition with it is אלהיך "thy Gods." From this passage it is argued that since אלהיך is in apposition with כמוש and since it is in the plural number, it is the plural of majesty, which conforms to the Semitic usage with reference to rulers. Therefore it is contended that אלהים אלהיך אלהינו etc., simply mean "God, thy God, our God," and are not to be taken in their primary, ordinary, literal meaning, the supposition being that when applied to the God of Israel they are the plural of majesty. In reply to this argument it is sufficient to note the fact that כמוש was not the name of one idol only, but it was the name of innumerable idols throughout the kingdom. Hence כמוש though in the singular form is a collective noun which embraced every idol of the realm. Hence אלהיך "thy gods" conforms strictly to the correct grammatical usage of the language and means "thy gods." The same explanation holds good with reference to Dagon in I Sam. 5:7 and like passages.

† Personality is not to be confounded with corporeality. One is as much of a personality after death as he is before. Angels who have not human bodies are personalities. Likewise, God is רוח "spirit" without a material body yet He is a personality.

this same fact is presented in Gen. 35:7, in which passage one
reads that Jacob built an altar to the Lord, and called the name
of the place אֵל בֵּית־אֵל, "For there the Gods revealed themselves
unto him when he fled from the face of his brother" (Author's
Tr.).   The verb נִגְלוּ is in the plural number and has for its
subject הָאֱלֹהִים.   There were more than one of the Divine Persons who revealed themselves to Jacob as indicated by the plural
noun and the plural verb.

III. THE SIGNIFICANCE OF THE PLURAL PRONOUNS

A fifth group of facts pointing toward the conclusion of a plurality of Divine Personalities is the use of the plural pronouns
in a number of passages which refer to God.

A. The first example where this usage is found is in Gen. 1:26
which gives a conversation introduced by the words וַיֹּאמֶר אֱלֹהִים
"God said," נַעֲשֶׂה אָדָם בְּצַלְמֵנוּ כִּדְמוּתֵנוּ, "Let US make man in
our image, and according to OUR likeness."   From this quotation
one is forced to the irresistible conclusion that the speaker, who
is God, and the one to whom He was speaking, are of the same
divine essence or nature, for he uses the words, דְּמוּת צֶלֶם, "image
and likeness" in the singular number and attaches the plural
personal pronoun "our" to these singular nouns. This fact in and
of itself shows that the speaker and the one addressed are of
the same image and substance.   Hence since the speaker is God,
the eternal God, the one spoken to is none less than the eternal
God.

B. A second use of the plural personal pronoun is found
in Gen. 3:22, in which God says after man's disobedience
וַיֹּאמֶר יְהוָֹה אֱלֹהִים הֵן הָאָדָם הָיָה כְּאַחַד מִמֶּנּוּ "Behold, the man
is become as one of us."   Again, it is evident that the speaker,
the self-existing God, speaks to another who is of the same nature
as Himself, by the use of the expression כְּאַחַד מִמֶּנּוּ "as one of
us." Such language as this God could not use in speaking to a
created being. The language unquestionably implies the equality
of the speaker and the one addressed.

C. This same usage is seen in the account of the destruction
of the Tower of Babel recorded in Gen. 11.   In verse 7 God

said הָבָה נֵרְדָה וְנָבְלָה שָׁם שְׂפָתָם "Come, let US go down, and there confound their language." The explanation of the two passages just discussed is the only satisfying interpretation of this passage.

Solomon, to whom God gave special wisdom (I Kings 3:12), urged young people in the days of their youth to וּזְכֹר אֶת־בּוֹרְאֶיךָ "remember now thy creators" (Author's Tr., Eccl. 12:1). To the Hebrew student it is very plain that בּוֹרְאֶיךָ is in the plural number, as is indicated by the accompanying vowel which joins the personal pronoun "thy" to the participle "creators." Again, in Psa. 149:2 יִשְׂמַח יִשְׂרָאֵל בְּעֹשָׂיו "Let Israel rejoice in his Makers." The personal pronoun יו "his" shows that the participle is in the plural number and refers to Israel's God. The facts noted in this paragraph confirm the interpretation of the significance of the pronouns in paragraphs A, B, and C.

CONCLUSION

With the facts noted in this chapter before an honest inquiring heart, the conclusion is borne irresistibly upon the soul that the Tenach unmistakably teaches the plurality*† of God.

---

* That the word אֱלֹהִים denotes a plurality of personalities is clearly seen in the translation by Isaac Leeser in Josh. 22:22: "The God of gods, the Eternal, the God of gods, the Eternal, He knoweth," etc. Leeser knew that this word is plural, hence he translated it as such, though he applied it to heathen gods. The translators of the Jew. Pub. Soc. render it thus: "God, God, the Lord, God, God, the Lord, He knoweth," etc. This translation correctly makes it in apposition with the word אֵל but fails to translate it correctly. The correct translation is: "God, Gods, the Lord," etc.

† All standard Hebrew lexicons define the word 'elohim as a masculine, plural noun; hence scholarship confirms the contention herewith set forth.

THOUGH there are more personalities than one in the Divine Being, they form a unity of which the Scriptures constantly assume. David, the great king of Israel, in his memorable prayer (II Sam. 7:22) declares the unity of God: עַל־כֵּן גָּדַלְתָּ יְהוָֹה אֱלֹהִים כִּי־אֵין כָּמוֹךָ וְאֵין אֱלֹהִים זוּלָתֶךָ כְּכֹל אֲשֶׁר־ שָׁמַעְנוּ בְּאָזְנֵינוּ: "Wherefore thou art great, O Lord God: for there is none like thee, neither is there any God besides thee, according to all that we have heard with our ears." Isaiah, who had to contend with insidious idolatry which had crept into the nation, repeatedly affirmed that God is one as is seen in the following passages: מִי־פָעַל וְעָשָׂה קֹרֵא הַדֹּרוֹת מֵרֹאשׁ אֲנִי יְהוָֹה רִאשׁוֹן וְאֶת־אַחֲרֹנִים אֲנִי־הוּא: "Who hath wrought and done it, calling the generations from the beginning? I, the Lord, the first, and with the last, I am He" (Isa. 41:4). אַתֶּם עֵדַי נְאָם־יְהוָֹה וְעַבְדִּי אֲשֶׁר בָּחָרְתִּי לְמַעַן תֵּדְעוּ וְתַאֲמִינוּ לִי וְתָבִינוּ כִּי־אֲנִי הוּא לְפָנַי לֹא־נוֹצַר אֵל וְאַחֲרַי לֹא־יִהְיֶה: אָנֹכִי אָנֹכִי יְהוָֹה וְאֵין מִבַּלְעָדַי מוֹשִׁיעַ: "Ye are my witnesses, saith the LORD, and my servant whom I have chosen; that ye may know and believe me, and understand that I am He: before me there was no God formed, neither shall there be after me. I, even I, am the LORD; and besides me there is no savior" (43:10, 11). כֹּה־אָמַר יְהוָֹה מֶלֶךְ־יִשְׂרָאֵל וְגֹאֲלוֹ יְהוָֹה צְבָאוֹת אֲנִי רִאשׁוֹן וַאֲנִי אַחֲרוֹן וּמִבַּלְעָדַי אֵין אֱלֹהִים: "Thus saith the LORD, the king of Israel, and his redeemer, the LORD of hosts: I am the first, and I am the last; and besides me there is no God."* (44:6).

I. UNITY SEEN IN THE GREAT CONFESSION

In harmony with the statements just quoted is the Great Confession of Israel found in Deut. 6:4, which is שְׁמַע יִשְׂרָאֵל יְהוָֹה

---

*The same teaching concerning God i. e., that there is none beside Him, is set forth in numerous passages, a few of which are as follows: Num. 15:41; Isa. 43:3, 11; 45:5; 44:6; Deut. 4:35, 39; 32:39; Ex. 20:23; Hosea 13:4; 2 Sam. 7:22; I Kings 8:23.

אֱלֹהֵינוּ יְהֹוָה אֶחָד: "Hear, O Israel: the Lord our Gods is the LORD a unity." The first thing noticed about this confession is אֱלֹהֵינוּ. "Elohim." According to all Hebrew grammarians this word is the construct form of אֱלֹהִים (gods) to which the personal possessive pronoun ־נוּ "our" in the plural number is added. To show that this form is in the plural and means "our Gods," only a few illustrations will be necessary. First, dear reader, examine Josh. 24 : 23 : וְעַתָּה הָסִירוּ אֶת־אֱלֹהֵי הַנֵּכָר אֲשֶׁר בְּקִרְבְּכֶם וְהַטּוּ אֶת־לְבַבְכֶם אֶל־יְהֹוָה אֱלֹהֵי יִשְׂרָאֵל: "Now therefore put away, said he, the foreign gods which are among you, and incline your heart unto the Lord, the God of Israel." Note the similarity of these expressions: אֶת־אֱלֹהֵי הַנֵּכָר and אֶל־יְהֹוָה אֱלֹהֵי יִשְׂרָאֵל:. The former אֱלֹהֵי נֵכָר is correctly translated "foreign gods," but the latter is translated "the Lord, God of Israel," though to be faithful to the text one must translate אֱלֹהֵי of both expressions in the same way, namely, "Gods of," the former being the gods of the foreigners, whereas the latter is the Gods of Israel. A perfect illustration of אֱלֹהֵינוּ "our Gods," which is, as stated above, the construct form of a plural masculine noun with the plural suffix "our," is found in Deut. 5 : 3 in the word אֲבוֹתֵינוּ "our fathers." The singular of this word is אָב, and the plural construct is אֲבֹתֵי which form with suffix is אֲבוֹתֵינוּ. Hence it is quite manifest that this word like אֱלֹהֵינוּ is a plural noun with the suffix "our." In Isa. 53 appear several examples of this same grammatical construction in verses 4 and 5. אָכֵן חֳלָיֵנוּ הוּא נָשָׂא וּמַכְאֹבֵינוּ סְבָלָם וַאֲנַחְנוּ חֲשַׁבְנֻהוּ נָגוּעַ מֻכֵּה אֱלֹהִים וּמְעֻנֶּה: וְהוּא מְחֹלָל מִפְּשָׁעֵינוּ מְדֻכָּא מֵעֲוֹנֹתֵינוּ מוּסַר שְׁלוֹמֵנוּ עָלָיו וּבַחֲבֻרָתוֹ נִרְפָּא־לָנוּ: "But our diseases did He bear Himself, and our pains He carried while we indeed esteemed Him, stricken, smitten of God and afflicted. Yet He was wounded for our transgressions, He was bruised for our iniquities: the chastisement of our peace was upon Him and through His bruises was healing granted to us (Author's Tr.)." The words עֲוֹנֹתֵינוּ פְּשָׁעֵינוּ מַכְאֹבֵינוּ חֳלָיֵנוּ are translated "our iniquities," "our transgressions," "our pains," and "our diseases." When one reads the entire chapter he can see clearly that the servant of the Lord, namely, "my righteous servant" צַדִּיק עַבְדִּי is suffering and is smitten of God because of the "diseases, pains, transgressions, and iniquities" of those to whom Isaiah refers as 'us' i. e., the Hebrew nation. From these examples and hundreds of others which might be given, it is very clear that אֱלֹהֵינוּ is in the plural construct form and means "our Gods."*

The next point in this confession to note is אֶחָד. This word is a numeral adjective meaning "one" and is derived from the verb הִתְאַחֲדִי which verb occurs only once in the Tenach (Ezek. 21:21). From this context one sees that God predicted the coming of a foreign invasion against Jerusalem, and Ezekiel was commanded to smite his hands together and to prophesy. In verse 21 it occurs in the hithpa'el form, as seen above, and means "to unite self, to gather one's strength or forces (of the sword)." From these facts he sees that it primarily means, not one in the absolute sense of the term, but one in the sense of a unity.

While the fundamental idea is that of a compound unity or the oneness of different elements or integral parts, it came to be used to express one in the absolute sense as the numeral one, which fact is seen by numerous examples throughout the Tenach. This fact being true, it becomes necessary to study the context wherever it occurs in order to ascertain which idea is conveyed in each particular case. To fail to observe this precaution and to read the idea of oneness in the absolute sense of the word into

---

* In connection with this study it is well to call attention to the fact that the word אלהיכם "your gods" appears in Josh. 3:3; 23:3; I Sam. 6:5; I Kgs. 18:25. (King James Tr.). In the first two passages it is translated "your God" because it applies to the God of Israel, but in the two latter passages the same identical word is translated "your gods" because it applies to heathen deities. A faithful translation of these words demands that they be translated the same in each instance.

In Deut. 6:5 appears the expression אלהיך "thy God" but in Gen. 31:32 the same expression is used by Jacob in his conversation with Laban in the former's speaking to the latter concerning the teraphim which Rachel had stolen and is translated "thy gods." The fact is that the word is plural with a singular suffix added and should be translated as the plural in both instances.

In Judg. 3:7 appears the expression אלהיהם and is translated "their God" because it refers to the God of Israel, but in the preceding verse the same word which applies to heathen gods is translated "their gods." The word is plural in both instances and should be thus translated.

every example where it occurs is to ignore logic, to smash grammar, and to outlaw ordinary intelligence and common sense.

As an illustration in which the inherent fundamental idea of a compound unity stands forth in bold relief, let the reader note the language of Gen. 1: 5, 8, 13, etc. In verse 5 Moses said: וַיְהִי־עֶרֶב וַיְהִי־בֹקֶר יוֹם אֶחָד: "And there was evening and there was morning, day one." This statement brings together two contrasting ideas—light and darkness—into a compound unity, which idea is normally expressed by אֶחָד. In verse 8 the same language occurs except the day was "day two"; the same thing is true with reference to verse 13 with the exception that the work just enumerated was done on the third day. In each instance עֶרֶב, בֹקֶר "evening" and "morning" together made a unity אֶחָד.

The union of evening and morning, in the first instance, constituted the first unit of time—day one; the union of evening and morning, in the second instance, constituted the second unit of time—day two. The same facts are true of each succeeding day. Next, note Gen. 2:24. Here God said עַל־כֵּן יַעֲזָב־אִישׁ אֶת־אָבִיו וְאֶת־אִמּוֹ וְדָבַק בְּאִשְׁתּוֹ וְהָיוּ לְבָשָׂר אֶחָד: "Therefore shall a man leave his father and his mother, and shall cleave unto his wife: and they shall be one flesh." In this passage one sees two individuals, man and woman, and yet God said that they constitute a unity—a unity made by joining two opposites into a real oneness.

That אֶחָד fundamentally carries the idea of a compound unity is seen in Gen. 27:44, וְיָשַׁבְתָּ עִמּוֹ יָמִים אֲחָדִים עַד אֲשֶׁר־תָּשׁוּב חֲמַת אָחִיךָ "And tarry with him a few days, until thy brother's fury turn away." The word translated "few" is אֲחָדִים which is the plural form of אֶחָד. Here the period of time elapsing until Esau's wrath subsided is considered as a unity consisting of integral parts, the idea of unity being expressed by the fundamental inherent idea of אֲחָדִים. It is put in the plural form to agree grammatically with the word יָמִים "days." The same usage appears again in 29:20 where seven years of time are thought of as a very short period, the unity of the period being expressed by the inherent idea of the same word, whereas it, like the illustration just mentioned, is in the plural number agreeing with "days" which is in the plural. Therefore these two examples show clearly that אֶחָד primarily means a compound unity.

Another illustration of this usage is found in Ezra 2:64. כָּל־הַקָּהָל כְּאֶחָד "And the whole assembly was as one" (Author's Tr.). Here forty-two thousand, three hundred and sixty people, each an individual and integral part of the gathering, were כְּאֶחָד "as one"—a unity. Another example where the fundamental idea of the word stands forth clearly is found in Gen. 11:1. וַיְהִי כָל־הָאָרֶץ שָׂפָה אֶחָת וּדְבָרִים אֲחָדִים: "And the whole earth was of one language and of one kind of words"; (literally translated) "one lip and oneness of words." Here the idea is that each person in the world spoke the same language and used the same words. There were many different people, and at the same time numerous words used by these various individuals, and yet all taken together constituted a unity אֶחָת, (feminine form of word) of language. Hence in this passage the original inherent idea shines forth vividly. Another striking example of this primitive idea is found in Ezek. 37:17.   וְקָרַב אֹתָם אֶחָד אֶל־אֶחָד לְךָ לְעֵץ אֶחָד וְהָיוּ לַאֲחָדִים בְּיָדֶךָ: "And joining them one to the other unto thee as one stick; and they shall become one in thy hand" (Isaac Leeser Tr.). From the context one sees that Ezekiel performed a symbolic act, namely, he took two separate sticks, one representing Judah, and the other representing Israel, and was commanded to join them into one bundle. Thus the two separate sticks being joined together are spoken of as a unity אֶחָד of sticks, that is, a union of the two separate sticks. This symbolic act symbolizes the fact that at some future time the two kingdoms of Israel and Judah will be joined and will constitute a single united kingdom.

Another most forceful illustration of this unity is found in Jer. 32:39 וְנָתַתִּי לָהֶם לֵב אֶחָד וְדֶרֶךְ אֶחָד לְיִרְאָה אוֹתִי כָּל־הַיָּמִים לְטוֹב לָהֶם וְלִבְנֵיהֶם אַחֲרֵיהֶם: "And I will give them one heart and one way, that they may fear me for ever, for the good of them, and of their children after them." Under the new covenant all Israel are promised "one heart" לֵב אֶחָד, that is, all will see, think, and feel alike: hence לֵב אֶחָד "unity of heart."

Since אֱלֹהֵינוּ grammatically can mean nothing but "our Gods," and since אֶחָד has as its primary meaning that of "unity," one is forced to the irresistible conclusion that the real meaning of Israel's Great Confession is that the Divine Personalities, who are referred to by the plural noun אֱלֹהֵינוּ, as has been shown above, constitute a real unity אֶחָד, just as man and woman form a unity אֶחָד. These Divine Personalities are one in essence, being, and nature, unity and co-operation in the highest degree existing between them. Such, fundamentally, is the real meaning of this fundamental dogma of Israel.

Proof which corroborates this interpretation of Israel's Great Confession is found in the fact that when the nation lapsed into idolatry and her inspired prophets endeavored to win her back to God, they emphasized the truth that there is but one God. In all of their utterances concerning the proposition that there is but one God, they never did use their great confession. *If it means what it is usually understood to mean, namely, that God is one in the absolute sense of the term, then it is unthinkable that the prophets never did use it in their fight against idolatry. Therefore, they understood it to refer to God's unity and not to His being One in the absolute sense.*

At the time that Moses gave this great confession he fore-warned Israel concerning other gods as is seen in Deut. 4:35, אַתָּה הָרְאֵתָ לָדַעַת כִּי יְהוָה הוּא הָאֱלֹהִים אֵין עוֹד מִלְּבַדּוֹ: "Thou hast been shown in order that thou mayest know that יְהוָה is the Gods; there is not any beside Him" (Author's Tr. here and in following one.). Again, in Deut. 4:39: וְיָדַעְתָּ הַיּוֹם וַהֲשֵׁבֹתָ אֶל־לְבָבֶךָ כִּי יְהוָה הוּא הָאֱלֹהִים בַּשָּׁמַיִם מִמַּעַל וְעַל־הָאָרֶץ מִתָּחַת אֵין עוֹד "And thou shalt know this day and shalt lay it to thine heart that יְהוָה is the Gods in the Heavens from above and upon the earth from beneath; there is none other."

The flood tide of idolatry seemed to reach its height in Israel in the days of Isaiah, the prophet, who was a contemporary of Uzziah, Jotham, Ahaz and Hezekiah. In his combating this error he constantly used the arguments based upon the Scriptures quoted in the last paragraph. Thus in Isa. 44:6 כֹּה־אָמַר יְהוָה

מֶלֶךְ־יִשְׂרָאֵל וְגֹאֲלוֹ יְהוָה צְבָאוֹת אֲנִי רִאשׁוֹן וַאֲנִי אַחֲרוֹן וּמִבַּלְעָדַי אֵין
אֱלֹהִים: "Thus saith the LORD, the King of Israel, and his Redeemer, the LORD of hosts; I am the first, and I am the last; and besides me there are no gods" (Author's Tr.). Verse 7 וּמִי־כָמוֹנִי יִקְרָא וְיַגִּידֶהָ וְיַעְרְכֶהָ לִי מִשּׂוּמִי עַם־עוֹלָם וְאֹתִיּוֹת וַאֲשֶׁר תָּבֹאנָה יַגִּידוּ לָמוֹ: "And who, as I, shall call, and shall declare it, and set it in order for me, since I established the ancient people? and the things that are coming, and that shall come to pass, let them declare." Verse 8 וְאַתֶּם עֵדַי הֲיֵשׁ אֱלוֹהַּ מִבַּלְעָדַי וְאֵין צוּר בַּל־יָדָעְתִּי: "And ye are my witnesses. Is there a God besides me? yea, there is no Rock; I know not any." Again, one sees Isaiah using a similar statement (Isa. 45:5) which, likewise, is based upon Deut. 4:35, 39, namely, אֲנִי יְהוָה וְאֵין עוֹד זוּלָתִי אֵין אֱלֹהִים "I am יְהוָה and there is none else; besides me there are no gods." Isa. 45:6, 7 לְמַעַן יֵדְעוּ מִמִּזְרַח־שֶׁמֶשׁ וּמִמַּעֲרָבָה כִּי־אֶפֶס בִּלְעָדַי אֲנִי יְהוָה וְאֵין עוֹד: יוֹצֵר אוֹר וּבוֹרֵא חֹשֶׁךְ עֹשֶׂה שָׁלוֹם וּבוֹרֵא רָע אֲנִי יְהוָה עֹשֶׂה כָל־אֵלֶּה: "In order that they may know from the rising of the sun and from the West, that there is none beside me; I am יְהוָה and there is none else; forming the light and creating darkness; making peace and creating evil; I am יְהוָה who doeth all these things." Again, in vs. 21, 22 one reads as follows: הַגִּידוּ וְהַגִּישׁוּ אַף יִוָּעֲצוּ יַחְדָּו מִי הִשְׁמִיעַ זֹאת מִקֶּדֶם מֵאָז הִגִּידָהּ הֲלוֹא אֲנִי יְהוָה וְאֵין־עוֹד אֱלֹהִים מִבַּלְעָדַי אֵל־צַדִּיק וּמוֹשִׁיעַ אַיִן זוּלָתִי: פְּנוּ־ אֵלַי וְהִוָּשְׁעוּ כָּל־אַפְסֵי־אָרֶץ כִּי אֲנִי־אֵל וְאֵין עוֹד: "Declare and bring forth, yet let them take counsel together; who hath shown this from ancient times? Who hath declared it from old? Is it not I, and there are still no gods beside me: a God righteous and one who delivers; there is not any beside me. Turn unto me and be ye saved, all ye ends of the earth; for I am God and there is none else" (Author's Tr., 45:21, 22). Once more, note the argument in Isa. 64:4 (3). וּמֵעוֹלָם לֹא־שָׁמְעוּ לֹא הֶאֱזִינוּ עַיִן לֹא־רָאָתָה אֱלֹהִים זוּלָתְךָ יַעֲשֶׂה לִמְחַכֵּה־לוֹ: "And from of old, men have not heard nor have they perceived with their ears, and eye hath not seen Gods beside thee, who work for the one waiting for him." As a last quotation from

Isaiah, note Chapter 26:13. יְהוָֹה אֱלֹהֵינוּ בְּעָלוּנוּ אֲדֹנִים זוּלָתֶךָ
לְבַד־בְּךָ נַזְכִּיר שְׁמֶךָ: "Oh Lord, our Gods, other lords besides
thee have had dominion over us, but by thee only will we make
mention of thy name" (Author's Tr.).

Hosea, whose ministry preceded that of Isaiah by some thirty-
odd years, combated idolatry as did his successors. In Hos. 13:4
one reads וְאָנֹכִי יְהוָֹה אֱלֹהֶיךָ מֵאֶרֶץ מִצְרָיִם וֵאלֹהִים זוּלָתִי לֹא
תֵדָע וּמוֹשִׁיעַ אַיִן בִּלְתִּי: "And I am the Lord thy Gods from the
land of Egypt; and you shall not know gods besides me, there is
no savior besides me" (Author's Tr.).

From the above quotations it is clear how the prophets met
the problem of idolatry and what statements of the Torah they
used to teach the lesson that there is but one true and living
God. Since they nowhere used the language of the Great Confession in their hard fight for monotheism (the teaching that
there is but one God), it is quite evident that they, *who were
guided and aided by the Lord, and to whom the Word of the
Lord came, understood that it had no bearing on the issue*. The
prophets knew how to use the Word of God, as one sees from
many illustrations which appear in their writings. Hence one
must conclude that a forced meaning has been placed upon it, and
that evidently the plain and obvious meaning of the words conveys
the correct teaching, which is, as stated above, that the Divine
Personalities revealed to Israel at Sinai constitute a Unity though
a Plurality.

Another group of facts supports the conclusions to which one
comes concerning the proposition that an erroneous interpretation
has been forced upon this Great Confession. One of these facts
is that יָחִיד is used which primarily, as an adverb, means "only,
altogether, surely" in numerous passages where everything is ex-
cluded, except the point at issue. Likewise, רַק is a synonym of
יָחִיד. Another word which commonly was used to emphasize the
idea of one to the exclusion of all others is that of בִּלְתִּי. An
excellent illustration of this usage is found in Ex. 22:20 (19)
זֹבֵחַ לָאֱלֹהִים יָחֳרָם בִּלְתִּי לַיהוָֹה לְבַדּוֹ: "He that sacrificeth
unto any gods save unto יְהוָֹה only shall be utterly destroyed."
אַף also is used with this same significance. These words, just

mentioned, are the usual ones to emphasize the idea that there is but one of the persons or things mentioned; hence one arrives at the conclusion that had Moses meant to teach by the Great Confession the doctrine that there is but one Divine Personality, he would have expressed himself differently and would have used one of the regular words, in its proper construction, that excludes from consideration all others except the true God whose existence and nature he proclaimed. Since he did not choose such a restrictive word, evidently he was not affirming God's oneness in the absolute sense.

II. Unity Seen in the Expression "In Our Image"

This unity is again seen in the quotation, already used, from Gen. 1:26 where it is said, "Let us make man in our image, after our likeness." In the words "image" and "likeness" is reflected the same unity, which words are in the singular number, since the speaker and the one spoken to are of the same image and likeness. These words could not truthfully be spoken to a being inferior to or less than God, the speaker.

III. Unity Seen In Expression אֶל אֱלֹהִים

From another angle the unity of the plurality of Divine Personalities may be seen in Gen. 33:20. Here appears a record of Jacob's erecting an altar at Bethel after his sojourn in Syria, which is stated in the following words: וַיַּצֶּב־שָׁם מִזְבֵּחַ וַיִּקְרָא־לוֹ אֵל אֱלֹהֵי יִשְׂרָאֵל׃ "And he erected there an altar, and called it El-Elohe-Israel." אֵל is in the singular number and means God, the Mighty One; אֱלֹהֵי is in the plural number, as noted above; hence the combination of the words, אֵל אֱלֹהֵי יִשְׂרָאֵל affirms the unity and the plurality of God at the same time. Again, the unity of the plurality of God is seen in the Second Commandment (Ex. 20:5). כִּי אָנֹכִי יְהוָה אֱלֹהֶיךָ אֵל קַנָּא פֹּקֵד יְהוָה "For I am עֲוֹן אָבֹת עַל־בָּנִים עַל־שִׁלֵּשִׁים וְעַל־רִבֵּעִים לְשֹׂנְאָי׃ thy Gods, אֵל קַנָּא a jealous God, visiting the iniquity of fathers upon sons, unto the third and fourth generation of them that hate Me" (Author's Tr.).

In one word אֱלֹהֶיךָ, thy Gods, the Lord speaks of His plurality and at the same time of His unity in His use of the word אֵל. The plurality and the unity of God's nature again is seen in a won-

derful statement made by the Israelites who settled on the East side
of the Jordan and who were upbraided by their kinsmen on
the West side for having set up a memorial altar, in the following
quotation (Josh. 22:22): אֵל אֱלֹהִים יְהוָה אֵל אֱלֹהִים יְהוָה הוּא
"God, Gods, the יֹדֵעַ וְיִשְׂרָאֵל הוּא יֵדַע אִם־בְּמֶרֶד וְאִם־בְּמַעַל בַּיהוָה
Lord, God, Gods, the Lord, He knoweth, and Israel he shall know;
if it be in rebellion, or in treachery against the Lord" (Author's Lit.
Tr.). The word אֵל declares God's unity, but אֱלֹהִים, which is in
apposition with it, affirms the plurality of the Divine Being, while
יְהוָה identifies this unity of Divine Personalities as the Covenant
God of Israel (Ex. 6:2,3). In the "Ten Commandments" God
says כִּי אָנֹכִי יְהוָה אֱלֹהֶיךָ אֵל קַנָּא "For I am the Lord thy Gods,
a jealous God." Here the plural and singular forms appear, the
former emphasizing the plurality of Divine Personalities while
the latter predicates their unity.

IV. Unity Seen In the Use of a Singular Verb With a Plural Noun

Another fact corroborating the unity of Divine Personalities
is the use in the Hebrew of the singular verb with the plural noun
אֱלֹהִים. Examples of this usage are seen throughout the entire
Tenach. For many illustrations, however, see Gen. 1. בְּרֵאשִׁית
בָּרָא אֱלֹהִים "In the beginning created Gods." This quotation
serves sufficiently to make the point clear.

CONCLUSION

The question doubtless has arisen in the mind of the reader:
Why, if Israel's confession is to be correctly translated, "Hear,
O Israel, the Lord our Gods is the Lord a unity," has Israel
throughout the centuries understood it to mean that God is one
in the absolute sense instead of a compound unity?

Prior to the days of Moses Maimonides, the unity of God was
expressed by אֶחָד which, as has been proved beyond a doubt,
has as its primary meaning that of a compound unity. Maimonides, who drafted the thirteen articles of faith, in the second
one sets forth the unity of God, using the word יָחִיד which in the
Tenach is never used to express God's unity. This word occurs

in twelve passages that the reader may examine for himself, which investigation will prove conclusively that it carries the idea of absolute oneness (Gen. 22:2, 12, 16; Amos 8:10; Jer. 6:26; Zech. 12:10; Prov. 4:3; Judg. 11:34; Psa. 22:20(21), 35:17; 25:16; and 68:6(7). From these facts it is evident that a new idea was injected into this confession by substituting יָחִיד which in every passage carries the primary idea of oneness in the absolute sense for אָחָד which primarily means a compound unity. Hence from the days of Maimonides on, an interpretation different from the ancient one was placed upon this most important passage. In the language of Jeremiah let the writer plead with every Hebrew reader, "Thus saith the Lord, Stand ye in the ways and see, and ask for the old paths, where is the good way; and walk therein, and ye shall find rest for your souls" (Jer. 6:16).

כֹּה אָמַר יְהֹוָה עִמְדוּ עַל־דְּרָכִים וּרְאוּ וְשַׁאֲלוּ לִנְתִבוֹת עוֹלָם אֵי־זֶה דֶרֶךְ הַטּוֹב וּלְכוּ־בָהּ וּמִצְאוּ מַרְגּוֹעַ לְנַפְשְׁכֶם וַיֹּאמְרוּ לֹא נֵלֵךְ: There-fore let Israel now return to the original meaning of her Great Confession: "Hear, O Israel! the Lord Our Gods, is the Lord a Unity."

Some people have had difficulty concerning the doctrine of the plurality and unity of the divine Personalities. The great theologian, Dr. Theodore Christlieb, stated the problem tersely in the following words:

"The objections stirred by these might have been avoided by anticipation, had a firm hold been taken from the first of the truth indicated by the Hebrew form of the divine name ELOHIM (as will be more fully shown presently), that in God unity and plurality consist as correlatives which mutually require one another; that, as we have already indicated, it is the essential characteristic of the true doctrine of the divine nature, in contradistinction to Polytheism on the one hand, and an abstract Monotheism on the other, that both elements of true Being, unicity and multiplicity, do in God meet and interpenetrate one another in a perfectly unique and transcendental way."

CHAPTER V

THE TRINITY OF GOD

HAVING seen in the preceding chapter that, though there is a plurality of Divine Personalities, they are one in nature and essence, let us now continue this investigation to ascertain, if possible, how many persons are mentioned in the Tenach.

I. THE SPIRIT OF GOD

In Gen. 1:1, 2 appear the words אֱלֹהִים and וְרוּחַ אֱלֹהִים. The first word refers to a plurality of Divine Persons, and the second expression singles out one of these and states the special work which He did. In Job 26:13 appears the following statement: בְּרוּחוֹ שָׁמַיִם שִׁפְרָה "By His Spirit the heavens are garnished." In this passage the personality of the Spirit is clearly seen. The Spirit of God is not an influence emanating from God as heat goes forth from fire, or coldness from ice; but is one of the Divine Personalities active in creation. In Psa. 51:11(13) David in his pleading for mercy and restoration to God's favor prayed, וְרוּחַ קָדְשְׁךָ אַל־תִּקַּח מִמֶּנִּי: "And take not Thy Holy Spirit from me." The Holy Spirit was dwelling in his heart "To revive the spirit of the humble and to revive the heart of the contrite" (Isa. 57:15). Once more, the personality of the Spirit may be seen in Isa. 11:1, 2, which is a passage concerning the מָשִׁיחַ Messiah. וְיָצָא חֹטֶר מִגֵּזַע יִשָׁי וְנֵצֶר מִשָּׁרָשָׁיו יִפְרֶה: וְנָחָה עָלָיו רוּחַ יְהֹוָה רוּחַ חָכְמָה וּבִינָה רוּחַ עֵצָה וּגְבוּרָה רוּחַ דַּעַת וְיִרְאַת יְהֹוָה: "And there shall come forth a shoot out of the stock of Jesse, and a branch out of his roots shall bear fruit, and the Spirit of the Lord shall rest upon him, the spirit of wisdom and understanding, the spirit of counsel and might, the spirit of knowledge and of the fear of the Lord." Here the prophet speaks of the Spirit of the Lord in terms of that which He does for and through the Messiah. Since to the Spirit are ascribed the very elements of personality—wisdom, understanding, counsel, might, knowledge and fear—the only conclusion to which one can reasonably come is that the Spirit mentioned here is the Spirit of God, a Divine Personality. That the Spirit is God, hence omniscient

41

and omnipresent is clearly set forth in Psa. 139:7, אָנָה אֵלֵךְ מֵרוּחֶךָ,
וְאָנָה מִפָּנֶיךָ אֶבְרָח: "Whither shall I go from thy Spirit? or
whither shall I flee from thy presence."

II. THE SON OF GOD

Another one of these Divine Beings is addressed as "my son" by
the Lord God of Israel. In Psa. 2 the writer, David, in order to
support the prediction that God will enthrone King Messiah upon
His holy hill of Zion, quoted a decree which the God of Israel spoke
to one whom He addressed as His son, which decree is as follows:
אֲסַפְּרָה אֶל־חֹק יְהֹוָה אָמַר אֵלַי בְּנִי אַתָּה אֲנִי הַיּוֹם יְלִדְתִּיךָ: שְׁאַל
מִמֶּנִּי וְאֶתְּנָה גוֹיִם נַחֲלָתֶךָ וַאֲחֻזָּתְךָ אַפְסֵי־אָרֶץ: תְּרֹעֵם בְּשֵׁבֶט בַּרְזֶל
כִּכְלִי יוֹצֵר תְּנַפְּצֵם: "The Lord said unto me, Thou art my son;
this day have I begotten thee. Ask of me, and I will give thee
the nations for thine inheritance, and the uttermost parts of the
earth for thy possession. Thou shalt break them with a rod
of iron; thou shalt dash them in pieces like a potter's vessel."
Hence this language was addressed not to an angel, but to the
Son of God.

According to parallel passages the reign of Messiah is to be
one of universal righteousness, justice, and peace (see Isa. 11
and parallel passages). Since He whom God calls "my Son" will
administer such a universal righteous reign, it is evident that He
is not an ordinary man who is a faithful servant of God, for no
man (even though he be a son of God in the sense of his being
a faithful servant of God), regardless of his qualifications intellectually, morally and spiritually, can administer a kingdom
in which absolute righteousness and justice is dealt out to everyone. The truthfulness of this statement is borne out by the
stubborn facts of history. Therefore this One whom God terms
"my Son" is THE SON OF GOD in a unique and peculiar
sense, the Son of God par excellence. This conclusion is cor-
roborated by other statements of this Psalm and parallel passages.
As will be seen in Psalm 2:1-3, in the "end time" there will be
a confederacy or a United States of nations. The peoples of
the world will oppose the worship of the God of the Hebrews
and the Messiah of the Christians. The governments of the

world will use all of their resources in order to enforce a reso-
lution, which shall be adopted by a world congress, to blot out
both Judaism and Christianity from the globe. Since man is
"incurably religious" he will have a ready substitute to take their
place which, doubtless, will be the worship of man, the beginnings
of which spiritually-minded Bible students for a number of years
have seen slowly but surely developing. The world consolidated
politically and economically, headed up into one mighty, colossal
organization and entrenched in its position by modern science
and "a knowledge, falsely so-called " together with a philosophy
and religion made to order, constitutes a most formidable antag-
onist to Him whom God calls "my Son."

In addition to the outward, visible organization of world power,
from other portions of the Tenach one learns that there is a
supernatural world of evil, malignant spirits under the leadership
of Satan, who inspires and instigates all opposition against God
and the people of God. The truthfulness of this position is seen
in the contest which Moses, the great law-giver, had with the
magicians of Egypt (Ex. 7-13). These magicians actually at
first duplicated the miracles of Moses, not by sleight-of-hand
tricks, nor wisdom, but by Satanic power. For instance, their
rods became serpents just as really as Moses' rod became a serpent.
Again, in answer to Daniel's prayer an angel was dispatched by
the Lord to him, who was delayed twenty-one days by "the
prince of the kingdom of Persia," and was not permitted to continue his journey until Michael, one of the chief princes, came
to his rescue (Dan. 10). From Psa. 106:34-38 one sees that
all idolatry, which is in opposition to the worship of the true God,
is inspired by demons. Again, from Isa. 24:21 it is evident that
there is a host of evil spirits who are opposed to God: "And
it shall come to pass in that day, that the Lord will punish the
hosts of the high ones on high, and the kings of the earth upon
the earth." The leader of this host is undoubtedly "the anointed
cherub" who was cast out of the presence of God, who is a most
bitter enemy of God, and who raises up opposition to Him on
every occasion.

The combined forces of Satan and his innumerable hosts of
servile spirits, uniting with the forces and resources of the world

confederacy, constitute the most amazing array of power against
God with which no human being can possibly, under any conditions, cope successfully. Only the Omnipotent God can handle
such a situation. Hence since he whom God calls "my son," at
whose right hand the Eternal God goes forth (Psa. 110:5-7),
does successfully overthrow and demolish such titanic opposition,
he is none other than one of the divine persons referred to by
אֱלֹהִים "Gods."*

In this connection the question arises "If the one referred to
by the expression 'my Son' is God, why is He called God's Son?"
This is indeed an intelligible question. The mention of "Son"
suggests the correlative term "Father." Humanly speaking, a
father is older than his son, but, as seen from the preceding argument, THE SON OF GOD is one of the Divine Personalities;
hence the Son co-existed with the Father from all eternity (Mic.
5:2). This fact being true, in what sense is He a Son? The
only interpretation, which to the writer appears to harmonize
with all of the data and which does not conflict with any Scriptural
teaching, is that the terms "Father" and "Son" are used, not to
express the relationship existing between these two Divine Persons
in the beginning, but are terms, adapted to man's understanding,
to express the relationship existing between them from the time
of the fulfillment and onward of the promise, "For unto us a child
is born, unto us a son is given; and the government shall be
upon his shoulder: and his name shall be called Wonderful,
Counsellor, Mighty God, Everlasting Father, Prince of Peace."
Therefore Isaiah, in this passage, looking forward toward the
future said that the Eternal God would come to earth and be
born in the form of a child. His birth is not according to
natural generation, but, according to Isa. 7:14, "Behold the virgin

---

*In this connection it is well to consider a counter interpretation which
is frequently placed upon this passage, namely, that the one addressed "Thou
art my son" is any faithful servant of God. In reply to this position it is
sufficient to note the fact that if the expression "my son" means any and
all of the righteous servants of God, then there will be many sons who will
have universal sway over the world. This conclusion, however, is contrary
to the teaching, not only of Psa. 2, but of all of the Tenach. In verse 6,
the expression "my king" refers to one, and it is to him that universal,
absolute authority is given. There can be but one absolute monarch at any
one time; therefore the interpretation under investigation conflicts with the
teaching of the passage. Hence it is incorrect.

shall conceive and shall bear a son and shall call his name
Immanuel," it is supernatural. All men have natural fathers
and mothers, but the Everlasting God in being born of the virgin
does not have an earthly father but is begotten by the miraculous
power of one of these Divine Eternal Persons; hence strictly
speaking, He, the GOD-MAN, is the Son of God. The inspired
writer in Prov. 30:4 had this same GOD-MAN in view when
he asked the following question: מַה־שְּׁמוֹ וּמַה־שֶּׁם־בְּנוֹ כִּי תֵדָע׃
"What is his name, and what is his son's name, if thou knowest?"

III. The Angel of the Lord

In Gen. 16, there appears an account of the appearance of
מַלְאַךְ יְהֹוָה "the angel of the Lord" to Hagar, the handmaid
of Sarah, when she had been driven away by her mistress. In
verse 7 this Divine Person is called מַלְאַךְ יְהֹוָה "angel of the
Lord"; but in verse 13 Moses makes the following statement:
"And she called the name of the Lord that spake unto her, THOU
ART A GOD THAT SEETH: for she said, Have I even here
looked after him that seeth me?" Moses here says that Hagar
called the Name of the Lord Who spoke with her "Thou art a
God that seeth." It is clear from what Moses says that this
angel of the Lord was none other than one of the Divine Beings.
Again, in the eighteenth chapter one reads of another marvelous appearance of God. In verse 1 the statement is made,
וַיֵּרָא אֵלָיו יְהֹוָה בְּאֵלֹנֵי מַמְרֵא "and the Lord appeared unto him
(Abraham) by the oaks of Mamre"; in verse 2 one reads, "three
men stood over against him." Abraham immediately ran from
the tent door to meet them and addressed them as אֲדֹנָי "Lord."
This term, as is known to all Hebrew scholars, is one of the
Divine Names. After the usual oriental hospitality had been
extended to the visitors, the Lord יְהֹוָה said, "I will certainly
return unto thee when the season cometh round; and, lo, Sarah
thy wife shall have a son." Sarah in unbelief laughed at the
idea, because of which conduct the Lord said unto Abraham,
"Wherefore did Sarah laugh, saying, Shall I of a surety bear a
child, who am old? Is anything too hard for the Lord יְהֹוָה? At
the set time I will return unto thee, when the season cometh round,
and Sarah shall have a son." From this quotation it is quite clear

that the speaker was the Lord יְהוָֹה who promised to return a year hence and to grant to Abraham and Sarah a son. וַיֹּאמֶר יְהוָֹה אֶל־אַבְרָהָם לָמָּה זֶּה צָחֲקָה שָׂרָה "And the Lord said unto Abraham, Wherefore did Sarah laugh?" Furthermore, He asked the question concerning Himself, "Is anything too hard for יְהוָֹה the Lord?"

In the last verse of the chapter appears the statement, "And the Lord יְהוָֹה went his way, as soon as he had left off communing with Abraham." From these facts is drawn the irresistible conclusion that one of these supernatural individuals who appeared in human form on this occasion was one of the self-existing Divine Personalities, one of the אֱלֹהִים "Gods."

The fact of the appearance of one of the Divine Personalities for the purpose of communicating with Abraham His friend, shows the possibility of His assuming human form whenever the occasion arises. Again, in Ex. 3 the Angel of יְהוָֹה "the Lord" appears to Moses in the wilderness in the burning bush. In verse 2 He is called מַלְאַךְ יְהוָֹה "the Angel of the Lord," but in verse 4 this statement occurs: "And when the Lord יְהוָֹה saw that he turned aside to see, אֱלֹהִים (God) called unto him out of the midst of the bush and said, 'Moses, Moses.'" In verse 2 the One appearing to Moses is called מַלְאַךְ יְהוָֹה "Angel of the Lord," but in the latter statement He is called both יְהוָֹה "Lord" and אֱלֹהִים "God." This identification of the Angel of the Lord with the יְהוָֹה "Lord" and אֱלֹהִים "God" is confirmed by the fact that this Angel of the Lord in speaking of His appearance to Moses said, "that they may believe that יְהוָֹה Lord, the God of their fathers, the God of Abraham, the God of Isaac, and the God of Jacob, hath appeared unto thee" (Ex. 4:5).

In Mal. 3:1,2: "Behold, I send my messenger, and he shall prepare the way before me: and הָאָדוֹן the Lord, whom ye seek, will suddenly come to his temple; and the messenger of the covenant, whom ye desire, behold, he cometh, saith the Lord of Hosts." The prophet, in the first place, predicts that the messenger of the Lord shall precede Him and prepare the way for Him; and, secondly, that He, הָאָדוֹן the Lord, will suddenly come to His temple. The messenger who goes before the face of the Lord and prepares His way is undoubtedly Elijah the prophet who is mentioned in the last two verses of Malachi's prophecy. When Elijah prepares the way, the Lord comes suddenly to His temple. As to who is referred to by הָאָדוֹן *"Lord,"* there is no doubt that he is speaking of one of the Divine Persons; but who is meant by the expression מַלְאַךְ הַבְּרִית "Angel of the Covenant?" If the law of Hebrew parallelism obtains here, the answer is plain, namely, that the names "Lord" and "Angel of the Covenant" refer to the same personality. The flow of thought points definitely and positively to the conclusion that such is the case; hence only one individual is here spoken of. From the facts which have been learned from the passages in which the מַלְאַךְ יְהוָה "angel of the Lord" occurs, there is but one conclusion to be drawn, namely, that this "angel of the Lord" is one of the Divine Persons.

IV. THE LORD GOD

Throughout the Tenach appear the words אֲדֹנָי יְהוָֹה which, from the context in which they appear, refer also to one of these Divine Persons. Furthermore, one of these Personalities is sometimes addressed as הָאָדוֹן "the Lord."

V. THE TRINITY OF DIVINE PERSONALITIES

Thus far one has seen that the following names, *the Lord, the Lord God, Spirit of God, Son of God,* and *the Angel of the Lord* are applied to one or more of these Divine Personalities. With these facts in mind the reader may advance a step by investigating Isa. 48:12-16. שְׁמַע אֵלַי יַעֲקֹב וְיִשְׂרָאֵל מְקֹרָאִי אֲנִי־הוּא אֲנִי רִאשׁוֹן אַף אֲנִי אַחֲרוֹן׃אַף־יָדִי יָסְדָה אֶרֶץ וִימִינִי טִפְּחָה שָׁמָיִם קֹרֵא אֲנִי אֲלֵיהֶם יַעַמְדוּ יַחְדָּו׃הִקָּבְצוּ כֻלְּכֶם וּשְׁמָעוּ מִי בָהֶם הִגִּיד אֶת־אֵלֶּה יְהוָֹה אֲהֵבוֹ יַעֲשֶׂה חֶפְצוֹ בְּבָבֶל וּזְרֹעוֹ כַּשְׂדִּים: אֲנִי אֲנִי דִבַּרְתִּי אַף־קְרָאתִיו הֲבִאֹתִיו וְהִצְלִיחַ דַּרְכּוֹ: קִרְבוּ אֵלַי שִׁמְעוּ־זֹאת לֹא מֵרֹאשׁ בַּסֵּתֶר דִּבַּרְתִּי מֵעֵת הֱיוֹתָהּ שָׁם אָנִי וְעַתָּה אֲדֹנָי יְהוָֹה שְׁלָחַנִי וְרוּחוֹ: "Hearken unto me, O Jacob, and Israel my called: I am he; I am the first, I also am the last. Yea, my hand hath laid the foundation of the earth, and my right hand hath spread out the heavens:

when I call unto them, they stand up together. Assemble yourselves, all ye, and hear : who among them hath declared these things?
He whom the Lord loveth shall perform his pleasure on Babylon,
and his arm *shall be on* the Chaldeans. I, even I, have spoken;
yea, I have called him; I have brought him, and he shall make
his way prosperous. Come ye near unto me, hear ye this; from
the beginning I have not spoken in secret; from the time that
it was, there am I : and now the Lord God hath sent me, and
his Spirit." Here are three Divine Beings: אֲדֹנָי יְהֹוָה "the Lord
God"; שְׁלָחַנִי (sent) "Me" (the speaker Who has created the
universe) ; and רוּחוֹ: "His Spirit." As to the divine nature of
the first one mentioned there can be no doubt. The speaker
refers to Himself as "Me" since the Lord God hath sent Him.
"Me" is attached to the verb of which "the Lord God" is the
subject, and as has already been seen, the context shows that He
(the speaker) created the world; hence He is God, since other
passages ascribed the creation of the world to God. The third one
is the Spirit of God, and, as seen above, possesses all the
characteristics of God; hence is the third of the Divine Beings.

The three Divine Persons forming the Trinity again appear in
Isa. 63 :8-10. וַיֹּאמֶר אַךְ־עַמִּי הֵמָּה בָּנִים לֹא יְשַׁקֵּרוּ וַיְהִי לָהֶם לְמוֹשִׁיעַ:
בְּכָל־צָרָתָם לֹא צָר וּמַלְאַךְ פָּנָיו הוֹשִׁיעָם בְּאַהֲבָתוֹ וּבְחֶמְלָתוֹ הוּא
גְאָלָם וַיְנַטְּלֵם וַיְנַשְּׂאֵם כָּל־יְמֵי עוֹלָם: וְהֵמָּה מָרוּ וְעִצְּבוּ אֶת־רוּחַ קָדְשׁוֹ
וַיֵּהָפֵךְ לָהֶם לְאוֹיֵב הוּא נִלְחַם־בָּם: "For he said, Surely, they are my
people, children that will not deal falsely : so he was their Savior.
In all their affliction he was afflicted, and the angel of his presence
saved them : in his love and in his pity he redeemed them; and
he bare them, and carried them all the days of old. But they
rebelled, and grieved his holy Spirit : therefore he was turned
to be their enemy, *and* himself fought against them." In verse 8
the prophet refers to what the Lord God said concerning Israel's
being His people. In verse 9 he states that "the angel of His
presence saved them." As seen in the preceding section, the
angel of the Lord is one of the Divine Personalities. In Ex. 23 :
20, 21 appears the angel who was to go before Israel in the
journey to the promised land. This angel is none other than
"the angel of the Lord," for, said God, "My Name is in Him."

To proclaim the Name of God is to set forth God's wonderful character (Ex. 34:6,7). Hence when God said that His Name was in this angel He was simply declaring that the angel was not an ordinary created being, but one of the Divine Personalities. In referring to this same Divine Person God said, "My presence shall go with thee and I will give thee rest. And he said unto Him, if Thy presence go not with me, carry us not up hence" (Ex. 33:14, 15). Therefore the angel of His Presence in the passage which is under consideration is one of these Divine Persons. In verse 10 the prophet said that Israel "rebelled, and grieved His Holy Spirit," Who, as seen above, is a Divine Person; hence this passage likewise teaches that there are three Divine Persons Who constitute a *Unity*.

The doctrine of the Trinity is not, therefore, a doctrine which the Christians have imagined and formulated but is the clear teaching of the Tenach. Not only do the Jewish Scriptures teach the doctrine of the Trinity, but a thoughtful consideration of the second article of the "Thirteen Principles of the Faith" to which Judaism subscribes shows that the unity of God is not an ordinary unity, for it states that "The Creator, blessed be His Name, is a Unity, and that there is no unity in any manner like unto His, and that He alone is our God, Who was, is, and will be." The word "Unity" in this article of faith does not affirm oneness in the absolute sense, i. e., a oneness to the exclusion of all others, but it connotes a compound unity for it is different from unity in the absolute sense, since there are millions of illustrations of unity in the absolute sense.

Furthermore, Zohar, in commenting on Deut. 6:4, says, "Hear, oh Israel, Jehovah our God, Jehovah is One," saying, "Why is there need of mentioning the Name of God three times in this verse?" Then follows the answer, "The first Jehovah is the Father of all; the second is the Stem of Jesse, the Messiah, Who is to come from the family of Jesse through David; and the third One is the Way, Who is the Lord (meaning the Holy Spirit, Who shows us the way, as pointed out before), and these three are One." Likewise, Mr. Claude Montefiore, an eminent Hebrew, says, "I am well aware that in the purest and most philosophical presentation of the Christian doctrine of *Trinity* no infraction of the Divine Unity is intended. It will be needful for the Jewish theologians to consider anew the interpretation of the *Trinity*."

CHAPTER VI

GOD'S COMING TO EARTH

I. EARLY APPEARANCES OF THE LORD ON EARTH

HAVING seen in the preceding chapters that there is a plurality of Divine Personalities, but that they constitute a divine unity consisting of three personalities, the reader is now requested to advance a step further in this investigation to consider the predictions concerning one of these Divine Persons who is to assume human form in order to bless mankind. An excellent approach to this phase of the subject is the record of the appearance of מַלְאַךְ־יְהוָה "the angel of the Lord," of which occurrence appears the record in Ex. 3:1-4:17. In 3:2 Moses said, "And the angel of the Lord appeared unto him in a flame of fire out of the midst of a bush: and he looked, and, behold, the bush burned with fire, and the bush was not consumed." It is apparent to all that this fire was not ordinary fire but was a manifestation of supernatural power and glory. Being attracted by this unusual phenomenon, Moses turned aside to investigate the same. As he approached the bush, אֱלֹהִים "God called unto him out of the midst of the bush," to which call Moses responded, "Here am I." He who is called the "angel of the Lord" in verse 2 is called יְהוָה "the Lord" and אֱלֹהִים "God" in verse 4. Having instructed Moses to remove his shoes, this angel of the Lord said to Moses, "I am the God of thy father, the God of Abraham, the God of Isaac, and the God of Jacob." The continuity of thought demands that one understand that the "angel of the Lord" is the God of Abraham, Isaac and Jacob. Continuing this conversation, according to verse 13, Moses asked the Lord or Angel of the Lord, if the children of Israel should ask concerning who commissioned him and what is God's Name, what reply should he make to them? To the first question God said to tell them "I AM hath sent me unto you." To the second question He said, "I AM that I AM." Giving him further instructions as to what he should say, God said, according to verse 15, that Moses should tell them,

יְהֹוָה אֱלֹהֵי אֲבֹתֵיכֶם אֱלֹהֵי אַבְרָהָם אֱלֹהֵי יִצְחָק וֵאלֹהֵי יַעֲקֹב שְׁלָחַנִי
אֲלֵיכֶם זֶה־שְּׁמִי לְעֹלָם וְזֶה זִכְרִי לְדֹר דֹּר: "The Lord, the God of
your fathers, the God of Abraham, the God of Isaac, and the
God of Jacob, hath sent me unto you: this is my name for ever,
and this is my memorial unto all generations." With all of
this data in hand there can be no doubt in the mind of any that
this appearance of the angel in the bush amid the supernatural
flames was an appearance of one of the Divine Personalities who
claimed that he is the one whom Abraham, Isaac and Jacob worshipped.

II. Appearance of Divine Presence At the Exodus

When Moses delivered Israel from Egyptian bondage, "The
Lord went before them by day in a pillar of cloud, to lead them
the way, and by night in a pillar of fire, to give them light"
(Ex. 13:21). These pillars of cloud and of fire are again visible
manifestations of the Divine Presence with Israel. This fact
becomes more apparent from the language of Ex. 14:19, "And
the angel of God, who went before the camp of Israel, removed
and went behind them; and the pillar of cloud removed from
before them, and stood behind them." This same "angel of the
Lord" in verse 24 is called the Lord Himself: "And it came
to pass in the morning watch, that יְהֹוָה the Lord looked forth
upon the host of the Egyptians through the pillar of fire and of
cloud, and discomfited the host of the Egyptians."

This "angel of the Lord" who appeared both in the burning
bush and at the exodus from Egypt is called by Isaiah the Prophet
"the angel of His presence" מַלְאַךְ פָּנָיו in Isa. 63:9. "In all
their affliction he was afflicted, and the angel of his presence
saved them: in his love and in his pity he redeemed them; and
he bare them, and carried them all the days of old." This
verse without doubt summarizes God's dealings with Israel from
the time of the deliverance from Egyptian bondage onward. These
facts being true, "the angel of his פָּנָי presence" is the Lord
Himself. Why, one may ask, is this one called "the angel of
his presence" (or, "of his faces")? There can be but one reasonable, plausible answer, namely, he is thus called because "He is
the only face or personal manifestation of God which man"

had ever seen up to that time. Furthermore, since it is in the face that character—the real person—is reflected, and since this "Angel of the Lord" is, as seen above, the Lord Himself, He is in a figure called "the face of the Lord."

III. APPEARANCE OF DIVINE PRESENCE AT MT. SINAI

On another occasion the Lord revealed Himself in a thick cloud of smoke and flames of fire when He descended to the heights of Mount Sinai in order to give the "ten words." From the mountain height thunder pealed, lightning flashed, and there sounded forth the voice of a great trumpet waxing louder and louder.

וְהַר סִינַי עָשַׁן כֻּלּוֹ מִפְּנֵי אֲשֶׁר יָרַד עָלָיו יְהֹוָה בָּאֵשׁ וַיַּעַל עֲשָׁנוֹ כְּעֶשֶׁן הַכִּבְשָׁן וַיֶּחֱרַד כָּל־הָהָר מְאֹד: וַיְהִי קוֹל הַשֹּׁפָר הוֹלֵךְ וְחָזֵק מְאֹד מֹשֶׁה יְדַבֵּר וְהָאֱלֹהִים יַעֲנֶנּוּ בְקוֹל:

"And mount Sinai, the whole of it, smoked, because the Lord descended upon it in fire; and the smoke thereof ascended as the smoke of a furnace, and the whole mount quaked greatly. And when the voice of the trumpet waxed louder and louder, Moses spake, and God answered him by a voice" (Ex. 19:18, 19). Now, after Moses returned to the people from his interview with God on the mountain, the Lord spake the "ten words" as is recorded in Ex. 20:1-17. To confirm further the thought that God was in the midst of the cloud which descended upon Mount Sinai and from it spoke the "ten words," note the statement of Moses in Deut. 5:22(19).

אֶת־הַדְּבָרִים הָאֵלֶּה דִּבֶּר יְהֹוָה אֶל־כָּל־קְהַלְכֶם בָּהָר מִתּוֹךְ הָאֵשׁ הֶעָנָן וְהָעֲרָפֶל קוֹל גָּדוֹל וְלֹא יָסָף וַיִּכְתְּבֵם עַל־שְׁנֵי לֻחֹת אֲבָנִים וַיִּתְּנֵם אֵלָי:

"These words (the "ten words") the Lord spake unto all your assembly in the mount out of the midst of the fire, of the cloud, and of the thick darkness, with a great voice: and he added no more. And he wrote them upon two tables of stone, and gave them unto me." It was necessary for God to hide His real presence from mortal eyes lest man should die, as is stated in Deut. 5:23-27.

IV. APPEARANCE OF DIVINE PRESENCE IN THE TABERNACLE

Another instance of God's veiling Himself with His glory occurred when Moses had set up the tabernacle at Sinai.

וַיְכַס הֶעָנָן אֶת־אֹהֶל מוֹעֵד וּכְבוֹד יְהֹוָה מָלֵא אֶת־הַמִּשְׁכָּן: וְלֹא־יָכֹל

מֹשֶׁה לָבוֹא אֶל־אֹהֶל מוֹעֵד כִּי־שָׁכַן עָלָיו הֶעָנָן וּכְבוֹד יְהוָה מָלֵא אֶת־
הַמִּשְׁכָּן׃ "Then the cloud covered the tent of meeting, and
the glory of the Lord filled the tabernacle. And Moses was not
able to enter into the tent of meeting, because the cloud abode
thereon, and the glory of the Lord filled the tabernacle" (Ex. 40:
34, 35). Thus in the tabernacle appeared the visible manifestation of the Presence of God which is called "the glory of the
Lord." That the God of Israel was in the midst of this glory
is certain from Lev. 1:1: וַיִּקְרָא אֶל־מֹשֶׁה וַיְדַבֵּר יְהוָה אֵלָיו מֵאֹהֶל
מוֹעֵד "And the Lord called unto Moses, and spake unto him
out of the tent of meeting . . ." This same outward manifestation of God's Presence is seen at the dedication of Solomon's
temple, according to I Kgs. 8:10, 11: וַיְהִי בְּצֵאת הַכֹּהֲנִים מִן־הַקֹּדֶשׁ
וְהֶעָנָן מָלֵא אֶת־בֵּית יְהוָה׃ וְלֹא־יָכְלוּ הַכֹּהֲנִים לַעֲמֹד לְשָׁרֵת מִפְּנֵי הֶעָנָן
כִּי־מָלֵא כְבוֹד־יְהוָה אֶת־בֵּית יְהוָה׃ "And it came to pass, when the
priests were come out of the holy place, that the cloud filled the
house of the Lord, so that the priests could not stand to minister
by reason of the cloud; for the glory of the Lord filled the house
of the Lord."

V. Appearance of Divine Presence in the Temple

This divine manifestation of God's presence in the temple
remained throughout the days of the monarchy until the Babylonian captivity, at which time, according to Ezekiel, Chapters 9-11,
"the glory of the God of Israel" reluctantly left the holy place
to tarry a-while over the threshold of the temple; then over the
court; next over the doomed city, and finally it departed to the
mount of Olives, east of Jerusalem, from which eventually it
left the nation. Israel's great abominations were the occasion
of God's leaving the temple as is seen in Ezek. 8:6;
וַיֹּאמֶר אֵלַי בֶּן־אָדָם הֲרֹאֶה אַתָּה מָהֵם עֹשִׂים תּוֹעֵבוֹת גְּדֹלוֹת אֲשֶׁר בֵּית־
יִשְׂרָאֵל עֹשִׂים פֹּה לְרָחֳקָה מֵעַל מִקְדָּשִׁי׃ "And he said unto me,
Son of man, seest thou what they do? even the great abominations that the house of Israel do commit here, that I should go
far off from my sanctuary?"

After the return from Babylonian captivity and after Zerubbabel
had completed the second temple there is no mention of the

Presence of the glory of God. Israel's house was left desolate. Her sin had separated between her and her God. Though He allowed them to remain in the land, God was not in their midst as in former days. "According to Jewish historians themselves there were five things present in the first temple which were lacking in the second: (1) the ark and its contents; (2) the holy fire which descended from heaven to consume the sacrifices in token of God's acceptance; (3) the Urim and Thummin; (4) the spirit of prophecy; (5) the *Shekhinah glory*. As a matter of fact, we know from Jewish as well as from heathen writers that the Holy of Holies in the second temple through the nearly five centuries of its existence was a vacuum—an empty place—waiting for God to come and take manifest possession of it." Finally, in the year 70 of the common era this second temple was destroyed and the nation was scattered to the four corners of the earth and it remains scattered to the present day. Thus God and His outward manifestation is not with Israel. This long period of dispersion and of being without God has been Israel's long, dark, dreary night which, in the Providence of God, shall be turned into day in the future. Let each reader hope and pray that that day may speedily come.

VI. FUTURE APPEARANCES OF THE DIVINE PRESENCE ON THE EARTH

There appear in the prophetic word numerous promises of the appearance of the glory of God upon this earth again in the midst of Israel. Among these promises is the glorious one in Isa. 40: 3-5:

קוֹל קוֹרֵא בַּמִּדְבָּר פַּנּוּ דֶּרֶךְ יְהֹוָה יַשְּׁרוּ בָּעֲרָבָה מְסִלָּה לֵאלֹהֵינוּ: כָּל־
גַּיְא יִנָּשֵׂא וְכָל־הַר וְגִבְעָה יִשְׁפָּלוּ וְהָיָה הֶעָקֹב לְמִישׁוֹר וְהָרְכָסִים
לְבִקְעָה: וְנִגְלָה כְּבוֹד יְהֹוָה וְרָאוּ כָל־בָּשָׂר יַחְדָּו כִּי פִּי יְהֹוָה דִּבֵּר:

"The voice of one that crieth, Prepare ye in the wilderness the way of the Lord; make level in the desert a highway for our God. Every valley shall be exalted, and every mountain and hill shall be made low; and the uneven shall be made level, and the rough places a plain: and the glory of the Lord shall be revealed, and all flesh shall see it together; for the mouth of the Lord hath spoken it." In verses 9-11 below, the prophet with his gaze steadfastly upon the future sees a messenger approach-

ing, a messenger of good tidings for Zion, and shouts to him:
עַל הַר־נָּבֹהַ עֲלִי־לָךְ מְבַשֶּׂרֶת צִיּוֹן הָרִימִי בַכֹּחַ קוֹלֵךְ מְבַשֶּׂרֶת יְרוּשָׁלַםִ
הָרִימִי אַל־תִּירָאִי אִמְרִי לְעָרֵי יְהוּדָה הִנֵּה אֱלֹהֵיכֶם: הִנֵּה אֲדֹנָי יֱהֹוִה
בְּחָזָק יָבוֹא וּזְרֹעוֹ מֹשְׁלָה לוֹ הִנֵּה שְׂכָרוֹ אִתּוֹ וּפְעֻלָּתוֹ לְפָנָיו: כְּרֹעֶה
עֶדְרוֹ יִרְעֶה בִּזְרֹעוֹ יְקַבֵּץ טְלָאִים וּבְחֵיקוֹ יִשָּׂא עָלוֹת יְנַהֵל: "O thou
that tellest good tidings to Zion, get thee up on a high
mountain; O thou that tellest good tidings to Jerusalem, lift up
thy voice with strength; lift it up, be not afraid; say unto the
cities of Judah, Behold, your God! Behold, the Lord יְהֹוָה will
come as a mighty one, and his arm will rule for him: Behold,
his reward is with him, and his recompense before him. He
will feed his flock like a shepherd, he will gather the lambs in his
arm, and carry them in his bosom, *and* will gently lead those that
have their young." From these verses it is very clear that the
prophet sees the time when the Lord God of Israel shall come to
Zion in a personal, visible manner as a mighty warrior. Furthermore, they show that He will rule there, dealing out justice and
righteousness to all and rendering a recompense to every one.
Though He shall be an absolute monarch, He shall have the ten-
derness of a good shepherd, for He will feed His flock and will
gently carry the lambs in His bosom.*

This personal coming of the God of Israel is to be attended
by the manifestation of divine glory (verse 5), similar to but
more glorious than on former occasions. This personal glorious
appearance of God in Zion shall be revealed to all flesh
(all nations). Then will be fulfilled the passage which says,
"The earth shall be full of the knowledge of the glory of
the Lord, as the waters cover the sea" (Hab. 2:14). At that
time everyone shall have a personal knowledge of God because
He will be in Zion in person and the nations will go to
Jerusalem constantly and will be taught of Him (Isa. 2:1-4).
הַדָּבָר אֲשֶׁר חָזָה יְשַׁעְיָהוּ בֶּן־אָמוֹץ עַל־יְהוּדָה וִירוּשָׁלָםִ: וְהָיָה בְּאַחֲרִית
הַיָּמִים נָכוֹן יִהְיֶה הַר בֵּית־יְהֹוָה בְּרֹאשׁ הֶהָרִים וְנִשָּׂא מִגְּבָעוֹת וְנָהֲרוּ
אֵלָיו כָּל־הַגּוֹיִם: וְהָלְכוּ עַמִּים רַבִּים וְאָמְרוּ לְכוּ וְנַעֲלֶה אֶל־הַר־יְהֹוָה

---

*In Verse 11 the Lord compares Himself to a shepherd and the house
of Israel to His flock which He tends.

אֶל־בֵּית אֱלֹהֵי יַעֲקֹב וְיֹרֵנוּ מִדְּרָכָיו וְנֵלְכָה בְּאֹרְחֹתָיו כִּי מִצִּיּוֹן תֵּצֵא
תוֹרָה וּדְבַר־יְהוָה מִירוּשָׁלָםִ: וְשָׁפַט בֵּין הַגּוֹיִם וְהוֹכִיחַ לְעַמִּים רַבִּים
וְכִתְּתוּ חַרְבוֹתָם לְאִתִּים וַחֲנִיתוֹתֵיהֶם לְמַזְמֵרוֹת לֹא־יִשָּׂא גוֹי אֶל־גּוֹי
חֶרֶב וְלֹא־יִלְמְדוּ עוֹד מִלְחָמָה: "The word that Isaiah the son of
Amoz saw concerning Judah and Jerusalem. And it shall come
to pass in the latter days, that the mountain of the Lord's house
shall be established on the top of the mountains, and shall be
exalted above the hills; and all nations shall flow unto it. And
many peoples shall go and say, Come ye, and let us go up to
the mountain of the Lord, to the house of the God of Jacob;
and he will teach us of his ways, and we will walk in his paths:
for out of Zion shall go forth the law, and the word of the
Lord from Jerusalem. And he will judge between the nations,
and will decide concerning many peoples; and they shall beat their
swords into plow-shares, and their spears into pruning-hooks;
nation shall not lift up sword against nation, neither shall they
learn war any more."

In Psa. 50:1-6 appears a wonderful prediction when God shall
come to Zion as Judge. אֵל אֱלֹהִים יְהוָה דִּבֶּר וַיִּקְרָא־אָרֶץ
מִמִּזְרַח־שֶׁמֶשׁ עַד־מְבֹאוֹ: מִצִּיּוֹן מִכְלַל־יֹפִי אֱלֹהִים הוֹפִיעַ: יָבֹא
אֱלֹהֵינוּ וְאַל־יֶחֱרַשׁ אֵשׁ־לְפָנָיו תֹּאכֵל וּסְבִיבָיו נִשְׂעֲרָה מְאֹד: יִקְרָא
אֶל־הַשָּׁמַיִם מֵעָל וְאֶל־הָאָרֶץ לָדִין עַמּוֹ: אִסְפוּ־לִי חֲסִידָי כֹּרְתֵי בְרִיתִי
עֲלֵי־זָבַח: וַיַּגִּידוּ שָׁמַיִם צִדְקוֹ כִּי־אֱלֹהִים שֹׁפֵט הוּא סֶלָה: "The
Mighty One, God, the Lord, hath spoken, and called the earth from
the rising of the sun unto the going down thereof. Out of Zion,
the perfection of beauty, God hath shined forth. Our God
cometh, and doth not keep silence: A fire devoureth before
him, and it is very tempestuous round about him. He calleth
to the heavens above, and to the earth, that he may judge
his people: Gather my saints together unto me, those that
have made a covenant with me by sacrifice. And the heavens
shall declare his righteousness; for God is judge himself."
Though in verse 2 the Psalmist speaks of the fulfillment of this
passage as if it had already transpired, the context shows clearly
that it is a prediction of the time when God shall come to Mount
Zion and shall enter into judgment with the nations.

This use of the perfect tense is known as the prophetic perfect. By the spiritual illumination of the Divine Spirit the prophet saw this coming of the Lord and judgment scene as vividly as if it had already occurred. The word הוֹפִיעַ "shine forth" in verse 2 is the same one which is used in Deut. 33:2 by Moses to describe God's appearance on Mount Sinai when He delivered the law to him.

The use of this word suggests the scenes at Sinai. It was there that God, to a certain limited extent, "shined forth," thus manifesting His Presence and power. When God shines forth out of Zion there will be a duplication of the scenes of Sinai, but on a vaster and more magnificent scale. Again in Psa. 80:1(2) the Psalmist prays: רֹעֵה יִשְׂרָאֵל הַאֲזִינָה נֹהֵג כַּצֹּאן יוֹסֵף יֹשֵׁב הַכְּרֻבִים הוֹפִיעָה: "Give ear, O Shepherd of Israel, Thou that leadest Joseph like a flock; Thou that sittest *above* the cherubim, shine forth." The Psalmist before whose mind the throne of judgment and glory stood in vision implored the God of Israel in behalf of the chosen people to fulfill His promises by coming and by leading the Hebrew people like a flock back to their ancestral home. Again in Psa. 94:1-3 the Psalmist pleads: אֵל-נְקָמוֹת יְהוָה אֵל נְקָמוֹת הוֹפִיעַ: הִנָּשֵׂא שֹׁפֵט הָאָרֶץ הָשֵׁב גְּמוּל עַל-גֵּאִים: עַד-מָתַי רְשָׁעִים יְהוָה עַד-מָתַי רְשָׁעִים יַעֲלֹזוּ: "O Lord, thou God to whom vengeance belongeth, Thou God to whom vengeance belongeth, shine forth. Lift up thyself, thou judge of the earth: Render to the proud *their* desert. Lord, how long shall the wicked, How long shall the wicked triumph?" It is apparent from this passage that the inspired Psalmist understood that when God does shine forth He will render vengeance and recompense to the wicked. Seeing the prevalence of wickedness he prays earnestly for God to appear in this capacity.

A close study of Psalm 50 which, as stated above, sees the prediction already fulfilled shows the extent of this judgment. Likewise, it gives an indication of the time when it will be fulfilled, namely, after God has kept His silence for a long time (see verse 3). In verse 5 appear those whom God terms "My saints," even "those that have made a covenant with Me by sacrifice" gathered together unto God. Hence they are protected and blessed by

Him at this time. In verses 7-15 is a description of how God will deal with the surviving remnant of Israel at the time when He appears in Zion. In verses 16-21 is God's judgment upon the wicked and rebellious of the world. This same appearance of God to judge the world is seen in Joel 3:12-17 (4:12-17) :

יֵעוֹרוּ וְיַעֲלוּ הַגּוֹיִם אֶל־עֵמֶק יְהוֹשָׁפָט כִּי שָׁם אֵשֵׁב לִשְׁפֹּט אֶת־כָּל־הַגּוֹיִם
מִסָּבִיב: שִׁלְחוּ מַגָּל כִּי בָשַׁל קָצִיר בֹּאוּ רְדוּ כִּי־מָלְאָה גַּת הֵשִׁיקוּ
הַיְקָבִים כִּי רַבָּה רָעָתָם: הֲמוֹנִים הֲמוֹנִים בְּעֵמֶק הֶחָרוּץ כִּי קָרוֹב יוֹם
יְהֹוָה בְּעֵמֶק הֶחָרוּץ: שֶׁמֶשׁ וְיָרֵחַ קָדָרוּ וְכֹכָבִים אָסְפוּ נָגְהָם: וַיהֹוָה
מִצִּיּוֹן יִשְׁאָג וּמִירוּשָׁלַם יִתֵּן קוֹלוֹ וְרָעֲשׁוּ שָׁמַיִם וָאָרֶץ וַיהֹוָה מַחֲסֶה לְעַמּוֹ
וּמָעוֹז לִבְנֵי יִשְׂרָאֵל: וִידַעְתֶּם כִּי אֲנִי יְהֹוָה אֱלֹהֵיכֶם שֹׁכֵן בְּצִיּוֹן הַר־
קָדְשִׁי וְהָיְתָה יְרוּשָׁלַם קֹדֶשׁ וְזָרִים לֹא־יַעַבְרוּ־בָהּ עוֹד: "Let the nations bestir themselves, and come up to the valley of Jehoshaphat;
for there will I sit to judge all the nations round about. Put
ye in the sickle; for the harvest is ripe: come, tread ye; for the
winepress is full, the vats overflow; for their wickedness is great.
Multitudes, multitudes in the valley of decision! for the day of the
Lord is near in the valley of decision. The sun and the moon are
darkened, and the stars withdraw their shining. And the Lord will
roar from Zion, and utter his voice from Jerusalem; and the heavens and the earth shall shake: but the Lord will be a refuge unto his
people, and a stronghold to the children of Israel. So shall ye
know that I am the Lord your God, dwelling in Zion my holy mountain: then shall Jerusalem be holy, and there shall no strangers pass
through her any more." Malachi in 3:1-3 describes this same coming of God in judgment when He shall come suddenly to His
temple, purge out all wickedness, and purify the remnant of Israel.

הִנְנִי שֹׁלֵחַ מַלְאָכִי וּפִנָּה־דֶרֶךְ לְפָנָי וּפִתְאֹם יָבוֹא אֶל־הֵיכָלוֹ הָאָדוֹן
אֲשֶׁר־אַתֶּם מְבַקְשִׁים וּמַלְאַךְ הַבְּרִית אֲשֶׁר אַתֶּם חֲפֵצִים הִנֵּה־בָא אָמַר
יְהֹוָה צְבָאוֹת: וּמִי מְכַלְכֵּל אֶת־יוֹם בּוֹאוֹ וּמִי הָעֹמֵד בְּהֵרָאוֹתוֹ כִּי־הוּא
כְּאֵשׁ מְצָרֵף וּכְבֹרִית מְכַבְּסִים: וְיָשַׁב מְצָרֵף וּמְטַהֵר כֶּסֶף וְטִהַר אֶת־
בְּנֵי־לֵוִי וְזִקַּק אֹתָם כַּזָּהָב וְכַכָּסֶף וְהָיוּ לַיהֹוָה מַגִּישֵׁי מִנְחָה בִּצְדָקָה:
"Behold, I send my messenger, and he shall prepare the way be-
fore me: and the Lord, whom ye seek, will suddenly come to his
temple; and the messenger of the covenant, whom ye desire, be-

hold, he cometh, saith the Lord of hosts. But who can abide the
day of his coming? and who shall stand when he appeareth? for
he is like a refiner's fire, and like fullers' soap: and he will sit as
a refiner and purifier of silver, and he will purify the sons of Levi,
and refine them as gold and silver; and they shall offer unto the
Lord offerings in righteousness." After God appears in judgment
in Zion and has executed His righteous indignation upon all of the
wicked, He, as seen in Joel's passage just quoted, will reign in
Zion. At that time Zion will be a peaceful, glorious habitation
from which God will reign over the earth.

Note the picture of blessedness in Isa. 33:17-24.

מֶלֶךְ בְּיָפְיוֹ תֶּחֱזֶינָה עֵינֶיךָ תִּרְאֶינָה אֶרֶץ מַרְחַקִּים: לִבְּךָ יֶהְגֶּה אֵימָה
אַיֵּה סֹפֵר אַיֵּה שֹׁקֵל אַיֵּה סֹפֵר אֶת־הַמִּגְדָּלִים: אֶת־עַם נוֹעָז לֹא תִרְאֶה
עַם עִמְקֵי שָׂפָה מִשְּׁמוֹעַ נִלְעַג לָשׁוֹן אֵין בִּינָה: חֲזֵה צִיּוֹן קִרְיַת מוֹעֲדֵנוּ
עֵינֶיךָ תִרְאֶינָה יְרוּשָׁלַ͏ִם נָוֶה שַׁאֲנָן אֹהֶל בַּל־יִצְעָן בַּל־יִסַּע יְתֵדֹתָיו לָנֶצַח
וְכָל־חֲבָלָיו בַּל־יִנָּתֵקוּ: כִּי אִם־שָׁם אַדִּיר יְהוָה לָנוּ מְקוֹם־נְהָרִים יְאֹרִים
רַחֲבֵי יָדָיִם בַּל־תֵּלֶךְ בּוֹ אֳנִי־שַׁיִט וְצִי אַדִּיר לֹא יַעַבְרֶנּוּ: כִּי יְהוָה שֹׁפְטֵנוּ
יְהוָה מְחֹקְקֵנוּ יְהוָה מַלְכֵּנוּ הוּא יוֹשִׁיעֵנוּ: נִטְּשׁוּ חֲבָלָיִךְ בַּל־יְחַזְּקוּ כֵן
תָּרְנָם בַּל־פָּרְשׂוּ נֵס אָז חֻלַּק עַד־שָׁלָל מַרְבֶּה פִּסְחִים בָּזְזוּ בַז: וּבַל־
יֹאמַר שָׁכֵן חָלִיתִי הָעָם הַיֹּשֵׁב בָּהּ נְשֻׂא עָוֹן:
"Thine eyes shall see
the king in his beauty: they shall behold a land that reacheth
afar. Thy heart shall muse on the terror: Where is he that
counted, where is he that weighed *the tribute?* where is he that
counted the towers? Thou shalt not see the fierce people, a
people of a deep speech that thou canst not comprehend, of a
strange tongue that thou canst not understand. Look upon Zion,
the city of our solemnities: thine eyes shall see Jerusalem a
quiet habitation, a tent that shall not be removed, the stakes whereof shall never be plucked up, neither shall any of the cords thereof be broken. But there the Lord will be with us in majesty, a
place of broad rivers and streams, wherein shall go no galley with
oars, neither shall gallant ship pass thereby. For the Lord is our
judge, the Lord is our lawgiver, the Lord is our king; he will save
us. Thy tacklings are loosed; they could not strengthen the foot
of their mast, they could not spread the sail: then was the prey of

a great spoil divided; the lame took the prey. And the inhabitant shall not say, I am sick: the people that dwell therein shall be forgiven their iniquity."

VII. THE PERSONAL GLORIOUS APPEARANCE OF MESSIAH IN ZION

From the predictions concerning God's coming both in judgment and glory which have been quoted one would conclude that only one of the Divine Personalities will appear upon the earth and will judge the peoples. In Dan. 7 appears additional light upon this future glorious event. In verses 1-14 appears the record of the series of visions which were shown to Daniel the prophet who was a high official at the court of Belshazzar, king of Babylon, and who was a faithful prophet of God. In verses 15-28 appears the record of the interpretation of the visions, which was made to him by an interpreting angel. After giving an account of the appearance of the four wild animals, namely, a lion, a bear, a leopard, and a nondescript beast, which came up out of the agitated sea in the order enumerated and each of which succeeded his predecessor, Daniel says:

חָזֵה הֲוֵית עַד דִּי כָרְסָוָן רְמִיו וְעַתִּיק יוֹמִין יְתִב לְבוּשֵׁהּ כִּתְלַג חִוָּר וּשְׂעַר
רֵאשֵׁהּ כַּעֲמַר נְקֵא כָּרְסָיֵהּ שְׁבִיבִין דִּי־נוּר גַּלְגִּלּוֹהִי נוּר דָּלִק: נְהַר דִּי־
נוּר נָגֵד וְנָפֵק מִן־קֳדָמוֹהִי אֶלֶף אַלְפִים יְשַׁמְּשׁוּנֵּהּ וְרִבּוֹ רִבְבָן קָדָמוֹהִי
יְקוּמוּן דִּינָא יְתִב וְסִפְרִין פְּתִיחוּ: חָזֵה הֲוֵית בֵּאדַיִן מִן־קָל מִלַּיָּא
רַבְרְבָתָא דִּי קַרְנָא מְמַלְּלָא חָזֵה הֲוֵית עַד דִּי קְטִילַת חֵיוְתָא וְהוּבַד
גִּשְׁמַהּ וִיהִיבַת לִיקֵדַת אֶשָּׁא: וּשְׁאָר חֵיוָתָא הֶעְדִּיו שָׁלְטָנְהוֹן וְאַרְכָה
בְחַיִּין יְהִיבַת לְהוֹן עַד־זְמַן וְעִדָּן: חָזֵה הֲוֵית בְּחֶזְוֵי לֵילְיָא וַאֲרוּ עִם־
עֲנָנֵי שְׁמַיָּא כְּבַר אֱנָשׁ אָתֵה הֲוָא וְעַד־עַתִּיק יוֹמַיָּא מְטָה וּקְדָמוֹהִי
הַקְרְבוּהִי: וְלֵהּ יְהִב שָׁלְטָן וִיקָר וּמַלְכוּ וְכֹל עַמְמַיָּא אֻמַיָּא וְלִשָּׁנַיָּא לֵהּ
יִפְלְחוּן שָׁלְטָנֵהּ שָׁלְטָן עָלַם דִּי־לָא יֶעְדֵּה וּמַלְכוּתֵהּ דִּי־לָא תִתְחַבַּל:

"I beheld till thrones were placed, and one that was ancient of days did sit: his raiment was white as snow, and the hair of his head like pure wool; his throne was fiery flames, and the wheels thereof burning fire. A fiery stream issued and came forth from before him: thousands of thousands ministered unto him, and ten thousand times ten thousand stood before him: the judgment was set, and the books were opened. I beheld at that time because of the voice of the great words which the horn spake; I beheld even till the beast was slain, and its body destroyed, and it was given to be burned with fire. And as for the rest of the beasts, their dominion was taken away: yet their lives were prolonged for a season and a time. I saw in the night-visions, and, behold, there came with the clouds of heaven one like unto a son of man, and he came even to the ancient of days, and they brought him near before him. And there was given him dominion, and glory, and a kingdom, that all the peoples, nations, and languages should serve him: his dominion is an everlasting dominion, which shall not pass away, and his kingdom that which shall not be destroyed" (Dan. 7:9-14).

It is generally agreed among Biblical scholars that these beasts are symbols of world empires, which position is supported by verse 17. The kingdoms thus represented by them are Babylon, Medo-Persia, Greece, and Rome. Wild animals were chosen as fit symbols to depict the selfish warring characteristics of human governments.

Verse 9, quoted above, is a description of the throne of judgment and of glory which is held in heaven, as is learned from the other predictions. This one who sits upon the throne is called "ancient of days." That he is a Divine Being is beyond question. That this is a throne of judgment is evident from verse 10. From verse 11 it is evident that this judgment scene is not set until the fourth empire, namely, Rome, is in its last stages; in fact the verse shows that when this throne of judgment is set, the fourth beast is slain. In non-figurative language this statement teaches that the Roman Empire ceases as a government at that time. Verse 12 shows that the three former beasts were not dealt with in the supernatural way in which the fourth one is disposed of.

The question doubtless has arisen in the mind of the reader, "How can such an interpretation be true since Rome as a government has ceased to exist centuries ago?" To this question the answer is very easy. Though the Roman empire has not functioned since the fifth century of the common era, it by no means is dead. In the days of Constantine the Great the empire was divided into the eastern and western divisions, the capital of the latter being Rome, and that of the former, Constantinople. The western half was destroyed by the invasion of the Teutons in 476 but was revived about 800 by Charlemagne and was called "The

Holy Roman Empire." About 963 Otto the Great of Germany transferred the seat of government to his dominion and renamed it "The Holy Roman Empire of the German Nation." All of the German emperors from that day until Kaiser Wilhelm in 1918 was deposed claimed to be successors of Caesar, the word "Kaiser" being Caesar spelled in German. The very civilization of the western world is that of the old Roman empire.

The seat of the government at Constantinople continued until 1453 when it was captured by the Turks. At that time the government was transferred to Russia. Since then the Russian nation has been the modern successor of the eastern division of the Roman empire. The word "Czar" is but the Russian way of spelling Caesar. In 1917, however, the Russian empire succumbed to the influence of the Bolsheviki. The civilization of Russia was likewise based upon that of old Rome.

Though Rome in the form of its modern successors, Germany and Russia, for the time being has been reduced to a subordinate position among the nations, it is destined to reappear as a world empire in the end-time which will be dealt with summarily by the appearance of God upon his throne of judgment in glory.

In verses 13 and 14 appears the record of the last of this series of visions. In it the prophet saw that "there came with the clouds of heaven one like unto a son of man" who came before the Ancient of Days. Upon his arrival the Almighty conferred upon him a "dominion, and glory, and a kingdom that all the peoples, nations, and languages should serve him: his dominion is an everlasting dominion, which will not pass away, and his kingdom that which shall not be destroyed." Who is this one "like unto a son of man" to whom universal dominion and power are granted? This question may be answered by another writer who says "The Jews understood this 'coming in clouds' to refer to a personal Coming, and hence, as various writers have noticed, named as we have noticed, the Messiah, anticipatory, 'the son of clouds'." This Jewish interpretation is confirmed by a comparison of this passage with parallel ones (see for example Isa. 9: 6, 7; Psa. 2; Zech. 9: 10). These passages teach that the Messiah is to have universal dominion; this one who is brought before the Ancient of Days is given **universal** dominion which does not pass away; therefore he is the Messiah.

Since the judgment scene of this passage is in heaven, and since he who is "like unto a son of man" comes before it "with the clouds of heaven," one immediately asks, "Why is the Messiah spoken of as 'like unto a son of man' and 'why is it that he comes from heaven to earth on this occasion?'" The answer to the question, "Why is the Messiah said to be like a son of man?" finds expression in the fact that he is a man as is set forth in Isa. 9:6, 7. He does not simply have the appearance of a man but is in reality a man, a descendant of the house of David; hence he is בֶּן־דָּוִד "son of David." (cf. Jer. 23:5, 6), "Behold, the days come, saith the Lord, that I will raise unto David a righteous Branch, and he shall reign as king and deal wisely, and shall execute justice and righteousness in the land. In his days Judah shall be saved, and Israel shall dwell safely; and this is his name whereby he shall be called: The Lord our righteousness" (Also see Ezek. 37:24-28). In regard to the other question, furthermore, let it be noted that no purely angelic being is anywhere spoken of thus. It is true, however, that on various occasions when "the angel of the Lord" appeared unto various patriarchs, he is spoken of as a man, but the context always makes it plain that he is not a man but that he simply for the occasion assumed the form of man for the purpose of communicating with man. In this passage of Daniel there is no indication that this one has for the occasion assumed a human form; therefore this case is different from all of the theophanies of earlier times.

Since the Messiah is a real man—the God-man—and since He comes with the clouds of heaven to this judgment seat of the Almighty in heaven, the suppositions underlying Dan. 7:13-28 are that He has been in the world before, and that He has gone back to heaven where He is invested at this time with absolute authority over the entire world. These presuppositions are lifted out of the realm of hypotheses by the facts stated in Isa. 9:6, 7 and Psa. 110. The former of these passages teaches that the Messiah is to be born to the Jewish nation and that He is "Wonderful, Counsellor,

Mighty God, Everlasting Father, Prince of Peace." The latter shows that when the Messiah is rejected by the inhabitants of Jerusalem, He is invited by the eternal God to ascend to "His right hand" and to remain there until the eternal God subjects these enemies under his feet.

CHAPTER VII

MESSIAH'S COMING TO EARTH

THE nations of antiquity looked backward to a golden era which they claimed was in the past. In violent contrast to them, the Hebrew nation has through the ages looked forward to its golden age which is commonly and Scripturally called "the Messianic Age," or the era during which Israel's Messiah shall reign.

I. MESSIAH IN THE TORAH

The first clear and definite prediction of the Messiah appears in Gen. 49:10: לֹא־יָסוּר שֵׁבֶט מִיהוּדָה וּמְחֹקֵק מִבֵּין רַגְלָיו עַד כִּי־יָבֹא שִׁילֹה וְלוֹ יִקְּהַת עַמִּים: "The sceptre shall not depart from Judah, Nor the ruler's staff from between his feet, Until Shiloh come; And unto him shall the obedience of the peoples be." The official interpretation of the ancient synagogue on this passage is that it looks forward to the coming of the Messiah Who is called "Shiloh" here. That this position is correct is seen from the fact that "Unto him shall the obedience of the nations be." This last statement viewed in the light of others which enter more into detail is seen to be a definite prediction of the Messiah Who shall rule all nations.

In the prophecies of Balaam recorded in Num. 23:19-24; 24:4-9, 16-24 appear some wonderful predictions concerning the Hebrew Messiah. At the solicitation of Balak, king of Moab, Balaam insisted upon the Lord's permitting him to respond to the call of Balak. Though God permitted him to go, He limited him in the predictions he made. His first oracle (chapter 23:7-10) pronounced a blessing upon Israel.

At the instance of Balak a second altar was built at another place on which sacrifices were offered. From this position Balaam issued his second prediction. In verse 19 of this chapter the prophet declared that God would neither lie nor change His plan and purpose but on the other hand would perform what He had said. Therefore declared the prophet, "Behold, I have received commandment to bless: and He hath blessed, and I cannot reverse

65

it." Continuing this prediction he said, "He hath not beheld iniquity in Jacob; Neither hath he seen perverseness in Israel: the Lord his God is with him, And the shout of a king is among them." It is clear from the historical record and from the context of this verse that the prophet was not speaking of a condition which then existed but had his face toward the future and spoke of a time when the children of Israel shall be free from iniquity and perverseness, at which time the Lord God will be with him, *i.e.*, with Israel. Since the lines, "The Lord his God is with him, And the shout of a king is among them," constitute a "Hebrew parallelism," it is quite clear that God is in the midst of Israel, according to this prediction, in the capacity of its king. Furthermore, it is clear from this passage that the presence of God as king in Israel is the efficient cause which has removed iniquity and perverseness from the nation. A glance at Jewish history shows that there has always been and is at the present time the presence of iniquity and sin within the nation; but when this prophecy is fulfilled she will have been purged from every taint of unrighteousness. These facts prove conclusively that in these lines the prophet is not speaking of God's dwelling either in the tabernacle or the temple in the form of the Shekinah glory but is there in person as Israel's king.

When Balak saw that Balaam pronounced a blessing instead of a curse upon Israel he changed his position again and requested that Balaam from this third position should pronounce a curse upon the chosen people. In this oracle instead of cursing he blessed the nation and spoke of the glory of its king and the extent of his kingdom. "Water shall flow from his buckets, And his seed shall be in many waters, And his king shall be higher than Agag, And his kingdom shall be exalted" (24:7). Agag was king of the Amorites, one of the most powerful tribes inhabiting Canaan at that time. Men think by comparisons; hence God in order to convey to Balak's mind the power and greatness of Israel's future king stated that he would be higher than Agag and that his kingdom should be exalted. History states with no uncertain sound that this prediction has never as yet been fulfilled.* This verse,

---

* David and Solomon did not fulfill it.

viewed in the light of verse 21 of the twenty-third chapter, is seen
to refer to God when He shall appear in Zion as Israel's king.

Having been disappointed in the three oracles uttered by the
prophet, which God required him to speak contrary to his desires,
Balak erected a fourth altar, hoping in vain that as a last attempt
he would obtain his desire. By the Spirit of God Balaam spoke
again, in which oracle he declared : אֶרְאֶנּוּ וְלֹא עַתָּה אֲשׁוּרֶנּוּ וְלֹא
קָרוֹב דָּרַךְ כּוֹכָב מִיַּעֲקֹב וְקָם שֵׁבֶט מִיִּשְׂרָאֵל וּמָחַץ פַּאֲתֵי מוֹאָב
וְקַרְקַר כָּל־בְּנֵי־שֵׁת: וְהָיָה אֱדוֹם יְרֵשָׁה וְהָיָה יְרֵשָׁה שֵׂעִיר אֹיְבָיו
וְיִשְׂרָאֵל עֹשֶׂה חָיִל: וְיֵרְדְּ מִיַּעֲקֹב וְהֶאֱבִיד שָׂרִיד מֵעִיר: "I see him,
but not now; I behold him, but not nigh: There shall come
forth a star out of Jacob, And a sceptre shall rise out of Israel,
And shall smite through the corners of Moab, And break down
all the sons of tumult. And Edom shall be a possession, Seir
also shall be a possession, *who were* his enemies ; While Israel doeth
valiantly. And out of Jacob shall one have dominion, And shall
destroy the remnant from the city" (Num. 24 :17-19). A careful
examination of these verses shows that the one whom the prophet
saw in the distance (in point of time) is the one who comes out of
Jacob to have dominion, and who conquers the surrounding nations
as is stated in the prophecy. This prediction in the light of Psa.
46 is seen to teach that this king who conquers these nations and
who reigns in Jacob is none other than the one of whom the
Psalmist spoke in the following words : אֱלֹהִים בְּקִרְבָּהּ בַּל־תִּמּוֹט
יַעְזְרֶהָ אֱלֹהִים לִפְנוֹת בֹּקֶר: הָמוּ גוֹיִם מָטוּ מַמְלָכוֹת נָתַן בְּקוֹלוֹ תָּמוּג
אָרֶץ: יְהֹוָה צְבָאוֹת עִמָּנוּ מִשְׂגָּב לָנוּ אֱלֹהֵי יַעֲקֹב סֶלָה: "God is in
the midst of her; she shall not be moved: God will help her,
and that right early. The nations raged, the kingdoms were
moved: He uttered his voice, the earth melted. The Lord of hosts
is with us ; The God of Jacob is our refuge" (Psa. 46: 5-7, 6-8).

A third passage in the Torah which undoubtedly is a reference
to King Messiah is Deut. 18:15-19:
נָבִיא מִקִּרְבְּךָ מֵאַחֶיךָ כָּמֹנִי יָקִים לְךָ יְהֹוָה אֱלֹהֶיךָ אֵלָיו תִּשְׁמָעוּן: כְּכֹל
אֲשֶׁר־שָׁאַלְתָּ מֵעִם יְהֹוָה אֱלֹהֶיךָ בְּחֹרֵב בְּיוֹם הַקָּהָל לֵאמֹר לֹא אֹסֵף
לִשְׁמֹעַ אֶת־קוֹל יְהֹוָה אֱלֹהָי וְאֶת־הָאֵשׁ הַגְּדֹלָה הַזֹּאת לֹא־אֶרְאֶה עוֹד

וְלֹא אָמוּת: וַיֹּאמֶר יְהֹוָה אֵלַי הֵיטִיבוּ אֲשֶׁר דִּבֵּרוּ: נָבִיא אָקִים לָהֶם
מִקֶּרֶב אֲחֵיהֶם כָּמוֹךָ וְנָתַתִּי דְבָרַי בְּפִיו וְדִבֶּר אֲלֵיהֶם אֵת כָּל־אֲשֶׁר
אֲצַוֶּנּוּ: וְהָיָה הָאִישׁ אֲשֶׁר לֹא־יִשְׁמַע אֶל־דְּבָרַי אֲשֶׁר יְדַבֵּר בִּשְׁמִי אָנֹכִי
אֶדְרֹשׁ מֵעִמּוֹ: "The Lord thy God will raise up unto thee a
prophet from the midst of thee, of thy brethren, like unto me;
unto him ye shall hearken; according to all that thou desiredst of
the Lord thy God in Horeb in the day of the assembly, saying,
Let me not hear again the voice of the Lord my God, neither let
me see this great fire any more, that I die not. And the Lord said
unto me, They have well said that which they have spoken. I will
raise them up a prophet from among their brethren, like unto thee;
and I will put my words in his mouth, and he shall speak unto them
all that I shall command him. And it shall come to pass, that whosoever will not hearken unto my words which he shall speak in my
name, I will require it of him."   In this prediction Moses promises
Israel a prophet who is to be like himself and who is to be a
Hebrew. A study of the life of Moses will give the picture,
though limited and more or less indistinct, of this future prophet.

A. Moses was born during the time when Israel was severely
oppressed by Gentile power.

B. Notwithstanding the miserable bondage into which he was
born, by the providence of God he was given every advantage and
opportunity which wealth and power could afford, being reared
and educated at the court of the Pharaoh of Egypt. Having been
adopted as the son of Pharaoh's daughter he possibly was an heir
to the throne.

C. Though highly educated he was very meek and humble. His
heart was overflowing with love for his brethren who were suffering such abject poverty and cruel bondage.

D. Upon visiting them in their sufferings he attempted to ad-
just a difference between one of his kinsmen and an Egyptian.
Thus he attempted to be a peacemaker. On the following day he
attempted to reconcile two of his brethren who were quarreling.
The one who was in the wrong reprimanded Moses, calling his
attention to the fact that the latter had killed an Egyptian on the
previous day. Whereupon Moses left the country and did not
reappear until God sent him back.

E. During this time there seems to have been no communication between Moses and his brethren for then he was in obscurity.

F. Upon his return he presented himself to his brethren, proving his call and commission from God by performing miracles.

G. After bringing ten plagues upon Egypt he delivered the downtrodden race from the cruel bondage.

H. When they were delivered from the servitude, he gave a law to them, which gives every evidence that it is the law of God.

I. He led the nation serving in the capacity of judge and prince. A disregard for his commandments and laws was punished by the Lord himself.

The points noted above are some of the outstanding characteristics and events in the life of Moses. It is quite certain that they are typical and foreshadow that One concerning whose coming he spoke, though Moses and his life typified him only in a most imperfect and limited manner.

Whenever God raises up the prophet who is the subject of this prediction everyone who does not accept his sovereignty nor obeys the words of God which he speaks, God requires it of him, *i.e.,* God metes out to each disobedient one the punishment which his sin merits. In view of this solemn warning it behooves each Hebrew, firstly, to be honest with himself, and, secondly, to be honest with his God, and to search the history of the Hebrew nation from the times of Moses until the present day to find out whether God has raised up this prophet. If God has already raised him up, the only reasonable thing for every Hebrew to do is to render absolute loyalty of heart to him and strict obedience regardless of circumstances or consequences. If He has not raised him up yet, he should keep his eyes, ears, and heart open watching and waiting for him. Such an attitude of heart and soul God honors by granting to one the true knowledge. Prov. 2:1-5:

בְּנִי אִם־תִּקַּח אֲמָרָי וּמִצְוֹתַי תִּצְפֹּן אִתָּךְ: לְהַקְשִׁיב לַחָכְמָה אָזְנֶךָ תַּטֶּה לִבְּךָ לַתְּבוּנָה: כִּי אִם לַבִּינָה תִקְרָא לַתְּבוּנָה תִּתֵּן קוֹלֶךָ: אִם־תְּבַקְשֶׁנָּה כַכָּסֶף וְכַמַּטְמוֹנִים תַּחְפְּשֶׂנָּה: אָז תָּבִין יִרְאַת יְהֹוָה וְדַעַת אֱלֹהִים תִּמְצָא: "My son, if thou wilt receive my words, And lay up my commandments with thee; So as to incline thine ear unto wisdom, And apply thy heart to understanding; Yea, if thou cry after discernment, And lift up thy voice for understanding; If thou seek her as silver, And search for her as for hid treasures: Then shalt thou understand the fear of the Lord, And find the knowledge of God."

From the quotations studied above it is quite clear that God's first and holiest plan for Israel was that He should be her King, and that some time in the future He would come in person, assuming the form of a man, a prophet like unto Moses (humanly speaking) and reign over the nation. But when men will not accept God's first and best gifts and plans, He gives them a secondary or subordinate one. Such was the case with reference to Israel in her clamoring for a king in order that she might be like other nations. Anticipating such a rebellion against God, Moses (Deut. 17:14-20) gave instruction as to their selection of a king.

II. MESSIAH IN THE FORMER PROPHETS

The occasion soon arose in the closing days of Samuel's life. Israel, being disgusted with the maladministration of affairs by Samuel's sons, insisted that a king be given her. Samuel protested, pointing out the sinfulness of the course which she was pursuing. Notwithstanding his warnings, the people demanded a king. Saul was selected and anointed and became "the anointed of the Lord" (I Sam. 26:9, 23). His personal appearance inspired great confidence and hopes in the minds of the people. It seems that they associated the great Messianic expectation with him and his kingship; but these expectations were soon blasted by Saul's disobedience.

In rejecting Saul the Lord said: "The Lord has sought Him a man after His own heart . . . hath appointed him to be prince over his people." Shortly after this Samuel anointed David who became the Lord's anointed, or Messiah. David began his reign well, which fact inspired the nation with enthusiastic expectation of the realization of the Messianic hope. But his great sin soon extinguished these radiant hopes. In the words of Delitzsch one may say, "We can also explain why it is that the victory gained over Ammon and the image of the Messiah have thus for David detached themselves from his person. In the midst of that war occurred the sin of David, which embittered the whole of his after-

life and which laid his typical glory in ashes. Out of these
ashes the phoenix of Messianic prophecy here arises. The type,
come to the consciousness of himself, here lays down his crown
at the feet of the Antitype." David in his swan song (II Sam.
23:1-7) admits his failure and points to another in the future:
וְאֵ֣לֶּה דִּבְרֵ֤י דָוִד֙ הָאַ֣חֲרֹנִ֔ים נְאֻ֤ם דָּוִד֙ בֶּן־יִשַׁ֔י וּנְאֻ֥ם הַגֶּ֖בֶר הֻ֣קַם עָ֑ל מְשִׁ֧יחַ
אֱלֹהֵ֣י יַעֲקֹ֗ב וּנְעִ֖ים זְמִר֥וֹת יִשְׂרָאֵֽל: ר֤וּחַ יְהוָה֙ דִּבֶּר־בִּ֔י וּמִלָּת֖וֹ עַל־
לְשׁוֹנִֽי: אָמַר֙ אֱלֹהֵ֣י יִשְׂרָאֵ֔ל לִ֥י דִבֶּ֖ר צ֣וּר יִשְׂרָאֵ֑ל מוֹשֵׁל֙ בָּֽאָדָ֔ם צַדִּ֔יק
מוֹשֵׁ֖ל יִרְאַ֥ת אֱלֹהִֽים: וּכְא֥וֹר בֹּ֖קֶר יִזְרַח־שָׁ֑מֶשׁ בֹּ֚קֶר לֹ֣א עָב֔וֹת מִנֹּ֥גַהּ
מִמָּטָ֖ר דֶּ֥שֶׁא מֵאָֽרֶץ: כִּֽי־לֹא־כֵ֤ן בֵּיתִי֙ עִם־אֵ֔ל כִּ֣י בְרִ֤ית עוֹלָם֙ שָׂ֣ם לִ֔י
עֲרוּכָ֥ה בַכֹּ֖ל וּשְׁמֻרָ֑ה כִּֽי־כָל־יִשְׁעִ֣י וְכָל־חֵ֔פֶץ כִּי־לֹ֖א יַצְמִֽיחַ: וּבְלִיַּ֕עַל
כְּק֥וֹץ מֻנָ֖ד כֻּלָּ֑הַם כִּֽי־לֹ֥א בְיָ֖ד יִקָּֽחוּ: וְאִישׁ֙ יִגַּ֣ע בָּהֶ֔ם יִמָּלֵ֥א בַרְזֶ֖ל וְעֵ֣ץ
חֲנִ֑ית וּבָאֵ֕שׁ שָׂר֥וֹף יִשָּׂרְפ֖וּ בַּשָּֽׁבֶת: "Now these are the last words
of David. David the son of Jesse saith, And the man who was
raised on high saith, The anointed of the God of Jacob, And
the sweet psalmist of Israel: The Spirit of the Lord spake by
me, And his word was upon my tongue. The God of Israel said,
The Rock of Israel spake to me: One that ruleth over men
righteously, That ruleth in the fear of God, *He shall be* as
the light of the morning, when the sun riseth, A morning
without clouds, *When* the tender grass *springeth* out of the
earth, Through clear shining after rain. Verily my house is not
so with God; Yet he hath made with me an everlasting covenant,
Ordered in all things, and sure: For it is all my salvation, and all
my desire, Although he maketh it not to grow. But the ungodly
shall be all of them as thorns to be thrust away, Because they cannot be taken with the hand; But the man that toucheth them Must
be armed with iron and the staff of a spear: And they shall be
utterly burned with fire in *their* place." He in vision saw Him
who will come and who will rule over man righteously and in the
fear of God. The beginning of his reign is compared to the dawn
of a perfect day, a day without clouds when the tender grass
shoots forth after genial showers. Being lashed by an outraged
conscience, because of his sins and failures, he frankly confesses
that his house "is not so with God," *i.e.,* he has not realized his
hopes nor has his reign met the expectations which its beginning

inspired in the hearts of the people. Following this confession, with an unswerving faith he predicts the fulfillment of the Messianic hope in the future because "He hath made with me an everlasting covenant, ordered in all things and sure." With a smiting conscience he realizes his dismal failure in bringing to fruition the expectations which his coronation promised, and looks forward for consolation to the perfect day of the Messiah "for it is all my salvation, and all my desire." "Although he maketh it not to grow" then, his strong faith in God and His faithfulness caused him to see its fulfillment in the distant future.

Solomon likewise is called "the Lord's anointed," a messiah (II Chron. 6:42). In many respects his reign surpassed that of David's but in no sense can it be said that it, even in a remote way, approximated the Messianic ideal. The brilliancy and outward splendor of the first part of his reign were overshadowed by the dark clouds of discontent, the evils which crept in with the introduction of idolatrous worship, and the poverty with its attendant evils caused by the burdensome taxation. "But the end of his reign was not equal to its beginning and the middle, the fair, the glorious, the pure image of the Messiah which he represented, became pale and with its waning, the development of the history of redemption took a new turn. In the time of David and of Solomon the hope of the faithful, which attached itself to the kingship of David, had not entirely broken with the present. At that time they knew, as a general rule, of no other Messiah save the anointed of God who is either David or Solomon himself."

After Solomon's day the kings of Judah are no longer called "the anointed of the Lord," for, doubtless, the blemishes and imperfections of the reigns of David and of Solomon had caused the people to divorce the idea of the Messiah and His glorious reign from the Davidic house. It is probable, however, that the suggestion of Delitzsch is correct, namely, that when such a king as Hezekiah mounted the throne, the Messianic hope settled down temporarily around his personality: but the nation was soon disillusioned by the inroads and aggressions of the mighty Assyrian empire and of the failures of the king. From his day on, it is quite certain that the Messianic hope, like the Shekinah glory

which departed from the temple, was thoroughly detached
from the fleshly descendants of David.   Isaiah, the latter part
of whose ministry fell during the reign of Hezekiah, in most
glowing terms pictures the glory of the Messiah's person and of
his reign.   With the failures and shortcomings of the house of
David serving as a background, he presented Israel's future
Messiah, according to the original representation in the Torah
(Num. 23:21), as God manifest in the flesh, Isa. 9:6,7 (5,6).

כִּי־יֶלֶד יֻלַּד־לָנוּ בֵּן נִתַּן־לָנוּ וַתְּהִי הַמִּשְׂרָה עַל־שִׁכְמוֹ וַיִּקְרָא שְׁמוֹ פֶּלֶא
יוֹעֵץ אֵל גִּבּוֹר אֲבִי־עַד שַׂר־שָׁלוֹם: לְםַרְבֵּה הַמִּשְׂרָה וּלְשָׁלוֹם אֵין־קֵץ
עַל־כִּסֵּא דָוִד וְעַל־מַמְלַכְתּוֹ לְהָכִין אֹתָהּ וּלְסַעֲדָהּ בְּמִשְׁפָּט וּבִצְדָקָה
מֵעַתָּה וְעַד־עוֹלָם קִנְאַת יְהוָה צְבָאוֹת תַּעֲשֶׂה־זֹּאת: "For unto us a
child is born, unto us a son is given; and the government
shall be upon his shoulder: and his name shall be called
Wonderful, Counsellor, Mighty God, Everlasting Father, Prince
of Peace.   Of the increase of his government and of peace there
shall be no end, upon the throne of David, and upon his kingdom,
to establish it, and to uphold it with justice and with righteousness
from henceforth even for ever.   The zeal of the Lord of hosts
will perform this."

As words are spelled with letters, thus God using the various
kings of Judah, though imperfect and marred their characters, as
His typical alphabet wrote upon the pages of the past clear and
definite messages concerning the future Messiah and His glorious
kingdom.

III. MESSIAH IN THE LATTER PROPHETS
Isa. 49:1-13:

שִׁמְעוּ אִיִּים אֵלַי וְהַקְשִׁיבוּ לְאֻמִּים מֵרָחוֹק יְהוָה מִבֶּטֶן קְרָאָנִי מִמְּעֵי
אִמִּי הִזְכִּיר שְׁמִי: וַיָּשֶׂם פִּי כְּחֶרֶב חַדָּה בְּצֵל יָדוֹ הֶחְבִּיאָנִי וַיְשִׂימֵנִי לְחֵץ
בָּרוּר בְּאַשְׁפָּתוֹ הִסְתִּירָנִי: וַיֹּאמֶר לִי עַבְדִּי־אָתָּה יִשְׂרָאֵל אֲשֶׁר־בְּךָ
אֶתְפָּאָר: וַאֲנִי אָמַרְתִּי לְרִיק יָגַעְתִּי לְתֹהוּ וְהֶבֶל כֹּחִי כִלֵּיתִי אָכֵן מִשְׁפָּטִי
אֶת־יְהוָה וּפְעֻלָּתִי אֶת־אֱלֹהָי: וְעַתָּה אָמַר יְהוָה יֹצְרִי מִבֶּטֶן לְעֶבֶד לוֹ
לְשׁוֹבֵב יַעֲקֹב אֵלָיו וְיִשְׂרָאֵל לֹא יֵאָסֵף וְאֶכָּבֵד בְּעֵינֵי יְהוָה וֵאלֹהַי הָיָה
עֻזִּי: וַיֹּאמֶר נָקֵל מִהְיוֹתְךָ לִי עֶבֶד לְהָקִים אֶת־שִׁבְטֵי יַעֲקֹב וּנְצִירֵי
יִשְׂרָאֵל לְהָשִׁיב וּנְתַתִּיךָ לְאוֹר גּוֹיִם לִהְיוֹת יְשׁוּעָתִי עַד־קְצֵה הָאָרֶץ:

כֹּה אָמַר־יְהֹוָה גֹּאֵל יִשְׂרָאֵל קְדוֹשׁוֹ לִבְזֹה־נֶפֶשׁ לִמְתָעֵב גּוֹי לְעֶבֶד מֹשְׁלִים
מְלָכִים יִרְאוּ וָקָמוּ שָׂרִים וְיִשְׁתַּחֲווּ לְמַעַן יְהֹוָה אֲשֶׁר נֶאֱמָן קְדֹשׁ יִשְׂרָאֵל
וַיִּבְחָרֶךָּ: כֹּה אָמַר יְהֹוָה בְּעֵת רָצוֹן עֲנִיתִיךָ וּבְיוֹם יְשׁוּעָה עֲזַרְתִּיךָ
וְאֶצָּרְךָ וְאֶתֶּנְךָ לִבְרִית עָם לְהָקִים אֶרֶץ לְהַנְחִיל נְחָלוֹת שֹׁמֵמוֹת:
לֵאמֹר לָאֲסוּרִים צֵאוּ לַאֲשֶׁר בַּחֹשֶׁךְ הִגָּלוּ עַל־דְּרָכִים יִרְעוּ וּבְכָל־
שְׁפָיִים מַרְעִיתָם: לֹא יִרְעָבוּ וְלֹא יִצְמָאוּ וְלֹא־יַכֵּם שָׁרָב וָשָׁמֶשׁ כִּי־
מְרַחֲמָם יְנַהֲגֵם וְעַל־מַבּוּעֵי מַיִם יְנַהֲלֵם: וְשַׂמְתִּי כָל־הָרַי לַדָּרֶךְ וּמְסִלֹּתַי
יְרֻמוּן: הִנֵּה אֵלֶּה מֵרָחוֹק יָבֹאוּ וְהִנֵּה־אֵלֶּה מִצָּפוֹן וּמִיָּם וְאֵלֶּה מֵאֶרֶץ
סִינִים: רָנּוּ שָׁמַיִם וְגִילִי אֶרֶץ וּפִצְחוּ הָרִים רִנָּה כִּי־נִחַם יְהֹוָה עַמּוֹ וַעֲנִיָּו
יְרַחֵם: "Listen, O isles, unto me; and hearken, ye peoples, from far:
the Lord hath called me from the womb; from the bowels of my
mother hath he made mention of my name: and he hath made my
mouth like a sharp sword; in the shadow of his hand hath he hid
me: and he hath made me a polished shaft; in his quiver hath he
kept me close: and he said unto me, Thou art my servant; Israel,
in whom I will be glorified. But I said, I have labored in vain, I
have spent my strength for nought and vanity; yet surely the justice *due* to me is with the Lord, and my recompense with my God.
And now saith the Lord that formed me from the womb to be his
servant, to bring Jacob again to him, and that Israel be gathered
unto him (for I am honorable in the eyes of the Lord, and my God
is become my strength); yea, he saith, It is too light a thing that
thou shouldest be my servant to raise up the tribes of Jacob, and
to restore the preserved of Israel: I will also give thee for a light
to the Gentiles, that thou mayest be my salvation unto the end of
the earth. Thus saith the Lord, the Redeemer of Israel, *and* his
Holy One, to him whom man despiseth, to him whom the nation
abhorreth, to a servant of rulers: Kings shall see and arise;
princes, and they shall worship; because of the Lord that is faithful, *even* the Holy One of Israel, who hath chosen thee. Thus
saith the Lord, In an acceptable time have I answered thee, and in
a day of salvation have I helped thee; and I will preserve thee, and
give thee for a covenant of the people, to raise up the land, to
make them inherit the desolate heritages; saying to them that are
bound, Go forth; to them that are in darkness, Show yourselves.

They shall feed in the ways, and on all bare heights shall be their pasture. They shall not hunger nor thirst; neither shall the heat nor sun smite them: for he that hath mercy on them will lead them, even by springs of water will he guide them. And I will make all my mountains a way, and my highways shall be exalted. Lo, these shall come from far; and, lo, these from the north and from the west; and these from the land of Sinim. Sing, O heavens; and be joyful, O earth; and break forth into singing, O mountains: for the Lord hath comforted his people, and will have compassion upon his afflicted." He who is called "son of David" in the book of Immanuel (Isa. 7-12) is in the latter part of Isaiah called "the servant of the Lord." A comparison of the "Servant" passages with the "Son of David" passages in the book of Immanuel proves beyond the shadow of a doubt the truthfulness of this position. Therefore it is of the Messiah* that the prophet speaks in the passage quoted above.

In verse 1 the personal individualistic note is so very clear that it is evident that the servant is an individual. "When the expression is applied in the fullest extent of its meaning, 'the servant of the Lord' signifies all Israel; when it is confined to its inner and narrower sense it signifies the true people of the Lord who are included in the entire nation, like the kernel within the husk (see the definition of this in Isa. 51:7; 65:10; Psa. 24:6; 73:15); here, however, the idea is restricted to its central thought and the idea becomes the ideal representation of an individual."† Therefore this verse speaks of Messiah's birth.

In Isa. 49:2, the prophet speaking for Messiah, uses two metaphors: first, he compares Messiah's tongue to a sharp sword which

---

* In Isa. 45:1 Cyrus, the Persian king, is called "his anointed" by the Lord. The context shows clearly that Cyrus was not "The Messiah." The Messiah, according to the testimony of the prophets, knows God and is in fellowship with Him whereas Cyrus did not know Him (vs. 5, 6); therefore "anointed" in this context is used with a secondary meaning. He was a messiah in that God used him to permit the Jews who were willing to return to the fatherland to do so. This partial and limited restoration was but a miniature, imperfect representation of the great, full, and final restoration of the nation to the fatherland under King Messiah (Jer. 23: 5-8).

† The prophets with one accord speak of the mother of Israel's Messiah and Redeemer but say nothing concerning an earthly father (See Gen 3: 15; Psa. 22:9, 10: Isa. 7:14; 49:1).

the Lord has hid in the shadow of his hand. The aptness of this figure is seen in the facts that in carnal war men are killed with swords, and that when God speaks the death sentence against any-one he is slain (see Psa. 33:9 which states that when God speaks, the decree is fulfilled). Secondly, he compares Messiah to a pol-ished arrow which He has hid in His quiver and which He at the proper time will place upon the bow string and shoot at His enemies. The predictions stripped of the figurative language and stated in plain words mean that Messiah is absent from the world, but that at the proper time God will send him to execute judgment upon the ungodly. That this interpretation is correct is seen from the fact that God speaks of Himself as a warrior who is armed with sword, bow, and arrow. Since the sword is hid in the warrior's hand in the first figure, and the arrow in His quiver in the second, these figures prove that the servant is present with God; hence is absent from the world.

It is evident that the first verse of Isa. 49 which speaks of the birth of the servant refers to Messiah's advent into the world whereas the second verse which compares him with the weapons of war in the hands of God, the warrior, refers to his being in heaven with God and his coming in vengeance to execute judgment upon a God-defying world. Hence the two verses are speaking of two different comings of the Messiah.* The first coming is when he enters the world through Virgin Birth; the second, when He returns from Heaven to execute the wrath of God upon the world in such a way that God will be glorified.

In the first half of verse 4 the Servant looking back over His labors when they are completed declares: "I have labored in vain, I have spent my strength for nought and vanity." Humanly speaking then, at the time of his giving utterance to these senti-ments it appears as if no results follow from his labors. This conclusion is confirmed by the latter half of the verse which is introduced adversatively, and which shows that the complaint is but a human estimate; "Surely (lit. nevertheless) the justice due to me is with the Lord, and my recompense with my God." He ex-presses the conviction that, notwithstanding the seeming failure of

---

* These two comings of the one Messiah are found in a number of pre-dictions.

the work, there are results from his labors, vindication of himself from the Lord, and a recompense for him which consists, as is seen from other passages, of satisfaction and joy in the triumph of his redemptive work.

With verse 5 there seems to be a new turn, as it were, in the career of the Messiah. Since his labor among his own people, as is expressed in the first part of verse 4, appears to be a failure, now the Lord lays before him a two-fold plan: (1) to bring Jacob again unto Himself (this statement presupposes that Jacob has departed from God), and to regather Israel back to the homeland; (2) to become "a light to the Gentiles, that thou mayest be my salvation unto the end of the earth." Upon his first appearance in Israel his labors bring little results; when he reappears as the "sword" of God and the "polished shaft" or "arrow" he restores Israel to God and becomes God's salvation to all nations, which fact will be the fulfillment of the promise to Abraham (Gen. 12:3).

In verse 7 the Lord, the Redeemer of Israel, in speaking to "him whom man despises, to him whom the nation (Israel) abhorreth, to a servant of rulers" who is Israel's Messiah, says: "Kings shall see and arise; princes, and they shall worship; because of the Lord that is faithful, *even* the Holy One of Israel, who hath chosen thee." The words "whom man despiseth, to him whom the nation abhorreth" throw a luminous light upon the prophecy in verse 4 which foretells the seeming failure of the work of the Messiah. When he appears to Israel the first time the nation despises and abhors him. He then withdraws from the scene and God hides him in His quiver; when the time is ripe for judgment upon Israel and the world he appears in his power and glory. Then "Kings shall see and arise; princes, and they shall worship." The nation will then see its mistake and will accept his sovereignty and Messiahship. So will the kings of the world.

According to verse 8 God makes this same Messiah whom the nation despised and abhorred "a covenant of the people (Israel)", *i.e.*, "the personal bond of connection uniting Israel and their God in a new fellowship." In 42:6 this same prophet emphasizes the same thought and in verse 4 he gives additional information which is: "He (the Servant of the Lord, the Messiah) will not fail nor

be discouraged until he have set justice in the earth and the isles
shall wait for his law." It is very clear from this statement that
this Servant is a prophet who delivers a law to Israel and acts as
a mediator between her and God, as did Moses at Sinai, in bringing Israel into the bonds of an everlasting covenant of which different prophets spoke. The fact that this Servant of the Lord
delivers a law for which the isles (nations of the world) wait, and
mediates an everlasting covenant between God and Israel, unmistakably identifies this Servant Prophet as The Prophet whom
Moses promised in the Torah. This conclusion is confirmed by the
promise found in Isa. 55:3,4: הַטּוּ אָזְנְכֶם וּלְכוּ אֵלַי שִׁמְעוּ וּתְחִי
נַפְשְׁכֶם וְאֶכְרְתָה לָכֶם בְּרִית עוֹלָם חַסְדֵי דָוִד הַנֶּאֱמָנִים: הֵן עֵד
לְאוּמִּים נְתַתִּיו נָגִיד וּמְצַוֵּה לְאֻמִּים: "Incline your ear, and come
unto me; hear, and your soul shall live: and I will make an
everlasting covenant with you, even the sure mercies of David.
Behold, I have given him for a witness to the peoples, a leader
and commander to the peoples." The context shows that the
prophet invites all of those who are thirsty and hungry,
spiritually speaking, to listen to his message, to incline the
ear and he will make an everlasting covenant with them. Though
he uses the first personal pronoun "I," it is evident that
it is God who is speaking and who is delivering a law and inviting
all who will listen to enter into an everlasting covenant, "even the
sure mercies of David." This statement refers to the oath of God
to David concerning the establishment of his throne for ever (II
Sam. 7). In verse 4 he speaks of this descendant of David as a
witness to the people and a leader and commander of the nations;
therefore this king of the Davidic dynasty is not only to be king
but also a law-giver. Besides his being both prophet and king he
will likewise, according to Psa. 110:4, be a priest after the order
of Melchizedek. Hence he shall function in three capacities: as
prophet, priest, and king. Zechariah in 6:13 speaks of this one,
King Messiah, as a priest sitting upon His throne. Therefore,
according to the warning of Deut. 18:15-19, everyone who does
not heed this prophet shall be held personally responsible.

According to this same verse Messiah when he returns will
"make them (the Hebrew race) inherit the desolate heritages."

No movement nor organization, regardless of finances, influence, power, etc. can restore the people to the land, and vice versa. Only this Servant, King Messiah, can do this thing.

Another glorious picture of Messiah and His work is given in Isa. 61:1-3: רוּחַ אֲדֹנָי יֱהוִֹה עָלָי יַעַן מָשַׁח יְהוָה אֹתִי לְבַשֵּׂר עֲנָוִים שְׁלָחַנִי לַחֲבֹשׁ לְנִשְׁבְּרֵי־לֵב לִקְרֹא לִשְׁבוּיִם דְּרוֹר וְלַאֲסוּרִים פְּקַח־קוֹחַ: לִקְרֹא שְׁנַת־רָצוֹן לַיהוָה וְיוֹם נָקָם לֵאלֹהֵינוּ לְנַחֵם כָּל־אֲבֵלִים: לָשׂוּם לַאֲבֵלֵי צִיּוֹן לָתֵת לָהֶם פְּאֵר תַּחַת אֵפֶר שֶׁמֶן שָׂשׂוֹן תַּחַת אֵבֶל מַעֲטֵה תְהִלָּה תַּחַת רוּחַ כֵּהָה וְקֹרָא לָהֶם אֵילֵי הַצֶּדֶק מַטַּע יְהוָה לְהִתְפָּאֵר: "The Spirit of the Lord יְהֹוָה is upon me; because the Lord hath anointed me to preach good tidings unto the meek; he hath sent me to bind up the broken-hearted, to proclaim liberty to the captives, and the opening *of the prison* to them that are bound; to proclaim the year of the Lord's favor, and the day of vengeance of our God; to comfort all that mourn; to appoint unto them that mourn in Zion, to give unto them a garland for ashes, the oil of joy for mourning, the garment of praise for the spirit of heaviness; that they may be called trees of righteousness, the planting of the Lord, that he may be glorified." In verse 1 the statement is made that Messiah shall be anointed, not with oil as were the ancient kings of Israel, but with the רוּחַ אֲדֹנָי, "Spirit of the Lord." The anointing with oil was simply symbolical and typical of the real spiritual anointing by the Spirit of God which the Messiah shall receive and which thus constitutes Him Israel's Messiah. In the succeeding verses appear the glorious results which follow the work of the Messiah. For glowing descriptions of the earth during the reign of the Messiah see Psa. 72; 132; Isa. 11 and 12.*

---

* In some quarters the Messianic prophecies are interpreted not as predictions of a personal Messiah but of an age or period of the world during which certain ideals and standards will prevail. During that age, according to this theory, the world will have evolved a civilization intellectually, ethically, culturally, and materially far superior to the present order: in other words, a golden age. In order to teach this lesson the most effectually to their contemporaries, the prophets personified the age, since, according to the current idea, a noble king was the very embodiment and personification of life's highest ideals and principles.

In reply to this position let the reader note the fact that the one fundamental principle for interpreting any language, oral or written, is that each word is to be taken in its ordinary, primary, literal meaning unless the context indicates otherwise. Whenever this rule is not observed, it is impossible for one to understand correctly what is said. Another important rule that is absolutely essential to proper understanding of language is that whenever the context points to a figurative or metaphorical meaning, that secondary or figurative meaning of the words or of the passage is to be chosen which accords with its symbolic or figurative meaning in passages about which there is no discussion. An examination of all of the Messianic passages in the Tenach points clearly to the conclusion that the literal meaning is to be chosen. Therefore the figurative interpretation of Messianic prophecies is purely arbitrary and gratuitous.

A second objection to this theory is that in the Messianic passages the Messiah is represented as coming and ushering in this golden age. Therefore the Messiah is distinguished in these prophecies from the age itself. (For examples see Isa. 11; 32; 33:17-23; Jer. 23: 5-8; Psa. 72; 132).

CHAPTER VIII

THE TIME OF MESSIAH'S COMING

THE time when God assumes human form in order to visit the world in its sorrows and distresses, which beset all on every hand, should be considered of the greatest importance not only by Israel but by all mankind.

I. ACCORDING TO THE PREDICTION OF THE TORAH (GEN. 49:10)

לֹא־יָסוּר שֵׁבֶט מִיהוּדָה וּמְחֹקֵק מִבֵּין רַגְלָיו עַד כִּי־יָבֹא שִׁילֹה וְלוֹ יִקְהַת עַמִּים: "The sceptre shall not depart from Judah, nor a lawgiver from between His feet, till Shiloh come, having the obedience of the peoples" (Author's translation). The person referred to as Shiloh is acknowledged by many Hebrew and Christian scholars to be the Messiah מָשִׁיחַ.

The position is sometimes taken that the translation of Gen. 49:10 is inaccurate. The following translation has been suggested by one author: "The sceptre shall not depart from Judah nor a lawgiver from between his feet forever. For Shiloh shall come, and to him shall be the gathering of the people." The translator then adds that the passage teaches "That Shiloh, by whom Messiah may be meant, shall restore the sceptre to Judah, and the right to make laws." This translation grammatically may be justified but it seems quite strained and awkward in this context. There is a contradiction between the translation and the translator's explanation. In the translation he states that the sceptre and a lawgiver shall never depart from Judah; in the comment he says that Shiloh, which expression may refer to Messiah, will restore the sceptre to Judah. If it has never departed from Judah, it cannot be restored; hence the contradiction. Even this translator admits that the passage may refer to the Messiah.

Isaac Leeser thus translates it: "The sceptre shall not depart from Judah, nor a lawgiver from between his feet; until Shiloh come, and unto him shall the gathering of the people be."

That the passage was anciently understood as of Messianic import is seen from the following quotation from Dr. Edersheim: "The expression 'Shiloh' is also applied to the Messiah, with

81

the curious addition, that in the latter days all nations would bring gifts to Him. Alike the Targum Onkelos, Pseudo-Jonathan, and the Jerusalem Targum, as well as Sanh. 98b, the Midrash on the passage, and that on Prov. 19:21, and on Lam. 1:16, where it is rendered *shelo,* 'whose it is,' refer the expression 'Shiloh,' and, indeed, the whole passage, to the Messiah."

Rab said, "The world was created only for the sake of David; Samuel said, It was for the sake of Moses; R. Yochanan said, It was only for the sake of the Messiah. What is his name? Those of the school of R. Shila say, Shiloh is his name, as it is said 'Until Shiloh come.'"

According to this prediction he comes before the sceptre (ruling power and authority) passes from Judah. Historically, the nation of Judah was completely destroyed and its governmental powers lost in the year 70 A. D. Hence according to the Torah, which is infallible, the Messiah has already come, but Israel did not recognize Him. See Isa. 53—the chapter which gives the picture of the Messiah suffering the agonies of death because of the transgression of Israel, His people, to whom the stroke was due.

II. ACCORDING TO THE PREDICTION OF DANIEL

The very year that מָשִׁיחַ Messiah, the Prince, should be cut off is definitely prophesied in Dan. 9:26. In order to understand this prediction let one note the context. In the first year of Darius the Mede (Dan. 9:1, 2) Daniel was reading the prophecy concerning the Babylonian captivity. Stirred by this reading he began to pray but was interrupted by the angel Gabriel who was dispatched from God to him. Daniel having read Jeremiah's prophecy, doubtless, concluded that the reign of "peace, plenty, and prosperity" for Israel was to follow immediately after the captivity. Since he was thinking in terms of years (see verse 2) the angel disabused his mind of the wrong conclusion which he had drawn from his reading and informed him that instead of the restoration of the kingdom to Israel in glory, which he assumed would be established at the end of the seventy years of captivity, there would be seven seventies (of years) "decreed upon thy people and upon thy holy city" before the inauguration of the glorious kingdom (Dan. 9:24). According to verses 25 and 26, at the conclusion of the sixty-ninth week (483rd year), the Messiah would be cut off and have nothing. The initial date of this period of four hundred and eighty-three years is the year of the issuing of the decree to the Jews to restore and to build Jerusalem, which, according to history, occurred in the year 538 B. C. Hence according to this prediction the Messiah was to be cut off four hundred and eighty-three years after Cyrus issued this decree.*

---

* The chronology of the Persian period of universal history is in great confusion; the inspired statement of Daniel is the only authenticated chronological statement which one has and in which he can put any dependence for these periods. Since the Tenach has proved to be accurate and absolutely trustworthy in every detail wherever it has been possible to test its statements by the acid tests of cold truthful scientific facts, one can be absolutely certain that the statement, "shall the anointed one be cut off, and have nothing" is trustworthy in the highest degree, and that the Messiah, the Prince, did come four hundred and eighty-three years after Cyrus issued his decree (Ezra 1:1-4) and was cut off.

CHAPTER IX

MESSIAH'S REDEMPTIVE CAREER

PSALM 110 is one of the highest mountain peaks of prophecy and sets forth in a most vivid and graphic manner the life and ministry of God's anointed King; hence a careful study of it will illuminate many of the questions connected with the nature and work of the Hebrew Messiah.

I. AUTHORSHIP OF THE PSALM

One of the first questions to be settled in approaching the study of this psalm is, Who was the human author whom God used in giving this revelation? In answer to this question various positions have been taken by scholars. In the superscription appear the words מִזְמוֹר לְדָוִד: "a Psalm of David." The writer is aware that in recent years rationalistic criticism has endeavored to throw doubt on the information given by the superscription of the psalms; but in the absence of clear, positive proof pointing in a different direction these superscriptions should be allowed to give their testimony unimpeached; hence one does well to accept the position that David, the King of Israel, was the human author.

Expositors endeavor, if possible, to place any document in its original historical setting in order to interpret it properly. In attempting to do so they seek for the historical facts which gave birth to the composition. Passing by the efforts made by some to find the setting of this psalm in the days of Hezekiah or some other prince of the house of David, the writer wishes the reader to note the fact that there are historical occurrences in the life of David sufficient to give birth or rise to this most magnificent ode. Among these events may be noted David's bringing the ark to Mt. Moriah; his making a sanctuary for it and his general oversight of things spiritual; and lastly his victories over the Syro-Ammonites. These events were of such moment as to give the typical background to this wonderful prophecy. At the beginning of David's reign, the hopes of the nation seemed to cluster

84

around his personality as the one through whom peace, blessings, and all the hopes promised to Israel would come. After his great sin (II Sam. 11), the Messianic hope seemed to detach itself from his personality and to take on a more definite form to be realized in the future in the coming of a king from his descendants who would rule in absolute righteousness, justice and in the fear of God.

וְאֵלֶּה דִּבְרֵי דָוִד הָאַחֲרֹנִים נְאֻם דָּוִד בֶּן־יִשַׁי וּנְאֻם הַגֶּבֶר הֻקַם עָל מְשִׁיחַ אֱלֹהֵי יַעֲקֹב וּנְעִים זְמִרוֹת יִשְׂרָאֵל: רוּחַ יְהוָה דִּבֶּר־בִּי וּמִלָּתוֹ עַל־לְשׁוֹנִי: אָמַר אֱלֹהֵי יִשְׂרָאֵל לִי דִבֶּר צוּר יִשְׂרָאֵל מוֹשֵׁל בָּאָדָם צַדִּיק מוֹשֵׁל יִרְאַת אֱלֹהִים: וּכְאוֹר בֹּקֶר יִזְרַח־שָׁמֶשׁ בֹּקֶר לֹא עָבוֹת מִנֹּגַהּ מִמָּטָר דֶּשֶׁא מֵאָרֶץ: כִּי־לֹא־כֵן בֵּיתִי עִם־אֵל כִּי בְרִית עוֹלָם שָׂם לִי עֲרוּכָה בַכֹּל וּשְׁמֻרָה כִּי־כָל־יִשְׁעִי וְכָל־חֵפֶץ כִּי־לֹא יַצְמִיחַ: "Now these are the last words of David. David the son of Jesse saith, And the man who was raised on high saith, The anointed of the God of Jacob, And the sweet psalmist of Israel: The Spirit of the Lord spake by me, And his word was upon my tongue. The God of Israel said, The Rock of Israel spake to me: one that ruleth over men righteously, That ruleth in the fear of God, *He shall be* as the light of the morning, when the sun riseth, A morning without clouds, *When* the tender grass *springeth* out of the earth, Through clear shining after rain. Verily my house is not so with God; Yet he hath made with me an everlasting covenant, Ordered in all things, and sure: For it is all my salvation, and all *my* desire, Although he maketh it not to grow" (II Sam. 23:1-5). From this quotation it is quite evident that David in the closing scenes of his life realized his own failures, but also the faithfulness of God in His raising up this righteous king of the future.

II. THE ORIGINAL TEXT AND TRANSLATION BY DELITZSCH.

לְדָוִד מִזְמוֹר נְאֻם יְהוָה לַאדֹנִי שֵׁב לִימִינִי עַד־אָשִׁית אֹיְבֶיךָ הֲדֹם לְרַגְלֶיךָ: מַטֵּה עֻזְּךָ יִשְׁלַח יְהוָה מִצִּיּוֹן רְדֵה בְּקֶרֶב אֹיְבֶיךָ: עַמְּךָ נְדָבֹת בְּיוֹם חֵילֶךָ בְּהַדְרֵי־קֹדֶשׁ מֵרֶחֶם מִשְׁחָר לְךָ טַל יַלְדֻתֶךָ: נִשְׁבַּע יְהוָה וְלֹא יִנָּחֵם אַתָּה־כֹהֵן לְעוֹלָם עַל־דִּבְרָתִי מַלְכִּי־צֶדֶק: אֲדֹנָי עַל־יְמִינְךָ מָחַץ בְּיוֹם־אַפּוֹ מְלָכִים: יָדִין בַּגּוֹיִם מָלֵא גְוִיּוֹת מָחַץ רֹאשׁ עַל־אֶרֶץ רַבָּה: מִנַּחַל בַּדֶּרֶךְ יִשְׁתֶּה עַל־כֵּן יָרִים רֹאשׁ:

"1 The oracle of the Lord unto my Lord:
    'Sit thou at My right hand,
    Until I make thine enemies
    The stool for thy feet.'

2 The sceptre of thine authority
    Shall the Lord stretch forth from Zion:
    'Rule thou in the midst of thine enemies.'

3 Thy people are most willing in the day of thy warfare;
    In holy festive garments,
    Out of the womb of the dawn
    Cometh to thee the dew of the young men.

4 The Lord hath sworn and will not repent:
    'Thou shalt be a priest for ever
    After the manner of Melchizedek.'

5 The Lord at thy right hand
    Dasheth kings in pieces in the day of His wrath;
6 He will judge among the nations;
    It becometh full of corpses.

    He dasheth in pieces the head over a wide land;
7 Of the brook shall he drink in the way;
    Therefore shall he lift up his head."

The poem falls into three strophes, each containing seven lines,
which fact bears "the threefold impress of the number seven,
which is the number of an oath and a covenant." There appears
in the hymn the Sacred Name of God יְהֹוָה three times, each of
which introduces the words of the Almighty.

III. WHO IS אֲדֹנִי? "MY LORD"

As to the meaning of אֲדֹנִי there has been much discussion to
no profit. One familiar with the Hebrew knows that this term
is frequently used by a servant when referring to his master
and occasionally by a subject when addressing his king, as is
seen in I Sam. 22:12, although the more correct form of address
is אֲדֹנִי הַמֶּלֶךְ, "My Lord the King" (I Sam. 24:8(9). That it
is used in addressing a Divine Being is seen in Josh. 5:14, 15.
To Joshua reconnoitering around Jericho a man suddenly appeared.
To his question as to whether he were for or against him, the
latter answered, saying, אֲנִי שַׂר־צְבָא־יְהֹוָה, "Prince of the Lord's
hosts am I." Joshua, recognizing that he was a Supernatural
Being, addressed him as אֲדֹנִי and worshipped. The statement that
he was the prince of the hosts of the Lord shows that he had con-

trol of all of the hosts of heaven, including all cherubim, seraphim, and angels of every rank and file. While this passage is not absolute proof that this one appearing to Joshua was God, the implications of the context point positively in that direction. These implications will be elevated to veritable proof by an examination of Judg. 6:13, 14.

In verse 11 of Judges 6 the statement is made that "The angel of the Lord came"; verse 12 states, "And the angel of the Lord appeared unto Him"; verse 13, "And Gideon said unto him, Oh, my Lord, if the Lord is with us . . . "; and in verse 14 appears this statement, "And the Lord looked upon him . . ." The Being Who is called "The Angel of the Lord" is, according to verse 14, the Lord Himself Whom Gideon addressed as אֲדֹנָי, the same form of the word which appears in Psalm 110. The position that אֲדֹנָי refers to a divine person in this Psalm is confirmed by the fact that it opens with the words נְאֻם־יְהוָה "the oracle of the Lord." These words, with very few exceptions, refer to a divine revelation; hence in the mouth of David, who occupied the highest position of honor and power in the kingdom, it signifies a divine revelation made to him concerning his superior. Since the only one known in Hebrew prophecy as superior to David is the Messiah, evidently David in the Spirit of God here spoke concerning Him.

A close study of Psalm 2 will show the truth seeker that it is seen clearly that the Messiah referred to in verse 3 is the same as is spoken of as "My King" in verse 6; that likewise the speaker of verses 7-9 who claims that God addressed Him as "My Son" and Who is to have universal dominion over the nations of the earth is the One referred to as מְשִׁיחוֹ "His anointed," and מַלְכִּי "My King"; and that hence the Messiah is both human and divine—God's Son. These facts being true, one is not surprised, when he reads in the Septuagint version, translated before 250 B. C., to see that the Hebrew translators used the same Greek word κύριος in translating both the word יְהוָה and אֲדֹנָי. This translation proves conclusively that the Hebrew scholars who made the Greek version understood that the One to Whom God spoke was likewise Divine.

IV. THE FIRST ORACLE

The words spoken by the Lord to David's Lord are, "Sit Thou at My right hand, until I make Thine enemies the stool for Thy feet." This language shows that there are enemies of the Messiah. It is impossible for anyone to be hostile to another unless in some way he has come in contact with the latter who has done something which displeases him. Therefore the assumption underlying this language is that the Messiah has come in contact with those who are hostile to Him. The following verse shows very clearly who these enemies are: "The sceptre of Thine authority shall the Lord stretch forth from Zion: rule Thou in the midst of Thine enemies." The first part of this Hebrew parallelism shows that the Messiah is to rule in Zion and the latter part points to the inhabitants of same as His enemies; therefore the inhabitants of Zion are His enemies. These two verses, therefore, presuppose that the Messiah comes to Zion and incurs the displeasure of the Hebrew people. When they become hostile to Him, the Lord invites Him, the Messiah, to leave the place of hostility and to sit at His right hand—in heaven. The period during which the Messiah is to remain in heaven with the Lord will be terminated by the latter's subduing the former's enemies. Therefore this passage assumes two comings of the Messiah: at His first coming the Hebrew people reject Him and He returns to the right hand of the throne of God awaiting the time (the length of which is not suggested here) when the Lord shall have brought the Hebrew people, those hostile to His Messiah, into a state of subjection. This conquest having been accomplished, the Messiah returns to Zion as its King and with divine authority and power rules in the very place where He formerly was rejected. At His first coming He comes in humiliation and, as Isa. 53 shows, He suffers and is rejected; He leaves the Hebrew people to suffer and to be driven from nation to nation because of the sin of their rejecting Him (which truth is taught in many other Scriptures); and finally He returns in the majesty and power of the Eternal God to restore the penitent remnant of the children of Israel to their own land, to make them the head of the nations instead of the tail, and to reign from sea to sea.

V. The Second Oracle

A. *Conversion of the Nation*

The second division of this psalm consists of verses 3 and 4. The words עַמְּךָ נְדָבֹת "Thy people are free-willingnesses" (i. e., "altogether cheerful willingnesses in the day of the marshalling of thy forces") answer the expectation that is aroused in verse 2, namely, since the Lord is to reign as a King He will have an army. The words "thy people " refer to the people of the Messiah, namely the Hebrew people. They are "free-willing-nesses." This translation is literal and is very graphic. One might call them free-willingness personified, free, voluntary willingness being the dominant, all-absorbing characteristic which eclipses all others at the time.

At this point the question arises, "Why will the Hebrew people accept their Messiah Whom they have formerly rejected, when He returns in the day of His power?" To many, such a thought is far beyond the realm of possibility; hence unthinkable. The answer to this question is found in Hos. 5:15, "I will go and return to my place, till they acknowledge their offence, and seek my face: in their *affliction* they will seek me earnestly." When one is in good health and has a sufficiency of material goods he feels, as a rule, very independent; but should he lose not only health, but property, he realizes for the first time how dependent he is. In this condition life takes on a different hue; he views everything from a different angle. Thus it shall be with Israel. When she enters the period which is called "the time of Jacob's trouble" (Jer. 30:7), she will suffer as she has never at any time. She will be reduced to such straits as at present are inconceivable. It is true that many of Israel at various times have suffered almost unthinkable horrors, but there have never been any such difficulties and times of trouble as will come to the nation in the future. Daniel in speaking of this very time says, "And there shall be a time of trouble, such as never was since there was a nation even to that same time: and at that time thy people shall be delivered, everyone that shall be found written in the book" (Dan. 12:1). According to the Torah, Pharaoh, king of Egypt, was most reluctant in permitting Israel to leave

the country in order to serve the God of Israel. Finally, after
God had sent ten different judgments upon him, he was willing
for them to go. Judgments similar to those which He brought
upon Egypt by Moses, but far more intense and severe, will be
visited during the time of trouble upon all nations. These judgments will, figuratively speaking, awake Israel to the fact that
something is very radically wrong not only with the world in
general, but with Israel in her relation to her God in particular.
Under the stress of these severe judgments those who have sur-
vived the calamities, according to Hosea's prophecy, will seek
God earnestly. In harmony with this statement appears one in
the Torah. In Deut. 4:29, after having forewarned Israel that
in the event they corrupted themselves in the land He would
scatter them among the nations, God promised that "From
thence ye shall seek the Lord thy God, and thou shalt find him,
when thou searchest after him with all thy heart and with
all thy soul." Thus Israel, like mankind in general, will only learn
her great lesson by bitter experience. God has chosen her "in
the furnace of affliction" (Isa. 48:10). In the midst of this distress
they come to the point that they will say בָּרוּךְ הַבָּא בְּשֵׁם יְהֹוָה
"Blessed be he that cometh in the name of the Lord" (Psa.
118:26). Thus they become "free-willingnesses."

The expression "free-willingnesses" is but another way of stating that the nation will repent of her having been enemies of
God's Messiah, and that she will whole-heartedly accept Him and
His leadership. This teaching is confirmed by the confession
which Israel, according to Isa. 53:1-9, will yet make in the future.
At the time of its national repentance Israel will confess that
she had misunderstood the mission and work of the Servant of
the Lord, having thought that He was smitten by the Lord for
His sins, whereas He was smitten for the transgression of the
nation. (A full discussion of the Servant of the Lord of Isa. 53
will be seen in Chapter X.) The unmistakable prediction that
Israel will repent and come back to God is seen in Jer. 3:20-23:

אָכֵן בָּגְדָה אִשָּׁה מֵרֵעָהּ כֵּן בְּגַדְתֶּם בִּי בֵּית יִשְׂרָאֵל נְאֻם־יְהֹוָה: קוֹל עַל־
שְׁפָיִים נִשְׁמָע בְּכִי תַחֲנוּנֵי בְּנֵי יִשְׂרָאֵל כִּי הֶעֱווּ אֶת־דַּרְכָּם שָׁכְחוּ אֶת־
יְהֹוָה אֱלֹהֵיהֶם: שׁוּבוּ בָּנִים שׁוֹבָבִים אֶרְפָּה מְשׁוּבֹתֵיכֶם הִנְנוּ אָתָנוּ לָךְ

כִּי אַתָּה יְהֹוָה אֱלֹהֵינוּ: אָכֵן לַשֶּׁקֶר מִגְּבָעוֹת הָמוֹן הָרִים אָכֵן בַּיהֹוָה אֱלֹהֵינוּ תְּשׁוּעַת יִשְׂרָאֵל: "Surely as a wife treacherously departeth from her husband, so have ye dealt treacherously with me, O house of Israel, saith the Lord. A voice is heard upon the bare heights, the weeping *and* the supplications of the children of Israel; because they have perverted their way, they have forgotten the Lord their God. Return, ye backsliding children, I will heal your backslidings. Behold, we are come unto thee; for thou art the Lord our God. Truly in vain is *the help that is looked for* from the hills, the tumult on the mountains: truly in the Lord our God is the salvation of Israel."

Verse 20 is the Lord's severe indictment of Israel in departing from Him. Verse 21 is a prediction of her having been convicted, returning in genuine repentance to God. Verse 22a is God's invitation to return to Him. In 22b and 23 is Israel's confession to God and her acknowledgment that He is the One Who brings deliverance. In Zech. 12:10-14 appears another prediction relative to this same national repentance, at which time God "will remove the iniquity of that land in one day." This last statement refers to the time and event mentioned in Isa. 66:8, which has tersely been expressed: "A nation born in a day."

Just as the "people offered themselves willingly" (Judg. 5:2) and the governors did likewise (verse 9), so will the entire nation offer herself to her long-rejected Messiah to serve in any capacity He chooses. The word חַיְלֵךְ, translated "warfare" refers to troops and frequently to the marshaling of forces or armies. As proof of these statements see Ex. 14:28; I Kgs. 20:1; II Chron. 26:13.

B. *A Nation of Priests*

The converted nation will really be a kingdom of priests (cf. Ex. 19:6), for they will be arrayed in בְּהַדְרֵי־קֹדֶשׁ "holy festive garments." These words are the regular ones used in the Torah to refer to the attire of an officiating priest. Hence the nation in reality will at that time become a nation of priests. מֵרֶחֶם מִשְׁחָר לְךָ טַל יַלְדֻתֶךָ "Out of the womb of the morning thou hast the dew of thy youthful ones." Though there are two figures of speech blended in these words, a careful examination of each idea will render the passage very intelligible. The morning of the great day of King Messiah is likened to a woman who gives birth to children. The use of this figure carries with it the correlative idea of the most severe suffering and pain. In Isa. 66:7-9 the prophet uses the same figure, but instead of personifying morning he compared Zion to the woman who is in travail bringing forth her children.

בְּטֶרֶם תָּחִיל יָלָדָה בְּטֶרֶם יָבוֹא חֵבֶל לָהּ וְהִמְלִיטָה זָכָר: מִי־שָׁמַע כָּזֹאת מִי רָאָה כָּאֵלֶּה הֲיוּחַל אֶרֶץ בְּיוֹם אֶחָד אִם־יִוָּלֵד גּוֹי פַּעַם אֶחָת כִּי־חָלָה גַּם־יָלְדָה צִיּוֹן אֶת־בָּנֶיהָ: הַאֲנִי אַשְׁבִּיר וְלֹא אוֹלִיד יֹאמַר יְהֹוָה אִם־אֲנִי הַמּוֹלִיד וְעָצַרְתִּי אָמַר אֱלֹהָיִךְ: "Before she travailed, she brought forth; before her pain came, she was delivered of a man-child. Who hath heard such a thing? Who hath seen such things? Shall a land be born in one day? Shall a nation be brought forth at once? For as soon as Zion travailed, she brought forth her children. Shall I bring to the birth, and not cause to bring forth? saith the Lord: shall I that cause to bring forth shut the womb? saith thy God." Here Zion is the name poetically given to the nation which is compared to a woman in travail. That this period of travail is most severe is seen from the fact that God punishes Jerusalem double for her sins (Isa. 40:1,2). The Child of which the nation is delivered is the faithful, penitent, God-fearing remnant of the nation who, seeing the mistake of the nation and thirsting after God with all of its heart, returns to God and the Messiah Whom the nation rejected at His first coming.

This remnant of the nation which is born in a day, appears again in Ezek. 20:33-39. Promising to gather the scattered nation from all the lands whither they have been dispersed and to bring them "into the wilderness of the peoples" and to "enter into judgment with you face to face," God makes the following promise: "And I will cause you to pass under the rod, and I will bring you into the bond of the covenant; and I will purge out from among you the rebels, and them that transgress against me; I will bring them forth out of the land where they sojourn, but they shall not enter into the land of Israel: and ye shall know that I am the Lord" (Ezek. 20:37, 38). Here appears the remnant that is born in a day when Zion is in travail after all of the rebels and transgressors have been slain.

This purified remnant is compared in the second figure of this statement to the dewdrops upon the vegetation in the early morning. Associated with the idea of dew is that of vigor, youth, and power. As the innumerable dewdrops on the vegetation are invisible while it is yet dark but are clearly seen in all of their beauty at the sunrise, so this penitent remnant at the close of Israel's dark night of trouble becomes manifest when King Messiah Who, according to Mal. 4:2, is "the Sun of Righteousness" arises with healing in His wings.

The fact that the converted nation is a kingdom of priests (cf. Isa. 61:6) presupposes that the leader likewise is a priest. This supposition is confirmed by verse 4: "The Lord has sworn and will not repent: thou shalt be a priest forever after the manner of Melchizedek." God's sworn statement is a sufficient guarantee of its fulfillment. The fact that the ruler, the hero of this psalm, is to be a priest after the order of Melchizedek, confirms the position taken at the beginning of the study of this psalm, namely, that David was not the subject but the author. Franz Delitzsch on this point remarks: "How could David be called a priest after the manner of Melchizedek, he who had no claim upon the tithes of the priests like Melchizedek, and to whom was denied the legal right to offer sacrifices (cf. II Chron. 26:20), a right which is inseparable in the Old Testament from the idea of the priesthood?" Jeremiah in making his prediction of the new covenant doubtless had this thought in mind when he spoke the following words: וְהָיָה אַדִּירוֹ מִמֶּנּוּ וּמֹשְׁלוֹ מִקִּרְבּוֹ יֵצֵא

וְהִקְרַבְתִּיו וְנִגַּשׁ אֵלַי כִּי מִי הוּא־זֶה עָרַב אֶת־לִבּוֹ לָגֶשֶׁת אֵלַי נְאֻם־יְהֹוָה:

"And their prince shall be of themselves, and their ruler shall proceed from the midst of them; and I will cause him to draw near, and he shall approach unto me: for who is he that hath had boldness to approach unto me? saith the Lord" (Jer. 30:21). Likewise, Zechariah, a post-exilic prophet, doubtless had this same Psalm in mind when he by inspiration declared,

כֹּה אָמַר יְהֹוָה צְבָאוֹת לֵאמֹר הִנֵּה־אִישׁ צֶמַח שְׁמוֹ וּמִתַּחְתָּיו יִצְמָח וּבָנָה

אֶת־הֵיכַל יְהוָה: וְהוּא יִבְנֶה אֶת־הֵיכַל יְהוָה וְהוּא יִשָּׂא הוֹד וְיָשַׁב וּמָשַׁל

עַל־כִּסְאוֹ וְהָיָה כֹהֵן עַל־כִּסְאוֹ וַעֲצַת שָׁלוֹם תִּהְיֶה בֵּין שְׁנֵיהֶם: "Thus
speaketh the Lord of hosts, saying, Behold, the man whose
name is the Branch: and he shall grow up out of his place; and
he shall build the temple of the Lord; even he shall build the
temple of the Lord; and he shall bear the glory, and shall sit
and rule upon his throne; and he shall be a priest upon his
throne; and the counsel of peace shall be between them both"
(Zech. 6:12, 13).   "The coming Prince of Israel requires no
priestly assistance, but is placed near to God as a Priest, and has
free access to Him."   This Man Who is called צֶמַח the Branch,
is recognized both among Jews and Gentiles as the promised
Messiah.   According to Zechariah He will wear not only the
regal crown, but the sacred mitre, being both King and
Priest.

VI. MESSIAH'S FINAL CONQUEST

In harmony with the statement of verse 1 that the Lord God
will subject the Messiah's enemies under Him, the psalmist in
Psa. 110:5-7 declares that the Lord God at the right hand of
the Messiah (assisting Him) strikes through kings in the day
of His wrath.   Hence though the Messiah does take personal
vengeance against His enemies as set forth in Isa. 63:1-6, the
Lord God assists in the subduing of the same.   The conflict in
which the Messiah will engage when He returns in glory is
graphically set forth in the prayer of Habakkuk, chapter 3.   Likewise, Joel in the third chapter of his prophecy sets forth the
judgment which the Messiah will bring upon the godless nations
when He returns.   These Scriptures, as well as many others,
simply set forth in graphic form the destruction of the armies
of the world as is suggested in verse 6 of this ode.   The expression "He dasheth in pieces the head over a wide land" has been
variously interpreted.   It is quite likely, however, that it is a
reference to the slaughter of the Ruler who reigns over wide
stretches of territory.   It is quite probable that this one is the
same one who is set forth as the little horn on the fourth beast
mentioned in Dan. 7, which is the same person as the one who
is spoken of as the king of Babylon in the end-time.

CONCLUSION

To sum up the information gathered from this psalm let the reader note that the One concerning Whom the psalmist is speaking is God manifest in the flesh (cf. Isa. 9:6(5)), Who is come to Zion and Who, having incurred her displeasure, is rejected; therefore, God invites Him to remain in His Presence until the subjection of said enemies. When they are subdued the Messiah returns in power and the remnant of those who rejected Him accept Him willingly, becoming a nation of priests who constitute His priestly army. He as their Leader is a Priest, not according to the Aaronic priesthood, but after the order of Melchizedek, being appointed to this office by an oath. When He returns to begin His reign in Zion with the assistance of the Lord, He smites all of His enemies and sets up His kingdom among men.

AUTHOR'S TRANSLATION WITH EXPLANATORY NOTES IN ITALICS

A Song of David *which the Spirit of God* spoke through him (II Sam. 23:1, 2).

A Divine Revelation of יְהֹוָה (The Lord) to my Lord, *King Messiah, God manifest in human form, concerning His relations to Israel*:

"Sit at my right hand *in the heavens, since the inhabitants of Jerusalem, to whom you went when you were born of the Virgin (Isa. 7:14) and whom you tried to lead back to God, have absolutely spurned your good offices and have rejected you. Continue in association with me in the Heaven of Heavens (Psa. 115:16)* until *the time arrives when* I shall make your enemies the footstool of your feet. *This subjugation of the children of Israel will be accomplished at the close of 'the time of Jacob's trouble' when they have made an end of breaking in pieces the power of the holy people (Dan. 12:7). Then,* the rod of your strength, will *I* יְהֹוָה (The Lord) send forth out of Zion, *which figurative language refers to your glorious reign in Jerusalem (Psa. 2). According to Our Eternal Purpose,* rule in the midst of your enemies, *since they in their great distress will then earnestly say, 'Blessed be he that cometh in the Name of the Lord.'*

"When you go to Zion the second time, the attitude of the nation will be exactly opposite from what it was when you went there

the first, for your people *will offer themselves to you as* free-will offerings *with their whole hearts* in the day of your power *when you muster all of your forces and resources and establish your universal reign of righteousness in their midst. The entire nation will then be a kingdom of priests (Ex. 19:5) arrayed* in the garments of holiness.   Out of the womb of the morning you will have the dew of your youthful ones.   *In these figures the time of your beginning to reign is spoken of as the mother of the remnant of the nation which, in turn, is compared to the early morning dew because of the youthful vigor of each one of your people and of the great number of them.*

"*Since the nation is to be a kingdom of priests, it is proper that you as her leader and King, likewise, be a Priest.*

"*Therefore, I* יְהוָה have sworn and will not repent, 'you are a Priest for ever after the order of Melchizedek.'   *You are the King of Glory (Psa. 24:8) and Priest, not of the Aaronic order, but of a higher type, Melchizedek, King of Salem (Jerusalem) in the days of Abraham to whom the latter paid tithes, being the pattern (Gen. 14:18; Zech. 6:13).*

יְהוָה   " 'the Lord' at your right hand will fatally wound kings in the day of His wrath.   He will judge among the nations, *when He assists you in establishing your throne;* He will fill *the battlefields* with dead bodies, *as is set forth in Isa. 63:1-6;* He will fatally wound the head *man who governs* a vast land, *and who is the Anti-Messiah* (cf. Dan. 7:8, 11).   *In this final conflict He,* the Lord, will drink of the brook by the way, *which language means that He will not stop, rest, and prolong the conflict, but, rather, will hastily complete His conquest.*   Therefore He will lift up *His* head *in triumph at the end of the battle.*

Chapter X

BEHOLD, THE LAMB OF GOD!

I. The Historical Setting of Isaiah 53

IN the latter half of Isaiah* (chapters 40-66) appear the great Servant Passages which reach the highest peaks of glory of the revelation contained in the Tenach.

These twenty-seven chapters divide into three sections of nine chapters each. In the first section (chapters 40-48) Israel is seen in Babylonian captivity and Cyrus, the king of Persia, appears upon the historical horizon as the one chosen of God through whom deliverance shall be brought to the captive exiles. In the same section also appears "the servant of the Lord" who, in a very limited and imperfect way, Cyrus typifies. In the second section (chapters 48-57) appears this Servant of the Lord as the principal actor upon the stage. Here Israel in the white light of spiritual illumination which comes from the Spirit of God is seen to be in a captivity of a far more serious nature than of being in exile in a foreign country, i.e., in the bondage and servitude to sin and unrighteousness. Here also the Servant of the Lord in the three central chapters of this middle division appears as the great deliverer of his people from this spiritual bondage. In the last section (chapters 58-66) the glorious result of the work of the Servant of the Lord has appeared, Israel has been delivered from her severe bondage to sin and is enjoying the covenant relation-

---

* By rationalistic critics the book of Isaiah has been dissected and apportioned to a number of different authors, the principle of dissection being determined by supposed changes in style, diction and subject matter. A close examination of the book as a whole, and a comparison of the parts after the process of dissection has been completed, prove positively that the grounds for such a dissection are purely imaginary, there being no positive data to justify such an apportionment of the contents to different authors who lived in a period of between 200 and 300 years. For every dissimilarity that may be discovered in the two sections, there are many more similarities. A scientific investigation of the supposed evidence pointing to various authors will cause the imaginary differences to vanish. On the contrary, a sound, sane exegesis of the contents of the book in its historical setting points definitely to its unity.

ship with her God under the personal rule and power of the Servant of the Lord.

In the central chapter of this central section of the second half of Isaiah the Servant stands forth in all His glory and beauty. This great passage (52:13-53:12) is the highest mountain peak of God's prophetic revelation.

II. The Text of the Great Servant Passage

הִנֵּה יַשְׂכִּיל עַבְדִּי יָרוּם וְנִשָּׂא וְגָבַהּ מְאֹד: כַּאֲשֶׁר שָׁמְמוּ עָלֶיךָ רַבִּים
כֵּן־מִשְׁחַת מֵאִישׁ מַרְאֵהוּ וְתֹאֲרוֹ מִבְּנֵי אָדָם: כֵּן יַזֶּה גּוֹיִם רַבִּים עָלָיו
יִקְפְּצוּ מְלָכִים פִּיהֶם כִּי אֲשֶׁר לֹא־סֻפַּר לָהֶם רָאוּ וַאֲשֶׁר לֹא־שָׁמְעוּ
הִתְבּוֹנָנוּ:

מִי הֶאֱמִין לִשְׁמֻעָתֵנוּ וּזְרוֹעַ יְהֹוָה עַל־מִי נִגְלָתָה: וַיַּעַל כַּיּוֹנֵק לְפָנָיו
וְכַשֹּׁרֶשׁ מֵאֶרֶץ צִיָּה לֹא־תֹאַר לוֹ וְלֹא הָדָר וְנִרְאֵהוּ וְלֹא־מַרְאֶה וְנֶחְמְדֵהוּ:
נִבְזֶה וַחֲדַל אִישִׁים אִישׁ מַכְאֹבוֹת וִידוּעַ חֹלִי וּכְמַסְתֵּר פָּנִים מִמֶּנּוּ נִבְזֶה
וְלֹא חֲשַׁבְנֻהוּ: אָכֵן חֳלָיֵנוּ הוּא נָשָׂא וּמַכְאֹבֵינוּ סְבָלָם וַאֲנַחְנוּ חֲשַׁבְנֻהוּ
נָגוּעַ מֻכֵּה אֱלֹהִים וּמְעֻנֶּה: וְהוּא מְחֹלָל מִפְּשָׁעֵינוּ מְדֻכָּא מֵעֲוֹנֹתֵינוּ
מוּסַר שְׁלוֹמֵנוּ עָלָיו וּבַחֲבֻרָתוֹ נִרְפָּא־לָנוּ: כֻּלָּנוּ כַּצֹּאן תָּעִינוּ אִישׁ
לְדַרְכּוֹ פָּנִינוּ וַיהֹוָה הִפְגִּיעַ בּוֹ אֵת עֲוֹן כֻּלָּנוּ: נִגַּשׂ וְהוּא נַעֲנֶה וְלֹא יִפְתַּח־
פִּיו כַּשֶּׂה לַטֶּבַח יוּבָל וּכְרָחֵל לִפְנֵי גֹזְזֶיהָ נֶאֱלָמָה וְלֹא יִפְתַּח פִּיו: מֵעֹצֶר
וּמִמִּשְׁפָּט לֻקָּח וְאֶת־דּוֹרוֹ מִי יְשׂוֹחֵחַ כִּי נִגְזַר מֵאֶרֶץ חַיִּים מִפֶּשַׁע עַמִּי
נֶגַע לָמוֹ: וַיִּתֵּן אֶת־רְשָׁעִים קִבְרוֹ וְאֶת־עָשִׁיר בְּמֹתָיו עַל לֹא־חָמָס עָשָׂה
וְלֹא מִרְמָה בְּפִיו: וַיהֹוָה חָפֵץ דַּכְּאוֹ הֶחֱלִי אִם־תָּשִׂים אָשָׁם נַפְשׁוֹ יִרְאֶה
זֶרַע יַאֲרִיךְ יָמִים וְחֵפֶץ יְהֹוָה בְּיָדוֹ יִצְלָח: מֵעֲמַל נַפְשׁוֹ יִרְאֶה יִשְׂבָּע
בְּדַעְתּוֹ יַצְדִּיק צַדִּיק עַבְדִּי לָרַבִּים וַעֲוֹנֹתָם הוּא יִסְבֹּל: לָכֵן אֲחַלֶּק־לוֹ
בָרַבִּים וְאֶת־עֲצוּמִים יְחַלֵּק שָׁלָל תַּחַת אֲשֶׁר הֶעֱרָה לַמָּוֶת נַפְשׁוֹ וְאֶת־
פֹּשְׁעִים נִמְנָה וְהוּא חֵטְא־רַבִּים נָשָׂא וְלַפֹּשְׁעִים יַפְגִּיעַ:

"Behold, my servant will deal wisely, he will rise and be exalted, and be very high. Just as many were astonished at thee,—so disfigured, his appearance was not like that of a man, and his form not like that of the children of men,—so will he make many nations tremble; kings will shut their mouths at him, for they see what has not been told them, and perceive what they have not heard. Who has believed what we have heard? And the arm of

the Lord,—over whom hath it been revealed? And he came up
like a layer-sprig before him, and like a root-sprout out of dry
ground; he had no form and no beauty, and we saw him and there
was no appearance that we could have found pleasure in him. He
was despised and forsaken of men, a man of sorrows and familiar
with sickness, and like one from whom men hide their face,
despised, and we esteemed him not. Verily our sicknesses he hath
borne, and our pains—he hath laden them; but we considered him
as one stricken, one smitten of God, and afflicted. Whereas he was
pierced because of our transgressions, bruised because of our iniquities; the punishment for peace to us lay upon him, and through
his stripes came healing to us. We all like sheep went astray; we
had each turned to his own way, and the Lord caused to fall on
him the iniquity of us all. He was ill-treated, while he suffered
willingly, and opened not his mouth; like the lamb that is led to the
shambles, and like a sheep that is dumb before her shearers, and he
opened not his mouth. Out of prison and out of judgment was he
taken; and of his contemporaries, who considered this: 'He was
snatched out of the land of the living, seeing that, on account of
the transgression of my people, vengeance fell on him?' And his
grave was assigned to him with transgressors, and with a rich man
was he in his death, because he had committed no unrighteousness, nor was there deceit in his mouth. And it pleased the Lord
to bruise him; he afflicted him with disease: if his soul were to pay
a trespass-offering, he should see posterity, live long days, and
the purpose of the Lord should prosper through his hand. Because
of the travail of his soul he will see, will refresh himself; through
his knowledge will he obtain righteousness, my righteous Servant,
for the many, and their iniquities will he take upon himself. Therefore I give him a share with the great, and with the strong will
he share spoil; because he poured out his soul unto death, and let
himself be numbered among transgressors, while he bare the sins
of many, and interceded for the transgressors" (Isa. 52:13-53:12).

The English translation quoted above is from the Fourth Edition
of "Commentary on Isaiah" by the late Franz Delitzsch. In order
to understand the message of this great servant passage, one must
study the text most carefully.

"But yet a connection must exist between the national sense in which 'Servant of the Lord' was used in 41:8 and the personal one here. The future Saviour is not described as the Son of David, as in chaps. 7-12 and elsewhere, but appears as the embodied idea of Israel, i.e., as its truth and reality in person. The idea of Servant of the Lord, to speak figuratively, is a pyramid. The lower basis is the whole of Israel; the middle section, Israel not merely after the flesh, but after the Spirit, the summit is the person of the Mediator of salvation arising out of Israel. The Mediator is the centre (1) in the circle of the kingdom of promise—the second David; (2) in the circle of the people of salvation—the true Israel; (3) in the circle of humanity—the second Adam. In these discourses, chaps. 40-66, the doctrine of salvation reaches its second stage. Israel's character as God's servant, rooted in the Lord's choice and call, and exhibited in bearing and action which harmonize with that call, is concentrated in Him, in Him alone, as its ripest fruit. God's gracious purpose in reference to humanity, which was the governing force in Israel's election, is carried by Him to full accomplishment."

III. WHO IS THIS SERVANT OF ISA. 52:13-53:12?

Having seen that the context in each instance must determine to whom or to what the expression "my servant" refers the reader is now invited to note carefully the context of chapters 52:13-53:12 to ascertain who is the servant here.

A. *Is Israel This Servant?*

In the first place, is the suffering servant a Personification of the nation of Israel? To this question some honest, conscientious scholars answer in the affirmative. To the writer, however, this position is untenable for six unmistakable reasons:

(1) The prophet speaks of the servant as "he," "him," and "his" and clearly differentiates him from the audience with which he identifies himself and of which he speaks as "we," "our," and "us" (See 53:1-6). Since it is to the nation that he addresses his discourse and since he distinguishes between the servant and the audience, the servant is not the nation.

(2) This servant suffers for the entire nation. In 53:6 the prophet declares that all Israel has gone astray, i.e., they have

gone off into sin. In verse 8 he affirms that the servant "was cut off out of the land of the living for the transgression of my [Isaiah's people, the Hebrews] people to whom the stroke was due." Since, therefore, the servant suffers for the guilt of the nation, he cannot be the nation.

(3) The servant submits to the suffering heaped upon him submissively offering NO resistance. From this standpoint it is clear that one other than the nation is the sufferer. It is a well known fact that, instead of submitting to the cruelties and atrocities heaped upon her, Israel has stubbornly resisted with physical force in innumerable instances those who persecuted her, and only submitted when overpowered by superior forces. As proof of this assertion it is well to note the following summary of some outstanding historical facts in the life of the nation, which is written by an eminent Hebrew who deals with this subject historically: "Here is one described, who bears all sorts of affliction and oppression, without making the slightest resistance, without even opening his mouth to utter reproach—one who has the meekness and gentleness of a lamb, the inoffensiveness of a sheep. Surely this does not apply to the Jews. A very hasty glance at this history is sufficient to convince us of that. As long as ever they had the power, they did resist bitterly and bloodily. We freely acknowledge that their provocations were great. We have no wish to defend the wickedness of Christian nations. We grant that their treatment of the Jews is a blot and a stain. But that is not the question. The question is, Did the Jews bear all the oppression heaped upon them like lambs? Did they suffer evil without resisting it? History answers in the negative. The history of the Jewish captivity for the first seven centuries is a history of a series of insurrections, fierce and violent, against the nations. How desperate was the resistance to the Roman power which brought on the destruction of the temple by Titus! But when that was destroyed, the spirit of resistance still remained. A. D. 115, the Jews of Cyrene rebelled and slew 220,000 Libyans; and it was not until after several bloody battles that they submitted. A. D. 132, Bar Cochba appeared in the character of the Messiah at the head of an army, ready to shake off the Roman yoke. R. Akiba, one of those looked upon by the Rabbis as most righteous, supported

his resistance to the Roman authority; a bloody war was the consequence, and it was only by force that this insurrection was put down. A. D. 415, the Jews of Alexandria revolted. A. D. 522, the Jews of Persia revolted under the conduct of R. Mid, or Miz, at their head, and declared war against the King of Persia. A. D. 535, the Jews in Caesarea rebelled. A. D. 602, the Jews at Antioch. A. D. 624, the Jews in Arabia took up arms against Mahomet. A. D. 613, they joined the armies of Chosroes, when he made himself master of Jerusalem, and put thousands to death."

(4) This servant suffers VOLUNTARILY but the nation has never thus suffered. "He poured out his soul unto death." This statement shows that he suffers willingly, which position is strengthened by the fact that when he suffers he is silent and resigned to his lot. Nowhere in the pages of Jewish history can it be shown that the nation or a remnant of the nation has voluntarily suffered in behalf of others. Therefore from this consideration it is clear that the nation is not the subject of the prophecy.

(5) The servant suffers UNTO DEATH, whereas the nation is to continue. According to 53:8, 12, the servant is cut off out of the land of the living, but, according to Jer. 30:11, Israel continues as a nation: "For I will make a full end of all the nations whither I have scattered thee, but I will not make a full end of thee; but I will correct thee in measure, and will in no wise leave thee unpunished." Therefore, since the servant goes to death, but the nation survives the catastrophe which blots out all other nations, Israel cannot be the servant of this passage.

(6) The servant is RIGHTEOUS whereas the nation, according to all of the prophets, is unrighteous and sinful. According to Isa. 53:11, God declares that he is righteous, and according to verse 9, which is a part of Israel's penitential confession, he does no violence, neither is deceit in his mouth. Since every man has to suffer for his own sins (Ezek. 18:20, "The soul that sinneth, it shall die"), and since the Servant does not suffer for his own sins but for the sins of others, he is free from sin; hence righteous in the absolute sense of the term. Such cannot be said of the nation for all like sheep have gone astray. In order to see the great abyss of sin and unfaithfulness into which the nation is plunged, see Isa. 59. THEREFORE ISRAEL IS NOT THE SERVANT.

B. *Is a Pious Remnant the Servant?*

Having seen conclusively that the nation cannot possibly be the subject of this prophecy, the reader is now asked to consider the question whether a pious remnant of the nation can be personified and presented as the righteous Servant. There are those who affirm that such is the case. To the writer, however, there are, again, six conclusive arguments which disprove most clearly and most positively this position.

(1) If a pious remnant is the servant, then the pronouns "he," "his," and "him" would refer to this remnant, and the pronouns "we," "us," and "our" would likewise refer to the rest of the nation. Since Isaiah identified himself with those referred to by the latter pronouns, he would not be numbered in that class referred to by the former pronouns which, according to this interpretation, refer to the pious remnant. Therefore this supposition is reduced to an absurdity since Isaiah, a righteous man, would not be classed among the pious remnant, but with the ungodly.

(2) A second consideration disproving this position is that no individual can make atonement for the sins of others since each one bears his own iniquity, according to Ezek. 18:20.

(3) A third consideration is that there has been no individual in the nation in the past of whom it can be said was free from sin; and hence able to atone for the sins of the people.

(4) The most pious and godly of the nation throughout its past history have whenever possible avoided suffering, which characteristic is common to mankind; but this servant suffers willingly.

(5) According to this passage the servant is cut off out of the land of the living; but if the servant is the remnant, it is to cease to exist; this conclusion is contrary to the predictions of the prophets, which declare that the faithful remnant will continue.

(6) The most pious and godly among the Hebrews have acknowledged their sinfulness, but this servant does not. Isaiah, when the Lord appeared to him, confessed his sinfulness (Isa. 6:5). In making a prediction concerning the nation in the "end time" Isaiah in 64:5-7 says: "Thou meetest him that rejoiceth and worketh righteousness, those that remember thee in thy ways: behold, thou wast wroth, and we sinned: in them have we been of

long time; and shall we be saved? For we are all become as one that is unclean, and all our righteousnesses are as a polluted garment: and we all do fade as a leaf; and our iniquities, like the wind, take us away. And there is none that calleth upon thy name, that stirreth up himself to take hold of thee; for thou hast hid thy face from us, and hast consumed us by means of our iniquities." It is very clear from this passage that even the most pious and godly of the nation of the future will make this great confession of their sinfulness.

From the six considerations just enumerated it is impossible to avoid the conclusion that this servant cannot be a pious remnant of the nation.

C. *Is The Messiah This Servant?*

Since the considerations noted above prove clearly that the servant is neither the nation personified nor a pious remnant of the nation thus considered, it is now in order to investigate a third interpretation, namely, that this servant is Israel's Messiah of whom the prophets spoke frequently. The evidence at hand is overwhelming that the ancient synagogue thus interpreted it as Messianic. Jonathan ben Uzziel (first century of the common era) begins his Targum on this passage: "Behold, my Servant, Messiah, shall prosper; He shall be high and increase, and be exceedingly strong." In this passage he interprets all of the statements which refer to an exalted Messiah to an individual, but those statements which refer to sufferings he applies to the nation. In order to do this he juggles with the words, not permitting them to speak for themselves. "The Babylonian Talmud likewise reflects this same ancient interpretation in *Sanhedrin:* "The Messiah—what is his name? . . . Rabbis say the 'leprous one'; (those) of the house of Rabbi (say), 'the sinful one,' as it is said 'Surely He hath borne our sicknesses.' "

Even Abarbanel admits the Messianic interpretation, though in a polemic against the Nazarenes he applies it to the Jewish nation. "The first question," says he, "is to ascertain to whom (this Scripture) refers: for the learned among the Nazarenes expound it of the man who was crucified in Jerusalem at the end of the second Temple, and who, according to them, was the Son of God and took form in the Virgin's womb, as is stated in their writings.

Jonathan ben Uzziel interprets it in the Targum of the future
Messiah; and *this is also the opinion of our learned men in the
majority of their Misrashim."* Likewise, Jafet, the Karaite, interprets the passage as Messianic in his presenting the career of the
Messiah from birth to the throne and appeals to Benjamin ha-
Nahawendi, of the same Jewish sect, as authority for his interpretation.

This Messianic interpretation of the passage seems to have been
universal up to the days of Rashi (Rabbi Solomon Yizchaki)
1040-1105, who applied it to the Jewish nation. In commenting on
the change of interpretation David Baron, the eminent Hebrew
scholar, says: "The Messianic interpretation of this chapter (Isa.
53) was most universally adopted by Jews, and his view, which we
shall examine presently, although received by Aben Ezra, Kimchi,
and others, was rejected as unsatisfactory by Maimonides, who is
regarded by the Jews as of highest authority, by Alshech (as stated
above) and many others, one of whom says the interpretation
adopted by Rashi 'distorts the passage from its natural meaning,'
and that in truth 'it was given of God as a description of the Messiah, whereby, when any should claim to be the Messiah, to judge
by the resemblance or non-resemblance to it, whether he were the
Messiah or not,' and another says: 'The meaning of "was wounded
for our transgressions, . . . bruised for our iniquities," is that
since the Messiah bears our iniquities, which produce the effect of
His being bruised, it follows that whosoever will not admit that
the Messiah thus suffers for our iniquities must endure and suffer
for them himself.' "

Not only have Hebrew scholars in the past interpreted this
passage as Messianic, but the liturgy for the Day of Atonement in
the Musaph Service confesses: "We are shrunk up in our misery
even until now! Our Rock hath not come nigh unto us; Messiah our Righteousness (or 'our righteous Messiah') has departed
from us: Horror hath seized upon us and we have none to justify
us. He hath borne the yoke of our iniquities and our transgressions and is wounded because of our transgressions. He beareth
our sins on His shoulders that He may find pardon for our iniquities. We shall be healed by His wound at the time the Eternal
will create Him (Messiah) as a new creature. Oh bring Him up

from the circle of the earth, raise Him up from Seir to assemble us the second time on Mount Lebanon, by the hand of Yinnon." This excerpt is conclusive proof that the writer of this section of the liturgy, who is said to have been Eleazer ben Katin, and who lived in the ninth century, likewise interpreted this passage as Messianic. In the Daily Prayer Book in Hebrew and English, published by the Hebrew Publication Society, on pages 250 and 251 the Messiah is called "the Son of David, Thy Servant." This use of the term is an echo of the Messianic interpretation of Isa. 53.

IV. THE CAREER OF THE MESSIAH 52:13-15

From the foregoing discussion it is clear to the reader that the subject of this prophecy is the personal Messiah of whom the prophets have spoken. In the three verses for consideration in this section appears an outline of the entire career of the Messiah. Verse 13, in the briefest manner, outlines his career from the time of his entrance into the world unto his exaltation at the right hand of God; verse 14 explains graphically his deep humiliation and suffering which are presupposed in verse 13; and verse 15 advances beyond verse 13 in that it speaks of his future glories when he shall return to the earth and become King of kings, and Lord of lords. The prediction begins with the exclamation הִנֵּה "Behold."* Thus God points out His servant to the nation.

He "deals wisely" or "prospers." His wisdom expresses itself in His action and He is successful in accomplishing the work which He has to do.

Next the statement is made, "He will rise, and be exalted, and be very high." The word יָרוּם translated by Delitzsch "He will rise" has as its inherent meaning the idea of rising but one has to learn from the context the nature of the rising. The English ver-

---

* This word God uses in calling attention to Himself and to His Messiah. In Isa. 40:9, 10 God says הִנֵּה אלהיכם "Behold, your God! behold, the Lord יהוה will come as a Mighty One, and His arm will rule for Him." Again, in Jer. 23:5 in introducing King Messiah he uses the same word: "Behold, the days come, saith the Lord, that I will raise unto David a righteous Branch, and he shall reign as king and deal wisely, and shall execute justice and righteousness in the land." In Zech. 6:12 God, viewing Messiah, speaks of him as "the man," and exclaims, "Behold, the man whose name is the Branch." Again, looking at King Messiah God says, "Behold, thy king cometh unto thee (Jerusalem)."

sions with which the author is acquainted translate it "be exalted." This translation is rather vague because one cannot learn from it whether the servant is exalted among men, i.e., he is highly esteemed by men, or he is exalted by the Lord who esteems him highly because "he deals wisely." The context precludes the idea that he is exalted by men for in 53:2, 3 the prediction is made that he is despised of men and rejected. Nor can it mean that he is exalted by the Lord in a providential way to a position of glory and power among men because he is cut off out of the land of the living. These statements being true, the context will have to be consulted to ascertain the meaning of יָרוּם, translated in most versions "be exalted," but by Delitzsch "will arise." Furthermore, since his life of rejection by his people terminates with an ignominious death (53:8, 9), there is no place for greatness prior to death; therefore the meaning of the term must be sought in the literal facts connected with the case. He is literally ill-treated (52:14) and put to death (53:8, 9, 12). These facts suggest that a literal resurrection from the dead may be the import of this word. This supposition ceases to be an hypothesis but becomes an established fact when viewed in the light of 53:10 which states that after he has made his soul an offering for sin "He shall prolong his days." Therefore a literal resurrection from a state of death accords best with all of the facts presented by the context.

After he rises he is "lifted up." Since the rising is literal, it is quite likely that the being lifted up is also literal. This supposition is lifted up into the category of probabilities by the prediction of Psa. 110:1, 2 which shows that after Messiah is rejected by the inhabitants of Jerusalem, the Lord God invites him to leave the earth and to ascend to His right hand. The word translated "lifted up" is נִשָּׂא which is the niphal stem and can be translated in a reflexive sense or passively, i.e., "lift himself up" or "be lifted up." In either sense this passage in the light of Psa. 110 refers to Messiah's ascension to the right hand of God. Finally, the statement is made "and shall be very high." This statement simply affirms that having ascended to the right hand of God he remains there in that position of honor and glory. On these three Hebrew words Delitzsch comments as follows: "If we consider that יָרוּם signifies not only to be high, but to rise up (Prov. 11:11) and become exalted, and also to become manifest as exalted (Psa. 21:13 (14), and that the word נִשָּׂא, according to the immediate and original reflexive of the niphal, signifies to raise one's self, whereas גָּבַהּ מְאֹד expresses merely the condition without the subordinate idea of activity, we obtain this chain of thought: he will rise up; he will raise himself still higher, he will stand on high. The three verbs (of which the two perfects are defined by the previous future), consequently denote the commencement, the continuation, and the result or climax of the exaltation; and Stier is not wrong in recalling to mind the three principal steps of the *exaltation* in the historical fulfillment, namely, the resurrection, the ascension, and the sitting down at the right hand of God. The addition of מְאֹד 'exceedingly,' shows very clearly that גָּבַהּ is intended to be taken as the final result; the Servant of יְהֹוָה rising from stage to stage, reaches at last the immeasurable height that towers above everything besides." Jalkut in commenting on Isaiah recognizes the three stages here mentioned but interprets them differently. הִנֵּה "Behold, my servant deals wisely; this is King Messiah; he will rise from (above) Abraham and be higher than Moses and exceedingly higher than the angels of service."

The sufferings of the Messiah appear in verse 14. It is quite evident that he is subjected to some form of very cruel torture which disfigures and mars his appearance to the extent that he no longer has the appearance of a man, or suffers more than any man has ever suffered. Furthermore, his sufferings are registered upon his countenance to such an extent that those who behold him are nonplussed, i.e., they are literally confounded because that has occurred which they would not have thought to be possible. This verse viewed in the light of 53:4-9 is seen to refer to torture and death at the hands of enemies.

In verse 15 the sufferings have passed and the Messiah stands forth in glory with authority and power. At the time of his torture and suffering many individuals were caused to wonder and to be confounded; at the time of his appearing in power and glory he confounds not simply many individuals but many nations.

The kings of the earth who, according to Psa. 2, rage both against God and King Messiah, appear here upon the scene in the most humble and submissive attitude, which fact is indicated by the statement: "Kings shall shut their mouths at him." The unexpected has occurred. They see things which they have never seen and understand things which have never been told them. Of course, it is clear that the things which they see and understand and which had never been told them are the exaltation, glory, and authority of this Servant of the Lord, Messiah, Son of David. It is evident that for some reason the Messiah has been veiled so that the kings of the world never see nor hear of him until he comes in glory and power. Upon whose shoulders rests the responsibility for not giving the message of the Messiah to the kings of the world? The answer is easy. Those to whom God gave His Word are primarily responsible for the failure. Secondly, each individual king and person is responsible because he has neither longed nor searched for the knowledge of God, since, according to Prov. 2:1-5, everyone who seeks shall know the truth of God.

V. Israel's Penitential Confession   Isa. 53:1-9

In these verses appears the confession which penitential Israel shall make when she sees her mistake and returns to the Lord her God. That this passage is a confession which the nation shall make is evident from the fact that the prophet repeatedly in these verses states that "He (the Servant) hath borne our (the Hebrew nation's) griefs, and carried our sorrows; yet we did esteem him stricken, smitten of God and afflicted." That the nation will do this thing is evident from a number of passages. In Psa. 110:3 God says that Messiah's people who reject him at first will become "free willingnesses" in the day of the latter's power. (For a discussion of this point see Chapter IX.) Both Jeremiah (3:20-22) and Zechariah (12:10-14) tell of this same national repentence. Again Jeremiah in 50:4, 5 declares: "In those days, and in that time, saith the Lord, the children of Israel shall come, they and the children of Judah together; they shall go on their way weeping, and shall seek the Lord their God. They shall inquire concerning Zion with their faces thitherward, *saying,* Come ye, and join yourselves to the Lord in an everlasting covenant that shall not be forgotten." Thus far Israel has never made this confession; but, since God says that she will, the time will come when the nation will be brought to that condition of heart and mind. For the sake of clearness let it be said that this national repentance will occur in the year 1928 plus X— that is, A. D. 1928 plus the number of years which intervenes between the present and the fulfillment of this prediction. (Original manuscript written in 1928.)

A. Messiah's Person Veiled Isa. 53: 1

The questions "Who has believed what we have heard? and the arm of the Lord,—over whom hath it been revealed?" are simply rhetorical ones to indicate that comparatively few have believed the reports which have been heard. The ones expressing these sentiments are the penitent nation in the "end time." They admit that they have heard the message concerning this Servant but very few of them, comparatively speaking, believed it. In the preceding verse this Servant is revealed to the kings who have never heard of him but in this verse he is now revealed to those who have heard of him and who disbelieved up until the time of this confession. Their amazement at their blindness is so very great that they are led to give expression to these questions. From 53:1-9 it is evident that the Messiah has been hidden from the nation as a whole, although a few individuals have seen the truth and accepted him, as is implied in the questions referred to above.

Who is responsible for Israel's not seeing the Messiah? Each individual Hebrew is responsible to God for his knowledge or lack of knowledge. Isaiah (29:13, 14) explains one reason for her failure to recognize him. "And the Lord said, Forasmuch as this people draw nigh *unto me,* and with their mouth and with their lips do honor me, but have removed their heart far from me, and their fear of me is a commandment of men which hath been taught *them;* therefore, behold, I will proceed to do a marvellous work among this people, even a marvellous work and a wonder; and the wisdom of their wise men shall perish, and the understanding of their prudent men shall be hid." According to this passage religion to the nation is reduced to a mechanical ritualistic performance which has been taught them *"by rote."* Though one subscribe to correct doctrinal statements and observe scrupulously divine precepts, he can never see the truth of God and the work-

ing of His power when his religion is simply mechanical and
lifeless. A little different aspect of the reason of Israel's failure
to recognize her Messiah is presented by Jeremiah (13:15-17):

שִׁמְעוּ וְהַאֲזִינוּ אַל־תִּגְבָּהוּ כִּי יְהוָֹה דִּבֵּר: תְּנוּ לַיהוָֹה אֱלֹהֵיכֶם כָּבוֹד
בְּטֶרֶם יַחְשִׁךְ וּבְטֶרֶם יִתְנַגְּפוּ רַגְלֵיכֶם עַל־הָרֵי נָשֶׁף וְקִוִּיתֶם לְאוֹר וְשָׂמָהּ
לְצַלְמָוֶת יָשִׁית לַעֲרָפֶל: וְאִם לֹא תִשְׁמָעוּהָ בְּמִסְתָּרִים תִּבְכֶּה נַפְשִׁי
מִפְּנֵי גֵוָה וְדָמֹעַ תִּדְמַע וְתֵרַד עֵינִי דִּמְעָה כִּי נִשְׁבָּה עֵדֶר יְהוָֹה:

"Hear ye, and give ear; be not proud; for the Lord hath spoken.
Give glory to the Lord your God, before he cause darkness, and
before your feet stumble upon the dark mountains, and, while ye
look for light, he turn it into the shadow of death, and make it
gross darkness. But if ye will not hear it, my soul shall weep in
secret for *your* pride; and mine eye shall weep sore, and run down
with tears, because the Lord's flock is taken captive." When God
calls to the nation or an individual and he fails to respond whole-
heartedly, He will send spiritual darkness as judicial punishment,
which will cause him to stumble.

The message which has formerly been rejected, but which now
penitent Israel accepts, is the message concerning "the arm of the
Lord." Who or what is referred to by this expression? It occurs
in various places. For instance, the Israelites in speaking of His
delivering them from Egyptian bondage say, "The Lord brought
us forth out of Egypt with a mighty hand, and with an out-
stretched arm, and with great terribleness, and with signs and with
wonders." The historical record shows that the one who brought
Israel out of bondage was "the angel of the Lord," or, as he is
called in other places, the Lord himself. Therefore those expressions are but figures of speech referring to the Lord. Isaiah was
fond of using this expression which in some of the contexts may
be interpreted as a reference to a manifestation of God's power;
but the question is what does it mean here? The context will have
to decide. The preceding verses undoubtedly refer to the Messiah,
an individual. The following verses continue that personal description and show that the Messiah was not recognized by the
nation. Therefore the context demands that it be understood as
a personal reference to the Messiah Himself.

B. *The Obscurity of the Messiah in Early Life Isa. 53: 2*

"The Lord's Servant does not burst upon the world all at once in sudden splendor of daring or achievement, dazzling eyes and captivating all hearts. He conforms to God's slow, silent law of growth." Another writer most effectually describes the obscurity of the Servant by the exclamation: "He grew up in obscurity and lowliness. Not as a prince royal on which the hopes and eyes of the nation are fixed, and whose movements are chronicled in Court Gazette or Circular. Here is one living a lowly life in lowlier environments. . . . Men expected 'a plant of renown' fairer and statelier than all the trees in the garden of God, with boughs lifted cedarlike in majesty; instead, there is a suckling, a sprout from the root of a tree that had been cut down, with nothing fair or majestic about it. It owes nothing to the soil in which it grows. The ground is dry, an arid waste without moisture." Notwithstanding this unfavorable environment the Servant grows, develops, and prospers in his work. Israel at the time of her return to God looks back over the desolate waste of the centuries, spiritually speaking, and confesses that "And he came up like a layer-sprig before Him and like a root-sprout out of dry ground; he had no form and no beauty, when we saw him and there was no appearance that we could find pleasure in him."

C. *Messiah Despised and Rejected of Men Isa. 53: 3*

Strange to say, this Servant is despised and rejected by the men of rank of his nation. The word נִבְזֶה "despised" occurs in 49:7 with נֶפֶשׁ "soul" added.* The significance of the addition of נֶפֶשׁ "soul" to נִבְזֶה "despised" is that the hatred toward him is rooted in the very depths of the being of these enemies. A usage similar to this one is found in Psa. 17:9 and is translated "deadly enemies"; hence the hatred which the men referred to have for him has permeated their entire being. Not only do they hate him, but they also stand aloof from him. The ones here referred to are evidently the leaders of the nation. For, by Isaiah especially, אִישִׁים is used to refer to the ruling, powerful class, and אָדָם to the masses of men. On this point see Isa. 5:15. Since the men of influence and power withhold their influence and support from him

---

* This verse has well been called Isa. 53 in an abridged form.

and oppose him, his influence is very much curtailed. Furthermore, since the masses of men are influenced entirely by the leaders and since they rejected him, it is not surprising that the entire nation, with few exceptions, likewise rejected him.

Not only is he despised and rejected of men, but he is acquainted with grief; or, literally, "familiar with sickness, and like one from whom men hid their face, despised, and we esteemed him not." The fact that he is acquainted with sickness is not to be understood that his body was frail and weak, and subject to every disease but, as Delitzsch explains, is to be understood that "the wrath instigated by sin, and the zeal of self-sacrifice, burnt like the fire of a fever in his soul and body."

Since he did not come as they expected—as a prince heralded with a blast of trumpets—but came in a humble, unobtrusive manner, his generation turned from him as one turns away the face from that which is disagreeable or which does not appeal to him. The entire race with the exception of a few has lightly esteemed him, thinking that he was unworthy of even the least consideration.

D. *The Servant Suffers for Others Isa. 53: 4, 5*

In violent contrast to the low estimate placed upon him by his race through the centuries, the penitent nation, in the future, will confess the serious mistake and blunder which was made by the forefathers and which has been continued through the years, when it declares: "Verily our sicknesses he hath borne, and our pains—he hath laden them; but we considered him as one stricken, one smitten of God and afflicted." The use of the words סָבַל נָשָׂא "bore *and* carried" immediately suggests the use to which they are put with reference to expiation and atonement in the Torah. Delitzsch in speaking of them says: "It is evident that both the verbs used in this verse, 'he hath borne,' and 'he carried,' are to be understood in the sense of an expiator bearing. . . . The meaning is not merely that the Servant of God entered into the fellowship of our sufferings but that He took upon Himself the sufferings which we had to bear, and deserved to bear, and therefore not only took them away . . . but bore them in His own person, that He might deliver us from them." In other words, He became the Lamb of atonement which bore Israel's sins.

In bearing the sins of the nation He was מְחֹלָל "pierced" "because of our transgression, bruised because of our iniquities." That מְחֹלָל means to "pierce" is seen by its use in 51:9 where it is translated both by Isaac Leeser and the translators of the Jewish Publication Society, "pierced." Even today in the Daily Prayer Book on page 18 the same word, in noun form, is used and translated "vessels" meaning the blood vessels. These facts show that the primary meaning of the word is to bore or make a hole. Therefore the penitent nation confesses that the Servant was pierced because of its transgressions and iniquities, and that the price of peace and health for it was purchased by Him.

E. *The Lost Nation Isa. 53: 6*

In continuing its confession the nation will admit that it has entirely strayed as wandering sheep away from The Shepherd, each man having turned to his own way. With its spiritual eyes open it will see the real reason for the suffering of the Servant, namely, "The Lord caused to light upon Him the iniquity of all of us." The verb used here means "to cause to meet." An illustration will make plain the thought. When a bi-convex lens is held in such a position that the sun may pass through it, all the rays striking the surface focus at one small point; thus the Lord "caused to meet on Him" or focused upon Him the sin of the entire race.

F. *The Submissiveness of the Servant Isa. 53: 7*

The word נִגַּשׂ literally means "mercilessly and tyrannically treated," indicating the most severe treatment to which one may be subjected. Likewise, He was afflicted but was non-resistant, not opening His mouth in protest. Again, in describing the submissiveness of the Servant the prophet compares Him to a lamb and a sheep which are led to the slaughter but which are dumb. These figures of speech suggest again the lamb which bears away the sins of the nation.

G. *Imprisonment, Trial, and Death of the Servant Isa. 53: 8*

In verse 8 the statement is made that "out of prison and out of judgment was he taken." This statement assumes the arrest of the Servant and of His being cast into prison. Since, according to verse 7, he is unmercifully treated by those in whose power he is, and since he is taken from prison and from judgment, it is most likely that the same harsh cruel treatment is given to him in taking him from prison and rushing him through a hasty trial.

The rest of this verse has been variously translated and interpreted. There are two possible translations which may be in accordance with the rules of grammar; hence it is difficult to determine which is the one in the prophet's mind. For the benefit of the reader both are given. (1) "And as to his generation, who protested or complained? for he was cut off out of the land of the living because of the transgression of my people to whom the stroke was due." (2) "And as to his generation, who considered that he was cut off out of the land of the living because of the transgression of My people to whom the stroke was due?" The former translation means that when the Servant was arrested and tried, no one protested against the injustice which was being done. The latter affirms, in the form of a rhetorical question, that no one of his generation realized the real significance of the suffering of the Servant, i.e., he was suffering not for his own sins, but for the sins of his nation to whom the stroke was due. Though one may not be positive and affirm which meaning was in the prophet's mind, he can be certain that no contemporary realized the significance of the suffering. Furthermore, since this Servant is so very unpopular and is in the hands of the ruling class which is hostile to Him, it is also most likely that no one offers a word of protest in His favor.

The sufferings thus depicted result in the death of the Servant for "He is cut off out of the land of the living." If justice and righteousness had been meted out to everyone, the death sentence would have fallen upon the entire nation, but the mercy of God interposed and allowed the stroke which was due to the race to fall upon Him.

The latter part of this verse likewise has been variously translated and about it a great discussion has raged. In the ordinary English version it is translated "for He was cut off out of the land of the living because of the transgression of my people to whom the stroke was due." This translation, grammatically speaking, is correct. Another rendering, however, is likewise correct, which is: "He was cut off out of the land of the living; on account of the transgression of My people, vengeance fell on Him." These two renderings yield the same net result, which accord with the facts of the context.*

Not being satisfied with the cruel death which they imposed upon Him, those in authority planned to heap disgrace and ignominy upon His name perpetually by burying Him with the wicked. According to Josephus, such was the custom among the Jews at that time. "He that blasphemeth God let him be stoned, and let him hang upon a tree all that day, and let him be buried in an ignominious and obscure manner." Since the plans and counsels of men are brought to nought while the counsels of God stand fast (Psa. 33:10, 11), and since this Servant is innocent "because He had done no violence and neither was deceit in His mouth," God providentially interposed by giving Him favor "with a rich man in His deaths" (Author's Tr.). Therefore He was not buried with the wicked, according to the plan of His enemies, but was in the hands of His friend.

VI. THE NECESSITY FOR ATONEMENT

"Yet it pleased the Lord to bruise him." It was in the great plan and purpose of God that the Messiah should suffer and die in order to make atonement. Three considerations render it obligatory.

A. *The Presence of Sin in the World*

That "sin" is in the world is evident from the wreckage seen on every hand. When God established the world, He created it "not a waste" (Isa. 45:18). According to Gen. 1:2, "the earth became a desolation and a waste" (Author's Tr.). During six

---

* The controversy, alluded to above, pertains to the word למו. Is this singular or plural? The position has been taken that it is plural and refers to the Hebrew nation; therefore the Servant is the nation personified. Kimchi is the first to have made this argument, claiming that למו is plural and equivalent to להם. But in his grammar he contradicted himself, for he says "מו (mo) occurs as an affix of the 3rd person singular as in Job 20:23; 22:2." Again, he affirms "מו (mo) is used both of many and of one." His statements in his grammar are correct for in poetry it may have the plural signification but in the passages referred to it is undoubtedly singular. Likewise in Isa. 44:15 it is singular. "He maketh it a graven image and falleth down thereto למו." Hence the context is to determine its significance. In this context it is clear that an individual suffers for the rest; therefore it is singular.

days God was "reconstructing" it preparatory to the creation of man. When God created him, He placed him in the most favorable surroundings in a garden eastward in Eden. By yielding to the temptation of הַשָּׂטָן "the Devil," man disobeyed God. This rebellion brought the curse upon the earth under which it has been groaning to the present time and will continue to do so until it is lifted when Messiah returns in glory (Zech. 14:11).

This disaster was not confined to the material world but reached unto man. God created man "in His own image, in the image of God created He him." From this statement it is clear that man, bearing the image of God, was in a perfect, healthy condition, both physically and spiritually. When he sinned, the curse likewise fell upon him (See Gen. 3:16, 19). David recognized the fallen condition of humanity: "Behold, I was brought forth in iniquity; And in sin did my mother conceive me" (Psa. 51:5). עָקֹב הַלֵּב מִכֹּל וְאָנֻשׁ הוּא מִי יֵדָעֶנּוּ: "The heart is deceitful above all things, and it is exceedingly corrupt: who can know it?" (Jer. 17:9).

Prior to Adam's transgression, sickness and disease were unknown. The day he sinned, the statement, "dying, thou shalt surely die" was fulfilled (Author's Tr.).*

Not only did man die on that day physically but also spiritually, for he was driven out from the presence of God, Who is the source of all spiritual life. This spiritual death terminates in eternal death. "The soul that sinneth, it shall die" (Ezek. 18:4). This statement refers not to physical, but to spiritual and eternal death. "There is no peace, saith my God, to the wicked" (Isa. 57:21). "And they (people living during the reign of the Messiah) shall go forth, and look upon the dead bodies of the men that have transgressed against me: for their worm shall not die†, neither shall

---

* This statement is scientifically correct. According to modern biology, the katabolic processes are functioning in the body of every individual from conception to death. Up to mid-life the anabolic processes, however, are in the ascendancy; after that time the former gain the ascendancy the result of which fact terminates in death.

† Throughout the Tenach the word שְׁאֹל occurs. Its origin is somewhat doubtful; some scholars, however, trace it back to the word "ask" while others trace it back to the word which means "to be hollow." Sometimes it is translated "grave" or "pit." In several passages the dead are said to be gathered in companies; hence the oft-recurring expression "gathered unto his fathers." This phrase, as the different contexts indicate, refers to something quite different and distinct from burial. Jacob was gathered

their fire be quenched; and they shall be an abhorring unto all flesh" (Isa. 66:24). From this verse it is clear that those living during the reign of Messiah and enjoying the unbounded spiritual blessings of that age will have spiritual vision and will see the wicked suffering in a place separated from God, from which place they can never go forth; hence spiritual death terminates in eternal banishment from the presence of God.

Such great wreckage and havoc as has been wrought throughout the entire realm of nature and in the human kingdom argues the presence of a force or power in the world antagonistic to God and capable of such unspeakable ruin. From different Scriptures it is evident that "the Devil" who is hostile to God was back of this disaster.

Moses and the prophets speak of עָוֹן וָפֶשַׁע וְחַטָּאָה "sin, trans-

---

unto his people; afterward his body was embalmed, and later buried. "Sheol" among the Hebrews was similar to "the realm of shades" in Babylonian mythology, to which Ishtar descended. It was a place of cessation from activity, and by Job is spoken of as a "place of rest," but not necessarily peaceful rest.

In Psa. 49 the writer, speaking of the irreligious wealthy class of people, said, in verse 14, that, "They are appointed as a flock for Sheol; Death shall be their shepherd: And the upright shall have dominion over them in the morning; And their beauty shall be for Sheol to consume, That there be no habitation for it." In the next verse the poet triumphantly declares, "But God will redeem my soul from the power of Sheol; For he will receive me." In the former verse the irreligious, godless ones are compared to a flock of sheep which is gathered into Sheol as its fold, there to remain and to be under the authority of the "upright" "in the morning"—the morning of eternity. The Psalmist affirms that God will not allow him to go to Sheol but rather will receive him into His fellowship. This passage most clearly teaches that there is a place of punishment to which the wicked go upon their departure from this life.

On this same subject Isaiah spoke as follows: "And it shall come to pass in that day, that the Lord will punish the host of the high ones on high, and the kings of the earth upon the earth. And they shall be gathered together, as prisoners are gathered in the pit, and shall be shut up in the prison; and after many days shall they be visited (punished)." The "host of the high ones on high," who are the evil spirits under Satan, according to this passage, will be gathered together with the kings of the earth, as prisoners are gathered into the pit, and shall be shut up; after many days punishment shall be administered to them. The duration of this punishment is not stated in this passage.

Daniel, however, in 12:2 answers that question. "And many of them that sleep in the dust of the earth shall awake, some to everlasting life, and some to shame and everlasting contempt." There will be two classes of people raised from the dead: first, those who are raised to everlasting life—unending; second, those to everlasting contempt—never-ending shame and punishment.

gression and iniquity." The first of these doubtless refers to what is known as "sin in the flesh" and is the cause of sin and transgression in the life. Sin in the flesh can be called spiritual gravitation. As there is the power of gravitation in the physical world, which, according to Newton's law, draws all physical objects toward the center of the earth, so there is a downward spiritual, evil force which pulls man down to a life of degradation and sin. Therefore the presence of this hostile deadly power of sin in the flesh which works itself out into a life of disobedience and transgression must be dealt with; hence the absolute necessity for the atonement of the Messiah.

B. *God's Character*

נַיַּעֲבֹר יְהֹוָה עַל־פָּנָיו נַיִּקְרָא יְהֹוָה יְהֹוָה אֵל רַחוּם וְחַנּוּן אֶרֶךְ אַפַּיִם וְרַב־
חֶסֶד וָאֱמֶת: נֹצֵר חֶסֶד לָאֲלָפִים נֹשֵׂא עָוֹן וָפֶשַׁע וְחַטָּאָה וְנַקֵּה לֹא יְנַקֶּה
פֹּקֵד עֲוֹן אָבוֹת עַל־בָּנִים וְעַל־בְּנֵי בָנִים עַל־שִׁלֵּשִׁים וְעַל־רִבֵּעִים:

"And the Lord passed by before him, and proclaimed, the Lord, the Lord, a God merciful and gracious, slow to anger, and abundant in lovingkindness and truth; keeping lovingkindness for thousands, forgiving iniquity and transgression and sin; and that will by no means clear the *guilty,* visiting the iniquity of the fathers upon the children, and upon the children's children, upon the third and upon the fourth generation" (Ex. 34:6, 7).

God, in proclaiming His name, declared His character. Since everything is related in some way to God, it is necessary to view each item in the light of this relationship.

In the above statement He affirms seven things concerning Himself: (1) "merciful and gracious"; (2) "slow to anger"; (3) "abundant in lovingkindness and truth"; (4) "keeping lovingkindness for thousands"; (5) "forgiving iniquity and transgression and sin"; (6) "that will by no means clear the guilty"; and (7) "visiting the iniquity of the fathers upon the children. . . ."

God's mercifulness and lovingkindness is sufficiently great to overlook any and all sins and to save every individual, if it were a matter purely of love. The characteristic of righteousness—absolute and uncompromising—demands that every sin shall be dealt with impartially upon the merits of the case. If it were purely a matter in which righteousness alone functioned, there would be no salvation for anyone since all have sinned, as declared the prophets. "They are corrupt, they have done abominable works; There is none that doeth good" (Psa. 14:1). God's righteousness is a check upon His love and vice versa.

He has to deal with Satan and sin because He is of "purer eyes than to behold evil, and that canst not look on perverseness" (Hab. 1:13). Therefore His holiness demands that they be dealt with adequately. In order to be true to Himself, He must deal with the problem. That He will be is seen in the statement which He made to Moses at the burning bush, אֶהְיֶה אֲשֶׁר אֶהְיֶה "I will be that I will be."

C. *Man's Good*

Since man's disobedience (Gen. 3), he has never been supremely happy as God originally intended that he should be. Into every life come more or less frequently—and usually most frequently— experiences that mar his happiness. Such are unavoidable.

The one thing which destroys happiness in the life of every man is the consciousness of sin. "They are all gone aside; they are together become filthy; There is none that doeth good, no, not one" (Psa. 14:3). With a heart from which flows such a life of sin, shame and unprofitableness, no man can experience real joy and satisfaction. Therefore it is imperative that an atonement sufficient to meet man's need and restore him to full and free fellowship with God must be made.

Having seen in this section that there is a spiritual downward pull of sin which has wrecked the material world and corrupted man's nature, that God's grace, righteousness, and holiness demand that the problem be dealt with adequately, and that man's good likewise demands the counteraction of sin and its removal in order that he may be supremely happy, one immediately recognizes that the sin question and its solution are vital not only to God but also to every individual who has ever lived, lives, or will live. Only God can grapple with and solve such a problem which concerns the happiness of each individual not only in time but throughout eternity.

VII. THE BLOOD OF THE ATONEMENT

"When his soul shall make an offering for sin." As seen above, since sin is such a mighty power, which has wrecked all of God's work in connection with this earth, the Messiah—God in the flesh —takes hold of the situation and solves it. The way he does it is by His soul's making itself an אָשָׁם "trespass offering" for sin. The principle of justice demands eye for eye, tooth for tooth, and life for life. Since "the soul that sinneth, it shall die," since God wishes to rescue every soul from eternal punishment, and since the animal sacrifices mentioned by Moses: "for it is the blood that maketh atonement by reason of the life" could not atone completely for man's sin, as is seen from the fact that this blood had to be shed yearly, it is the good pleasure of God to bruise Messiah whose blood is able to counteract all of the evil effects which resulted from man's sin. His "pouring out His soul unto death," since He is the Infinite God, is adequate to meet all of the demands of righteousness and to make complete atonement for man's sin.

"And the blood shall be to you for a token upon the houses where ye are: and when I see the blood, I will pass over you, and there shall no plague be upon you to destroy you, when I smite the land of Egypt. 14. And this day shall be unto you for a memorial, and ye shall keep it a feast to Jehovah: throughout your generations ye shall keep it a feast by an ordinance forever" (Ex. 12:13, 14). If the blood of the Passover lamb—a mere animal—was efficacious in protecting the first-born of the children of Israel from death when they screened themselves behind it by sprinkling it upon the door-posts and lintels, much more can the Blood of King Messiah protect the one who hearkens to His voice from the stroke of the death angel and save him from eternal death. Only those who were protected by the blood of the Passover lamb were safe; in every house of the Egyptians the first-born lay dead. The reason for sparing the first-born of Israel and the slaying of the first-born of the Egyptians was not that Israel morally was better than the Egyptians, but the explanation of the difference is to be found in the fact that there was power in the blood. Thus it will be when God comes to judge the living and the dead: Only those who have screened themselves behind the Blood of Messiah by accepting His atonement will be saved from eternal wrath and indignation. There is power, eternal cleansing power in the Blood of King Messiah.

One may not understand how the blood of the lamb upon the door-posts protected the first-born of the Israelites. The fact is that it did the work. A person who is sick with some deadly disease may not understand how a certain kind of medicine will enter the life-stream of the blood and destroy the death-dealing germs, but when he by faith takes the medicine, it does the work. One does not understand how food which is eaten is assimilated and is built into the protoplasm of the cell tissues but he knows that such is true. Likewise, he may not understand how the Blood of Messiah can cleanse from all sin, can break evil habits of long standing, and can make one acceptable in the sight of God. It is not necessary in order to enjoy some blessings to understand the whys and the wherefores. A knowledge of the fact that it does the work is all that is necessary. Being fully assured that there is power in the Blood, one can by faith—unwavering and unfaltering—accept this only way of approach to God and can enjoy the fullness of blessing with God not only in time but in eternity.

The power of the Blood of Messiah can break and crush the power of sin in the flesh of all those who accept Him. It was a matter of free choice and faith on the part of the Israelites when they protected themselves by the blood of the Passover lamb. It is a matter of free choice and faith with one today as to whether he accepts or rejects the Blood of Messiah. To accept in faith and abiding trust is to be in absolute security and safety; to refuse or to neglect to accept the atonement of Messiah is to reject God's ONLY way of redemption and salvation.

In society, when it has been proved that one is incurably insane, or a criminal, he is segregated to an institution for that purpose for the good of said society. God will be just as careful for the society of the redeemed in the eternal world. Those who do not accept Messiah's atonement and permit Him to cleanse them from all sin but choose rather to have Satan to be their master will be separated from the redeemed family of God in eternity and segregated in a place from which there shall be no escape and to which no hope can ever come. The justice of God and the redeemed, cleansed, and glorified society demand such an institution throughout eternity.

VIII. THE SUFFERING OF THE SERVANT IN THE PLAN OF GOD

In the words of Delitzsch, one may say "the supreme *causa efficiens* was God Who made the Son of Man subservient to His pleasure, His will, and predetermined counsel." Since God does not delight in the suffering of any of His creatures, He caused the stroke of judgment to fall upon His Servant that they may go free.

A. *The Voluntary Sacrifice of the Servant*

The words אִם־תָּשִׂים אָשָׁם נַפְשׁוֹ are variously translated by different ones. That translation which appears to the writer to be in harmony with the context is "When His soul shall make a trespass offering." There were various offerings in the Levitical system, but the one referred to here is the trespass offering concerning which Dr. Culross remarks "That while the sin-offering looked to the sinful state of the offerer, the trespass-offering was appointed to meet *actual transgressions,* the fruit of the sinful state. The sin-offering set forth propitiation, the trespass-offering set forth satisfaction. It was brought by the transgressor 'to make amends for the harm that had been done.'" The use in this passage of the Levitical terms connected with the sacrifice points definitely to the thought that this suffering Servant is the One Who was typified by the sacrifices which were required of Israel. In Lev. 17:11 God declares that the life of an animal is in the blood, and that it is "the blood that maketh atonement by reason of the life." Evidently, the Levitical sacrifices were insufficient to atone for the sins of the people; therefore this Servant of the Lord, being one of the Divine Personalities in human form, is the One Who makes complete satisfaction and atonement for the sins of man.

On the eve of the ninth of *Tishri* pious Hebrews provide themselves with a *Kapporah*—"means of atonement—a rooster for the male and a hen for the female." After he has recited the prayers the man swings the fowl three times around his head and devoutly recites: "This is my change, this is my redemption, this rooster is going to be killed and I will be admitted to a long, happy, and peaceful life." In the law God did not command that a rooster or a hen should be used as an atonement for the soul; He prescribed two goats; one for the Lord and one for Azazel (see Lev. 16).

The blood of those goats, however, could not atone for sin, but in a symbolic way rolled the sins of the pious worshipper forward one year when another sacrifice had to be offered. The importance of obeying the Lord implicitly may be seen in the case of the death angel's passing over Egypt the night Israel left. In strict obedience to the demand of the Lord, the blood of the Passover lamb was sprinkled upon the door-posts and lintels of every Hebrew home. The Egyptians had no passover with its blood. When the death angel passed over the land he slew the first-born of the Egyptians, whereas the first-born of the Israelites, being screened behind the blood, was spared. No substitute on the part of Israel would have saved the first-born; neither will it today.

Since the blood of the goat could not make atonement for sins, God, according to this prediction, allowed His Righteous Servant, the Messiah—the Spotless, Sinless Son of God—to offer His soul as a sacrifice for the sins of the people. Dear friend, no substitute will suffice. You must accept this sacrifice made by the Servant and offered freely to you, without money and without price, or be banished eternally from the presence of God into a place of anguish and misery.

Though this Servant before His death seems to have "labored in vain" and "have spent My strength for nought and vanity" (Isa. 49:4), He sees results from His labors and the sacrifice of Himself. Having been slain, He rises from the dead and, "prolongs His days" (see Psa. 16:10f). In another Messianic psalm (21:4) the inspired writer, speaking of King Messiah, said: "He asked life of thee, thou gavest it him, Even length of days for ever and ever." That אֹרֶךְ יָמִים refer to the future life is seen in the Targum of Jonathan and in the commentary of Kimchi, who interpret them to refer to "the life of the world to come." Hence this Servant lives for ever and ever.

His sacrifice is not in vain, for He "shall see seed," not in a literal fleshly posterity, for He is cut off out of the land of the living, but a spiritual seed—those who accept His atonement and His righteousness. That זֶרַע "seed" is used in the figurative sense is clear from Isa. 1:4, which refers to the children of Israel: "A seed of evil-doers, children that deal corruptly!" Again, in 57:4 the same prophet indicted the nation by saying: "Are ye not chil-

dren of transgression, a seed זֶרַע of falsehood?" Therefore the
"seed" is the one to whom the Psalmist David (Psa. 22:30)
referred: "A seed shall serve him."

Not only does He make atonement for man's redemption, but
the entire plan, purpose, "and the pleasure of the Lord shall prosper in His hand." Part of this plan and pleasure of God may be
seen in the following quotation: "Behold, my servant, whom I
uphold; my chosen, in whom my soul delighteth: I have put my
Spirit upon him; he will bring forth justice to the Gentiles . . .
I, the Lord, have called thee in righteousness, and will hold thy
hand, and will keep thee, and give thee for a covenant of the
people, for a light of the Gentiles; to open the blind eyes, to bring
out the prisoners from the dungeon, and them that sit in darkness
out of the prison-house." "And now saith the Lord that formed
me from the womb to be his servant, to bring Jacob again to him,
and that Israel be gathered unto him . . . yea, he saith, It is
too light a thing that thou shouldest be my servant to raise up the
tribes of Jacob, and to restore the preserved of Israel: I will also
give thee for a light to the Gentiles, that thou mayest be my salvation unto the end of the earth" (Isa. 42:1-7; 49:5, 6).

B. The Righteous Servant

God declares that this Servant is righteous. No individual could
make an offering for the sins of others except a righteous one.
That He is righteous in the absolute sense of the term is obvious
from the fact that this Servant is Messiah, the Son of David, Who
is God manifest in the flesh (Isa. 9:6, 7 (5, 6). This conclusion
is confirmed by Jeremiah who in speaking of the Messiah said that
God "will raise unto David a righteous Branch" and He shall be
called יְהֹוָה צִדְקֵנוּ "the Lord our Righteousness" (Jer. 23:5, 6).
Hence this king is King Messiah, is God in the flesh, and is the
righteous One Who justifies those who accept Him and His atonement. Notwithstanding the fact that not all are made righteous but
that "many" are—i.e., all are not willing to accept His atoning sacrifice for their sins; hence are not made righteous—all who do accept
Him genuinely will be clothed in His Righteousness (Isa. 61:10).

שׂוֹשׂ אָשִׂישׂ בַּיהֹוָה תָּגֵל נַפְשִׁי בֵּאלֹהַי כִּי הִלְבִּישַׁנִי בִּגְדֵי־יֶשַׁע מְעִיל צְדָקָה

יְעָטָנִי כֶּחָתָן יְכַהֵן פְּאֵר וְכַכַּלָּה תַּעְדֶּה כֵלֶיהָ:   "I will greatly rejoice

in the Lord, my soul shall be joyful in my God; for he hath
clothed me with the garments of salvation, he hath covered me
with the robe of righteousness, as a bridegroom decketh himself
with a garland, and as a bride adorneth herself with her jewels."

This righteous Servant makes those who accept Him righteous
"by his knowledge." Grammatically, this expression may refer to
the knowledge which this servant possesses and which enables him
to work out the perfect plan of God and thus make it possible for
many to become righteous by accepting him; or, it may mean that
by learning of the sacrifice which the servant has made and by accepting Him, one has not only the mental concept of Him but has
an experimental, spiritual, heart knowledge of Him. One cannot
be dogmatic here. From other Scriptures it is clear that both positions are correct. Since the Word of God is so very replete with
meaning it is quite probable that both meanings are expressed.

Not only does He make an atonement for those who accept Him
and bring them to a condition of righteousness and acceptance with
God, but He intercedes with God both for transgressors and for
those who in loving faith and obedience accept His sacrifice.

The sufferings and sacrifice of the Servant are richly rewarded
for He shall "see of the travail of his soul and shall be satisfied."

C. *The Servant's Supreme Sacrifice*

"Because he poured out his soul unto death." This is a voluntary, willing submission to death. Neither circumstances nor individuals force Him to such a tragic death; but He through love
for lost man willingly drinks the cup of death, even its very dregs.
In submitting to the ignominious death which He suffers He is
by His executers "numbered with the transgressors." In this verse
the two great fundamental doctrines of the sovereignty of God,
on the one hand, and the freedom of mankind, on the other, flow
into a single stream. Man can never harmonize these two seemingly contradictory teachings of Holy Scripture. He must, however, accept them as true because such is the teaching of the entire
Tenach and such is the case as is seen by every spiritually minded
person who seriously studies life and its problems. Thus the
sufferer voluntarily offers His life a ransom for the sins of the
world and at the same time His executers voluntarily, of their own
free-will and accord, put Him to death. Hence they in executing

Him, are simply carrying out the divine program. Though carrying out these purposes, they are responsible to God for their wickedness because they upon their own initiative put Him to death.

In His bearing the sin—the sin of many—at the time of pouring out His soul unto death, He makes "intercession for the transgressors," i.e., during His sufferings which are caused by the ill-treatment accorded to Him and His having been "pierced," He makes fervent intercession to God in behalf of His executers. In other words, the dying Servant of the Lord, free from all malice, envy, and hatred toward His persecutors and executers, prays God's forgiveness of them. What marvelous grace, what outpouring of love! My dear Hebrew friend, this dying, bleeding Messiah, as He dies, pleads to God for your salvation and forgiveness.

As a concluding remark it is well to call attention to the excellent summary of the chapter by Dr. Alexander who observes that these "frequent repetitions so far from being rhetorical defects or indications of another author, are used with obvious design, namely, that of making it impossible for any ingenuity or learning to eliminate the doctrine of vicarious atonement from this passage by presenting it so often, and in forms so varied and yet still the same, that he who succeeds in expelling it from one place is compelled to meet it in another. Thus in this verse, which fills up the last particulars of the humiliation and sufferings of the Messiah even unto death, it is once again repeated that it was 'for the transgression of my people' that the stroke fell upon Him."

IX. AUTHOR'S TRANSLATION WITH EXPLANATORY NOTES

Behold, my Servant, *King Messiah* מָשִׁיחַ, shall deal wisely *during His life; notwithstanding His purity and innocence He shall be put to death, but* shall rise *from the dead,* and be lifted up *when He accepts the invitation of God to sit at His right hand according to Psa. 110:1, 2* and shall be very high. Like as many were confounded at Thee *because of the horrifying appearance of thy mutilated body* (His visage was so marred more than the sons of men), so shall He startle many nations *by His appearing in glory as King of kings and Lord of lords;* kings *who have renounced Him and thrown off His authority in the World Conference (Psa. 2)* shall shut their mouths at Him, *and together with*

Princes render Divine worship (Isa. 49:7); for that which had not been told them, *by those who had the Word of God and who should have proclaimed it to the world,* shall they see; and that which they had not heard shall they understand clearly.

Who *among us Hebrews* hath believed our message *which was told to us by faithful competent witnesses?* And to whom has the arm of the Lord, *who is the Messiah,* been revealed? For He, *the Messiah,* grew up before Him, *i.e., God* as a tender plant, and as a root out of dry ground, *which figures of speech indicate the low spiritual condition of the people among whom Messiah grew up;* He had no form nor comliness, *i.e., He did not have the appearance and bearing of an earthly king;* and when we saw Him, He had no beauty that we desired Him *as our Messiah.* He was despised *with the greatest possible contempt* and lacked men *of influence and power among those who followed Him;* a man of sorrows *because of the lost spiritual condition of the world, and especially the dearth of spiritual life among the Hebrews,* and acquainted with sickness, *both spiritual and physical;* and like one from whom men hide their faces *in disgust* He was despised, and we considered Him as nothing, *yea as a dreamer and a poor fanatical peasant whose opinions amounted to nothing.*

But now after the lapse of many weary centuries of suffering and persecution in the worst of which we now are and which is called "the Time of Jacob's trouble" (Jer. 30:7) we, having turned to God in our distress and having been brought to the point where we truly say "Blessed be he that cometh in the name of the Lord," now see the great mistake which our forefathers made in rejecting the Messiah when he came and which our nation has made from that time to the present by refusing to listen to his claim to being our Messiah. Now we see the situation clearly, which is this, "Surely our sicknesses *both spiritual and physical* he bore and our griefs he *as our scape-goat* carried, but *at that time* we thought that he was plagued, smitten by God and afflicted *because of His own sins and transgressions. The fact is that* He was pierced, *as the Prophets by the Spirit foretold (Psa. 22:16; Zech. 12:10)* because of our transgressions and wounded because of our iniquities, and the chastisement of our peace, *i.e., the suffering which had to be borne in order that we might enjoy peace* was upon Him, and by the stripes, *which he endured for us,* healing is brought to us. *We now confess that* all of us, *i.e., our entire Hebrew race* like sheep strayed away *from God and His Word;* everyone of us turned to his own way; and *yet* the Lord caused to meet on Him the iniquity of all of us *like rays of light focused on a single spot. When He thus suffered for us,* those, *who were in authority,* violently treated Him and He was afflicted but He did not open His mouth *in protest against such treatment;* as a lamb to the slaughter is led and as a sheep before her shearers is dumb, He did not open His mouth.   Out of prison and away from trial He was taken; and as to His generation, *i.e., His contemporaries, who complained against such a miscarriage of justice, or* who realized that He was cut off out of the land of the living because of the transgression of My people to whom the stroke *of judgment* was due, (or on account of the transgression of My people, the stroke *of judgment* fell on Him)?   They, *in their plans* made His grave with the wicked *intending by so doing to heap ignominy and shame upon His name throughout all future generations, but by the overruling providence of God Who says* 'thus far shalt thou go and *no farther;' and who* "hath His way in the whirlwind and in the storm" *(Nahum 1:3), the wicked plan of His enemies was frustrated;* hence with a rich man was He in His death because He had done no violence, neither was deceit in His mouth.

The Prophet having foretold the full and voluntary confession which the nation shall make when her blindness is removed, explains the great facts of the death of the Servant by saying that, in keeping with His Eternal Plan, the Lord was pleased to bruise Him; He has put Him to grief; when His soul shall make a trespass offering for sin, *not His own but that of the world,* He shall see seed, *i.e., a spiritual seed, a host of redeemed men and women;* He shall prolong His days *after His death and resurrection;* and the pleasure of the Lord shall prosper in His hand, *a reference to His making atonement for lost man, and to His regathering Israel into her own land and into fellowship with God.*   He shall see of the travail of His soul, *i.e., results from His atoning suffering,* and be satisfied; by the knowledge of Himself, *both His knowledge of how to atone for man's sins and the knowledge of those who learn of Him and accept His sacrifice,* shall My Righteous

Servant, *Who is the Lord our Righteousness (Jer. 23:6),* bring righteousness to the many, *i.e., His righteousness shall be accredited to those who accept His sacrifice;* and He shall bear, *as the scape-goat,* their iniquities.   Therefore will I divide Him a portion with the great, and He shall divide the spoil with the strong, *when He returns with glory and power to rule the world in righteousness;* because He *voluntarily* poured out His soul unto death and was numbered with the transgressors, *though He was pure and holy;* yet He bore the sin of the many, and, *in love* made intercession for the transgressors *while He thus suffered.*

Chapter XI

THE ETERNAL GOD REVEALING HIMSELF,
ACCORDING TO THE NEW TESTAMENT

MOSES and the prophets raised many expectations and hopes which, according to the Tenach, were never realized during Old Testament times. Since the God of Israel is a God of truth and righteousness He never made any promises which He cannot and will not fulfill. Furthermore, it follows from the above statement that what He has not already fulfilled He will in the future at the proper time bring to pass.

In order that the Hebrew reader may realize that the New Testament is THE WORD OF THE GOD OF ISRAEL in the same sense in which the TORAH is, hence of equal importance, it is well for him to note some indisputable facts connected with it and its teaching.

I. The New Testament is the Continuation of the Old Testament

This fact is seen by a study of the contents of both. Both Testaments, as admitted by all scholars, are oriental. The Hebraic spirit breathes through all their pages; the diction, phraseology, idiomatic expressions, and concepts are likewise Hebraic.

The outstanding doctrines of both Testaments are the same. In both appears a pure monotheistic conception of God, which doctrine is peculiar to the sixty-six books (thirty-nine of the Old, twenty-seven of the New). The doctrine of the Trinity appears in both Testaments; but in the New Testament it is fully elaborated. The expectation of the Messiah raised in the Old is fulfilled, according to the New Testament, in the person of Jesus of Nazareth. In both Testaments the origin and nature of man are the same. In both appears the teaching of an evil, malignant spirit known as Satan, or the Devil, who is the leader of a mighty army of fallen spirits that are opposed to God and the children of

God. In both appears the doctrine of the lost condition of humanity. In both the doctrine of salvation (deliverance) is taught; in the Old Testament, however, the teaching is given in the form of types, symbols, and brief statements; whereas in the New Testament it is developed fully. By the prophets predictions were made of the restoration of the kingdom of God to the Davidic household; by the writers of the New Testament the same conception of the kingdom is set forth. In the Old Testament appear a few brief statements of the punishment of the wicked and the blessed condition of the righteous; in the New Testament these doctrines are fully developed. The mention of these doctrines will suffice to show that the New Testament is but a continuation of the Old.

The book of Genesis has been called "the seed plot of the Bible." By this statement the affirmation is made that all of the doctrines throughout the Tenach and the New Testament are to be found in the embryonic or undeveloped form in the book of Genesis. A careful study of this collection of sixty-six books by an unprejudiced truth-seeker produces the profound conviction that a unity pervades them, which fact proves beyond a doubt that the same Spirit Who spoke through the prophets likewise spoke through the writers of the New Testament.

II. THE NEW TESTAMENT FULFILLS THE OLD TESTAMENT EXPECTATION

As has already been seen in Chapter VIII, Israel's Messiah was scheduled to appear before the governmental powers departed from Judah. The meaning of Genesis 49:10, where such a promise is made, is explained by Dr. McCaul in the following words: "A chief tribal governor shall not cease from Judah nor a subordinate magistrate from His posterity until He Who is Peace shall come, and to Him shall be the obedience of the nations." In commenting upon this paraphrase of Dr. McCaul's, John Wilkinson says: "In short, that whatever might become of other tribes, Judah must retain his separate existence as a tribe, and also his independent government until the coming of Shiloh to Whom the heathen should yield obedience." Since it is an historical fact that the government passed away from the tribe of Judah in the year

70 A. D. and since the Word of God cannot be broken but is fulfilled to the very letter, Messiah came before that event.

To this fact the Talmud bears witness (in Sanhedrin, fol. 97, col. 2):

"Rav says, 'the appointed times are long since past'", in which quotation the word קֵץ is taken from the quotation of Daniel and means literally "end," as is seen from a study of the prophet's use of that term. Additional corroborative proof of this position is likewise found (in Sanhedrin, fol. 97. col. 1):

"The tradition of the school of Elijah. The world is to stand 6000 years, 2000 confusion, 2000 the Law, 2000 the days of Messiah." Rashi, commenting upon this Talmudical passage, states:

"After the 2000 years of the Law, according to the decree, Messiah ought to have come, and the wicked kingdom should have been destroyed and Israel's state of servitude should have been ended." The Talmud and Rashi both are correct in stating that the Messiah should have come at the expiration of the period of Law, though their reasons for making such statements are based upon tradition. According to the incontrovertible evidence presented in the New Testament, Jesus of Nazareth was the One of Whom the prophets spoke in the Messianic predictions and Who was to come before the collapse of the Jewish state.

We learn from the Scriptures that Messiah was scheduled to come in humility, to suffer, to make atonement for mankind, and to ascend to the right hand of the throne of God. According to the Gospel records, Jesus of Nazareth came at the proper time and fulfilled these predictions to the letter. At present He is at the right hand of the throne of God interceding for those who believe in Him, and awaits the time to come to restore Israel to fellowship with God.*

The fact that the Virgin Birth, pure life, ministry of service to others, death, burial, resurrection, and ascension to the right

---

* The inquiring mind might ask why it was that the Messiah, according to Old Testament schedule, after His rejection returned to heaven. To this question it is sufficient to reply that God never forces anyone's will. Israel refused to accept Him as her King and said: "We have no king but Caesar." Being rejected by His nation, He accepted the invitation of God to sit at His right hand where He will remain until the nation in real repentance confesses her error and reaches the point when she will say: "Blessed be He that cometh in the name of the Lord."

hand of the throne of God of Jesus of Nazareth answer in the minutest details to the predictions of the coming of the Messiah, as found in the Old Testament, which predictions were made during a period of from 1500 to 500 years prior to the birth of Jesus, proves beyond a doubt that He was and is the Hebrew Messiah. The force of this statement may be illustrated as follows: Suppose that in Europe were found a white crystal stone of certain composition through the center of which a streak of colored mineral deposit runs and one of whose surfaces is rough and convex, which facts prove that it was broken off another. Again, suppose that another like stone were found in America, one of whose surfaces was also rough and concave, and through which a similar deposit runs. Upon comparison of these stones it is seen that the convex surface of the one fits most accurately, to a hair's breadth, the concave surface of the other, while the streak of mineral deposit is alike in both. These facts would point most definitely to the conclusion that these at one time formed a single stone and that after the original stone was broken, one of the pieces was carried by some agent to the other continent. This most highly probable conclusion would be lifted from the realm of an hypothesis into that of an established fact when the chemist by his accurate tests proves that they are of the same chemical analysis. Thus Christ and the New Testament correspond exactly to the minute detailed picture of the Old Testament, as, dear reader, you can learn for yourself by a careful study of the New Testament and the comparison of the same with the predictions of the Old.

III. THE EVIDENCE OF THE EMPTY TOMB

A. *The Fact of the Empty Tomb*

The facts concerning the empty tomb, briefly stated, are these: Jesus having been crucified, after six hours on the Cross the Spirit departed from the body. By permission of Pilate, the Roman governor, Joseph of Arimathaea took the corpse and laid it in his new tomb. A heavy stone was rolled across the doorway and the Roman seal was placed upon it, while Roman guards watched. These events occurred late on the day before the Sabbath. According to the Jewish law both Jews and the disciples of Jesus rested on the Sabbath. Early on the first day of the week certain of the disciples found that the stone had been rolled away and that the tomb was empty. In vain they looked for the lifeless body.

B. *The Witnesses to the Empty Tomb*

About these facts there can be no question. The one question arising is this, "What became of that lifeless body which late on the day before the Sabbath was placed in the tomb but which was not there early on the first day of the week?" Various theories have been advanced by skeptics concerning this matter. To examine these speculative theories would consume much space and unnecessary time. The only rational, scientific method of approach is to weigh the evidence of the witnesses who testified that notwithstanding the presence of the Roman soldiers and seal, the stone was rolled away and the tomb was empty. Among these principal witnesses are Matthew and John who were of the twelve original apostles, who associated personally with Jesus during His ministry, and who were associated, as they testify, with Him after the time when the tomb was found empty. Another witness whose testimony is preserved is that of John Mark, whose mother was Mary of Jerusalem (Acts 12:12) and who was a cousin of Barnabas of Cyprus, but later of Jerusalem. He was in the most intimate touch with Simon Peter, the leader of the Apostolic Band, whose interpreter, according to early tradition, he was. Another witness is Luke, the physician. This witness was a very highly educated man as is evident by his writings which compare most favorably with the Greek masters. As evidence of this fact the prologue to his record of the Gospel is admitted by the scholarship of the world to be in the same class with Thucydides. Another bit of evidence of his scholarship is seen in the accurate use of medical terms (see Hobart's: "Medical Terms in Luke"). He was a scientist of the first magnitude, who did extensive research work, gathering his information from every available source before he attempted to write his history of the life of Jesus Christ (Lk. 1:1-4).

While it is true that Luke as a real scientist gathered his data from all available sources, tracing most accurately all information, it is to be understood that he was a saved, regenerated man, enjoying the fullness of the blessings of Christ and especially the guidance and illumination of the Spirit of God as he was engaged in his scientific research work. When he wrote his account, however, of the life of our Lord and the Acts of the Apostles, he enjoyed the full and complete inspiration of the Holy Spirit. Without controversy he enjoyed the fullness of inspiration of which Paul spoke: "Which things also we speak, not in words which man's wisdom teacheth, but which the Spirit teacheth; combining spiritual things with spiritual *words*" (I Cor. 2:13). Therefore his writings meet every test to which a scientific history may be subjected. To the reliability of these scientifically written documents is added the infallibility of the omniscience of the Holy Spirit of God. Therefore every statement of his can be accepted by the scientific man with absolute confidence.

Rationalistic critics have attempted to discredit him as a reliable historian. During the last century on several points to which he alone bore testimony they attempted to discredit his narrative. What Bryant, the poet, said was true in his case:

> "Truth crushed to earth shall rise again:
> Th' eternal years of God are hers;
> But error, wounded, writhes in pain,
> And dies among his worshippers."

The faithful research work of Dr. William Ramsay and others has in the last few decades brought to light historical facts which corroborate the statements of Luke which hitherto were unsupported by secular historians and which were questioned by the critics. These newly discovered facts prove that Luke was correct and now give him a standing of a reputable, trustworthy, firstrate historian. (See such works as "Was Christ Born in Bethlehem?" by Sir William Ramsay, and "Luke the Physician" by Prof. A. T. Robertson, etc.). These four witnesses have written accounts of the life of Jesus Christ in which each of them elaborates the details concerning His death, burial, and resurrection.

In addition to the twelve Apostles, Mark, and Luke, there were above 500 eye-witnesses who testified to the fact that Jesus after His death appeared to them alive. Twenty-odd years after the death of Christ, when the resurrection of the dead was called in question at Corinth, Paul, the Hebrew, met the challenge of his opponents by affirming that Christ appeared alive in His Resurrection body to above five hundred people, the greater part of whom were alive at that time to whom his opponents could go and verify his assertion. He never would have made such a statement if it were not true; for his enemies, who were very bitter, would have gone to any length in discrediting him in the eyes of the church at Corinth, had his assertion been assailable. Paul's being able to silence his opponents by challenging them to consult the then-living witnesses to whom Christ had appeared after His Resurrection, the number of which was above two hundred and fifty, proves conclusively that even his enemies were convinced of the truthfulness of his assertions concerning the Resurrection.

C. *The Competency of These Witnesses*

Before the written testimony of a witness to an historical fact can be accepted as true, it must be subjected to a rigid test by the "canons of historical criticism." According to these a witness must qualify clearly and unmistakably on six different points. (1) He must be a contemporary, i.e., living at the time of the event to which he bears witness. (2) He must be within reach of the occurrence. (3) He must give evidence that he is sufficiently interested in the event to give it sufficient attention. (4) Likewise, he must give sufficient evidence of mental grasp, i.e., he must be able to understand the things which he sees and hears. (5) He must give evidence of a memory which is able to reproduce that which he has seen and heard. (6) He must have established a record for unswerving veracity, i.e., he will speak the truth frankly regardless of consequences.

Witnesses qualifying on these six different points give testimony of the highest class, which cannot be questioned, and which establishes a fact as true. The cloud of witnesses referred to above unmistakably qualify on every point. That they do qualify is evident to every candid reader who will honestly and conscientiously, with an unbiased mind, read their testimony.

That the records which contain their testimony (the new Testament) are trustworthy and reliable may be seen when they are tested by "the historical canons of credibility" as formulated by Geo. Rawlinson in his Bampton lectures for 1859 on "The Historical Evidence of the Truth of Scripture Records." These witnesses were so absolutely sure of that which they believed that they were willing to lay down their lives for their faith, which many of them were compelled to do. (See any standard Church History).

D. *The Convincing Proof of the Resurrection*

The witnesses to the Resurrection of Christ relied upon the testimony of their (1) eyes, (2) ears, (3) sense of touch, and (4) spiritual recognition. During a period of forty days after the tomb was found empty Jesus appeared to various disciples, and once, at least, to above 500 who were gathered together. (1) When He appeared to them He permitted them to scrutinize Him in the most minute and thorough manner. The testimony of their eyes was that the One Whom they were examining was the same Individual Who had been crucified and buried. They listened to Him as He conversed with them of "things concerning the kingdom of God." On the evening of the first day of the week after the tomb had been found empty Jesus appeared to ten of the disciples and convinced them that He was the same individual. Evidently, He Who appeared in their midst was like Jesus Whom they had followed for approximately three and one-half years. He appeared to their eyes as the same individual. On this occasion Thomas was absent. When informed that Jesus had appeared he strongly expressed his doubts concerning their story, affirming that he would not believe unless he saw the print of the nails in His hands, and thrust his hand into His side which had been pierced by the soldier's spear. A week later when the ten were gathered together with Thomas, Jesus appeared; His personal appearance was the same as formerly. The proof was overwhelming and the doubts of Thomas yielded to facts and logic. Thomas was not the only one who doubted. The facts are that none of the disciples thought that He would rise from the dead; hence when He was placed in the tomb their hopes were buried with His lifeless body. But when they saw Him with their own eyes the evidence was so very overwhelming that an audience consisting of more than five hundred people ceased to doubt and was thoroughly convinced that Jesus was alive again and in their midst.

(2) Not only did they have the testimony of their eyes, but the testimony of their ears bore witness to the fact that the One Who came to them and claimed that He was Jesus raised from the dead

was really Jesus. It might be conceived possible for some individual to imitate the voice of another and thus deceive a few, even of close friends, for a while, but it is entirely incredible to think that anyone could have, during a period of forty days, been such an adept at the art of imitating Jesus as to deceive above five hundred reasonable, sane people. Therefore since these five hundred people had the testimony not only of their eyes but of their ears, and since they were thoroughly convinced that Jesus had arisen from the dead and had appeared to them, there is but one logical conclusion to which one may come, namely, that it was Jesus Who appeared to them alive after His Resurrection.

"Him God raised up the third day, and gave him to be made manifest, not to all the people, but unto witnesses that were chosen before of God, *even* to us, who ate and drank with him after he rose from the dead" (Acts 10:40, 41).

(3) In addition to the testimony of the eyes and of the ears the disciples had the testimony of the sense of touch for they actually took hold of His body with their hands, being thoroughly convinced by such an examination that there was no optical illusion, no hallucination on their part, and no spiritualistic appearance, but that Jesus of Nazareth actually appeared there in a body of flesh and bones. Therefore the testimony of three of the five senses through which men know facts of the external world agreed that Jesus had actually risen from the dead (Luke 24:39).

"That which was from the beginning, that which we have heard, that which we have seen with our eyes, that which we beheld, and our hands handled, concerning the Word of life (and the life was manifested, and we have seen, and bear witness, and declare unto you the life, the eternal *life,* which was with the Father, and was manifested unto us) ; that which we have seen and heard declare we unto you also, that ye also may have fellowship with us: yea, and our fellowship is with the Father, and with his Son Jesus Christ: and these things we write, that our joy may be made full" (I Jno. 1:1-4).

(4) Additional proof to that of the three senses noted above, which they had, was that of the sense of psychic or soul recognition. Personality, according to psychologists of standing, is a complex bundle of idiosyncrasies. There are no two personalities

exactly alike. Let one imagine that there was some individual who was of the same physique as Jesus, whose voice was as nearly like his as is possible, who had scars in both hands that were caused by the driving of nails through them, and who attempted to deceive these numerous disciples who had associated with Jesus in the most intimate way for approximately three and one-half years. Such an impostor, though successful in convincing the disciples through the testimony of seeing, hearing, and touching, would have been unable to convince them on the point of psychic or soul recognition. It is admitted by all who have studied conscientiously the records of the life of Jesus that His was a unique personality. Every thought and attitude of an individual manifests itself in some outward expression. To every situation each personality experiences a certain reaction. Those who had been associated with Jesus most intimately during His ministry had, as it were, felt His very heart throb in innumerable instances. Never did a heart beat and throb as His. Therefore it would have been impossible for a deceiver to play the role of the risen Jesus for any length of time without detection.

For the sake of showing the force of the above facts, let one imagine that some impostor could have deceived all of the people on all four of the above points for a few days. It is absurd in the extreme to imagine that such a one could have concealed his identity from the multitude during a period of forty days. These well-known lines confirm this conclusion: "You can fool all of the people some of the time; and some of the people all the time, but you can't fool all the people all of the time." From all the indisputable facts, noted in this section, there can be no reasonable doubt concerning the proposition that Jesus, the Hebrew Messiah, arose from the grave and appeared alive (fulfilling the Old Testament predictions) to a large company of credible, unimpeachable witnesses, many of whom expressed their convictions and sealed the testimony of their faith with their life-blood.

The Apostle John, an eyewitness of the life of Jesus, affirmed, "That which was from the beginning, that which we have heard, that which we have seen with our eyes, that which we beheld, and our hands handled, concerning the Word of life . . . declare we unto you . . ." (I John 1:1-3).

Without the Resurrection of Jesus the Gospel narrative would have been very imperfect. It is the sequel of the life presented throughout the records. According to the Old Testament and the New, He was God in human form. He was born of the virgin, lived a sinless life, performed miracles, and died in a super-human way. Therefore the Gospel picture, in order to be symmetrical, must have as its sequel the Resurrection and Ascension.

Without the Resurrection there would have been no Christian Church. Without it there would have been no Lord's Day. Without it there would be no hope of eternal life. It is related to these things as cause and effect. A religion that does not include a heart belief in the personal and bodily resurrection of the Lord Jesus Christ is not the true religion revealed in the New Testament.

IV. THE EVIDENCE OF PAUL'S CONVERSION
A. *The Man Saul*

Born about the same time as was Jesus were three outstanding Hebrew men: Philo Judaeus in Alexandria, Egypt; John the Baptist in Judea; and Saul of Tarsus in Cilicia. This section, however, shall deal with Saul of Tarsus. Passing hurriedly over the facts of his early life, one notes that Saul was born in Tarsus of Cilicia, a great university town. It is absolutely certain that he received an excellent education in the Greek schools (probably in the University of Tarsus), which fact is seen by a study of the thirteen books which he wrote and which are found in the New Testament. He finished his education, however, in the rabbinical school in Jerusalem, sitting at the feet of the great גַּמְלִיאֵל Gamaliel (Acts 22:3).

He in all probability was a member of the Sanhedrin for he states: "I advanced in the Jews religion beyond many of mine own age among my countrymen, being more exceedingly zealous for the traditions of my fathers" (Gal. 1:14). At the stoning of Stephen the witnesses laid down their garments at his feet (Acts 7:58), which fact indicates that he was in charge of the execution. He was a most promising young leader of his people, for he was "circumcised the eighth day, of the stock of Israel, of the tribe of Benjamin, a Hebrew of Hebrews; as touching the law, a

Pharisee; as touching zeal, persecuting the church; as touching the righteousness which is in the law, found blameless" (Phil. 3:5, 6). He was absolutely certain that religiously he was right and the Christians who worshipped Jesus as the Son of God were wrong. With this conviction he attempted to blot out Christianity not only from Jerusalem but from adjacent territory. He felt that by so doing he was rendering a true service to the God of his fathers. Having armed himself with letters of authority from the high priest at Jerusalem, he and his party started for Damascus in order to clear that city of the Christians (heretics). According to his statement in two public speeches (Acts 22, 26) and the statement of Luke, the noted historian (Acts 9), there occurred an event on the way just before the party arrived at Damascus. This occurrence was the turning point of his life.

B. *The Conversion of Saul*

From this time on instead of being a bitter opponent of the Christians he identified himself with them and became the chief exponent of the doctrine of the Christians. These facts are indisputable. Why did he change his religious affiliation, identifying himself with those whom he had persecuted? Various answers have been given to this question. In order to answer it satisfactorily let the reader now pursue the scientific method by studying the various motives which prompt men to change their religious affiliation. A careful survey of such motives yields the following list: (1) weakmindedness; (2) unstable character; (3) lack of knowledge and independent thought; (4) a disgruntled spirit; (5) monetary considerations; (6) popularity; (7) persecution; (8) conviction. By "weakmindedness" is meant a subnormal mental condition. In the class of "unstable character" may be placed those individuals whose sentiment and emotions predominate over purpose, reason, and will. In the third class are those who do not know facts but who depend upon others to point out the way in which they are to go. In the class of "disgruntled spirit" are those who are unhappy in a certain environment or position and who imagine that some other place will yield greater happiness, advantages, opportunities and the like. In the classification of "monetary considerations" are those who are insincere and who having very low standards of right and wrong, make wealth and pleasure the supreme object of life. In the "popular-ity" group are classed those individuals who prefer the praise and honor of men to that of God and act accordingly. In the "persecution" group are those who change their affiliation rather than be persecuted for their conscientious convictions. In the last class, namely, that of "conviction," are those who think for themselves and, being convinced that they are wrong, accept that which they know is right.

No one for a moment would class Saul among the weakminded for his epistles reveal the fact that he was an intellectual giant. It is admitted by logicians that the Book of Romans, which he wrote, is one of the most logical and powerful documents extant from all antiquity. Neither can he be classed among those of unstable character, for his entire life showed that sentimentality and emotionalism while present in his make-up were subordinate to reason, plan, and will. Again, he cannot be classed among those who lacked knowledge and who looked to others for leadership because he was a leader of men and gave evidence of a very broad culture and acquisition of knowledge. Neither can he be classed among the disgruntled spirits for in the Jewish religion he was most powerful and influential. There was nothing that caused him to be agitated, disturbed and disquieted because of factions or trouble in the ranks of Judaism. Money consideration never entered into his life. Had he chosen money he would have remained where he was. By making the change he gave up the prospects of acquiring wealth and the luxuries of life. Neither did popularity have any allurement for him. Had he desired it he would have remained in Judaism, but by identifying himself with the Christians he, like Moses who gave up the wealth of Egypt and who identified himself with his persecuted brethren, stepped over into the ranks of the extremely unpopular. He did not change his religious association because he feared persecution. While he remained in Judaism he was on the persecuting side; by identifying himself with the Christians he joined the ranks of the persecuted.

Having seen that it is impossible to classify Saul with any of the first seven groups the reader is now asked to consider thoughtfully placing him in the last group, namely, those who change their religious affiliation because of honest, conscientious convictions which are based upon absolute and overwhelming proof. In this connection it is best to let him speak for himself and relate why he changed his conviction concerning Jesus and identified himself with the Christians.*

The following speech was made by Paul† in the Hebrew language from the steps of the castle in Jerusalem: "Brethren and fathers, hear ye the defence which I now make unto you. And when they heard that he spake unto them in the Hebrew language, they were the more quiet: and he saith, I am a Jew, born in Tarsus of Cilicia, but brought up in this city, at the feet of Gamaliel, instructed according to the strict manner of the law of our fathers, being zealous for God, even as ye all are this day: and I persecuted this Way unto the death, binding and delivering into prisons both men and women. As also the high priest doth bear me witness, and all the estate of the elders: from whom also I received letters unto the brethren, and journeyed to Damascus to bring them also that were there unto Jerusalem in bonds to be punished. And it came to pass, that, as I made my journey, and drew nigh unto Damascus, about noon, suddenly there shone from heaven a great light round about me. And I fell unto the ground, and heard a voice saying unto me, Saul, Saul, why persecutest thou me? And I answered, Who art thou, Lord? And he said unto me, I am Jesus of Nazareth, whom thou persecutest. And they that were with me beheld indeed the light, but they heard not the voice of him that spake to me. And I said, What shall I do, Lord? And the Lord said unto me, Arise, and go into Damascus; and there it shall be told thee of all things which are appointed for thee to do. And when I could not see for the glory of that light, being led by the hand of them that were with me I came into Damascus. And one Ananias, a devout man according to the law, well reported of by all the Jews that dwelt there, came unto me, and standing by me said unto me, Brother Saul, receive thy sight.

---

* These speeches are preserved in Acts of the Apostles, which was written by Dr. Luke who, as stated above, has been vindicated by archaeological facts to be an historian thoroughly reliable in the most minute and detailed matters. Therefore he has accurately preserved these great testimonials of this great Hebrew scholar. Hence they contain a truthful account of the facts as they actually occurred.

† Saul's name was changed to Paul, which is Roman, on his first missionary journey (Acts 13:9).

And in that very hour I looked up on him. And he said, The God of our fathers hath appointed thee to know his will, and to see the Righteous One, and to hear a voice from his mouth. For thou shalt be a witness for him unto all men of what thou hast seen and heard. And now why tarriest thou?* arise, and be baptized, and wash away thy sins, calling on his name. And it came to pass, that, when I had returned to Jerusalem, and while I prayed in the temple, I fell into a trance, and saw him saying unto me, Make haste, and get thee quickly out of Jerusalem; because they will not receive of thee testimony concerning me. And I said, Lord, they themselves know that I imprisoned and beat in every synagogue them that believed on thee: and when the blood of Stephen thy witness was shed, I also was standing by, and consenting, and keeping the garments of them that slew him. And he said unto me, Depart: for I will send thee forth far hence unto the Gentiles" (Acts 22:1-21).

Before King Agrippa II Paul delivered his second speech in which he explains why he became a Christian. "And Agrippa said unto Paul, Thou art permitted to speak for thyself. Then

---

* As we learn from the Scriptures, it is not pleasing to the Lord for one to be simply a secret believer. He who is thoroughly convinced that Jesus is the Hebrew Messiah and Saviour of the world, of Whom the prophets spoke, must come out boldly and confess Jesus "in this adulterous and sinful generation." The Lord Himself said, "Be not afraid of them that kill the body, and after that have no more that they can do. But I will warn you whom ye shall fear: Fear him, who after he hath killed hath power to cast into hell; yea, I say unto you, Fear him" (Lk. 12:4, 5). One can never enjoy his fellowship with Jesus Christ and walk with God by faith as long as he pleases man. Dear friend, launch out boldly into the midst of the great sea of God's promises. If you stay close to the shore you will be continually in danger of being bombarded by men.

Paul realized that fact. He had no fear of men. He launched out immediately as soon as he was convinced that Jesus was his Messiah. He came out in the most public and open way and confessed his faith in Jesus by being baptized immediately. Wherefore, "why tarriest thou" O secret believer?

Elijah in his great warfare against Baalism at the Carmel contest urged the secret believers in God to cease "limping between the two sides." To them he declared, "If יהוה be God, follow him; but if Baal, then follow him" (I Kgs. 18:21). Again, my Hebrew friend, in this language let the author plead with you, if you are convinced that Jesus Christ is the Hebrew Messiah, to come out boldly in the light and blessings of the Lord and follow Him, obeying Him in every thing. You then can claim the promise that "every one that hath left houses, or brethren, or sisters, or father, or mother, or children, or lands, for my name's sake, shall receive a hundredfold, and shall inherit eternal life" (Matt. 19:29).

Paul stretched forth his hand, and made his defence: I think myself happy, king Agrippa, that I am to make my defence before thee this day touching all the things whereof I am accused by the Jews: especially because thou art expert in all customs and questions which are among the Jews: wherefore I beseech thee to hear me patiently. My manner of life then from my youth up, which was from the beginning among mine own nation and at Jerusalem, know all the Jews; having knowledge of me from the first, if they be willing to testify, that after the straitest sect of our religion I lived a Pharisee. And now I stand *here* to be judged for the hope of the promise made of God unto our fathers: unto which *promise* our twelve tribes, earnestly serving *God* night and day, hope to attain. And concerning this hope I am accused by the Jews, O king! Why is it judged incredible with you, if God doth raise the dead? I verily thought with myself that I ought to do many things contrary to the name of Jesus of Nazareth. And this I also did in Jerusalem: and I both shut up many of the saints in prisons, having received authority from the chief priests, and when they were put to death I gave my vote against them. And punishing them oftentimes in all the synagogues, I strove to make them blaspheme; and being exceedingly mad against them, I persecuted them even unto foreign cities. Whereupon as I journeyed to Damascus with the authority and commission of the chief priests, at midday, O king, I saw on the way a light from heaven, above the brightness of the sun, shining round about me and them that journeyed with me. And when we were all fallen to the earth, I heard a voice saying unto me in the Hebrew language, Saul, Saul, why persecutest thou me? it is hard for thee to kick against the goad. And I said, Who art thou, Lord? And the Lord said, I am Jesus whom thou persecutest. But arise, and stand upon thy feet: for to this end have I appeared unto thee, to appoint thee a minister and a witness both of the things wherein thou hast seen me, and of the things wherein I will appear unto thee: delivering thee from the people, and from the Gentiles, unto whom I send thee, to open their eyes, that they may turn from darkness to light and from the power of Satan unto God, that they may receive remission of sins and an inheritance among them that are sanctified by faith in me. Wherefore, O king Agrippa, I was not disobedient unto the heavenly vision: but declared both to them of Damascus first, and at Jerusalem, and throughout all the country of Judaea, and also to the Gentiles, that they should repent and turn to God, doing works worthy of repentance. For this cause the Jews seized me in the temple, and assayed to kill me. Having therefore obtained the help that is from God, I stand unto this day testifying both to small and great, saying nothing but what the prophets and Moses did say should come; how that the Christ must suffer, *and* how that he first by the resurrection of the dead should proclaim light both to the people and to the Gentiles. And as he thus made his defence, Festus saith with a loud voice, Paul, thou art mad; thy much learning is turning thee mad. But Paul saith, I am not mad, most excellent Festus; but speak forth words of truth and soberness. For the king knoweth of these things, unto whom also I speak freely: for I am persuaded that none of these things is hidden from him; for this hath not been done in a corner. King Agrippa, believest thou the prophets? I know that thou believest. And Agrippa *said* unto Paul, With but little persuasion thou wouldest fain make me a Christian. And Paul *said*, I would to God, that whether with little or with much, not thou only, but also all that hear me this day, might become such as I am, except these bonds" (Acts 26:1-29).

Dr. Luke gives the following account of Saul's conversion to Christianity in Acts 9:1-22: "But Saul, yet breathing threatening and slaughter against the disciples of the Lord, went unto the high priest, and asked of him letters to Damascus unto the synagogues, that if he found any that were of the Way, whether men or women, he might bring them bound to Jerusalem. And as he journeyed, it came to pass that he drew nigh unto Damascus: and suddenly there shone round about him a light out of heaven: and he fell upon the earth, and heard a voice saying unto him, Saul, Saul, why persecutest thou me? And he said, Who art thou, Lord? And he *said*, I am Jesus whom thou persecutest: but rise, and enter into the city, and it shall be told thee what thou must do. And the men that journeyed with him stood speechless, hearing the voice,* but beholding no man. And Saul arose from the

---

* To the casual reader there appears to be a contradiction in the statement of Luke in Acts 9:7 "And the men that journeyed with him stood speech-

earth; and when his eyes were opened, he saw nothing; and they led him by the hand, and brought him into Damascus. And he was three days without sight, and did neither eat nor drink. Now there was a certain disciple at Damascus, named Ananias; and the Lord said unto him in a vision, Ananias. And he said, Behold, I *am here,* Lord. And the Lord *said* unto him, Arise, and go to the street which is called Straight, and inquire in the house of Judas for one named Saul, a man of Tarsus: for behold, he prayeth; and he hath seen a man named Ananias coming in, and laying his hands on him, that he might receive his sight. But Ananias answered, Lord, I have heard from many of this man, how much evil he did to thy saints at Jerusalem: and here he hath authority from the chief priests to bind all that call upon thy name. But the Lord said unto him, Go thy way: for he is a chosen vessel unto me, to bear my name before the Gentiles and kings, and the children of Israel: for I will show him how many things he must suffer for my name's sake. And Ananias departed, and entered into the house; and laying his hands on him said, Brother Saul, the Lord, *even* Jesus, who appeared unto thee in the way which thou camest, hath sent me, that thou mayest receive thy sight, and be filled with the Holy Spirit. And straightway there fell from his eyes as it were scales, and he received his sight; and he arose and was baptized; and he took food and was strengthened. And he was certain days with the disciples that were at Damascus. And straightway in the synagogues he proclaimed Jesus, that he is the Son of God. And all that heard him were amazed, and said,

---

less, hearing the voice, but beholding no man," and the statement of Paul in Acts 22:9 "And they that were with me beheld indeed the light, but they heard not the voice of him that spake to me." This seeming discrepancy vanishes in the light of a knowledge of the use of the Greek cases. In 9:7 Luke puts the word "voice" in the genitive case, which, as all Greek grammarians know, is the case which designates "kind" or "species"; hence it is the case which is regularly used to describe an object or thing. Therefore its use excludes everything except that which is mentioned. In other words his use of the genitive case emphasized the fact that they heard an articulate voice and not some inarticulate sounds.

In 22:9 Paul put the word "voice" in the accusative case, which case is known by grammarians as that of "extension," inclusiveness, comprehensiveness. Paul's use of the accusative case here assumes what was stated by Luke, namely, that they actually heard the voice in the sense of receiving an audible impression, but shows that they were unable to understand the import of the words. Hence the agreement between the two statements in the light of the grammar is perfect.

Is not this he that in Jerusalem made havoc of them that called on this name? and he had come hither for this intent, that he might bring them bound before the chief priests. But Saul increased the more in strength, and confounded the Jews that dwelt at Damascus, proving that this is the Christ."

From Paul's own testimony and the historical statements of Luke one learns why Paul became a Christian. The facts, briefly stated, are these: as he in company with others was journeying toward Damascus, Jesus, the ascended Christ, caused a miraculous light to shine round about Saul, which was brighter than the noon-day sun. Out of heaven He spoke to him. Saul, being brought in touch* with Jesus Christ and being in full possession of his mental faculties, realized that Jesus of Nazareth Whose followers he was persecuting was the Christ, the Hebrew Messiah. Being fully persuaded of his error in rejecting Jesus, he surrendered fully and completely to Him, accepting Him as his Lord and Saviour. Being blinded by the brilliancy of the light, and being led by others of his party, he entered the city of Damascus, where he remained three days in prayer and fasting. At the expiration of this time the Lord sent Ananias who laid his hands upon him, thus imparting the Holy Spirit to him and restoring his sight. He also baptized him. From that day Saul became a most ardent and powerful preacher of the Gospel.

Paul's sudden "right about face," spiritually speaking, may be

---

* Vain attempts have been made by skeptics to break the force of Paul's testimony concerning his seeing Jesus in glory when he was on his way to Damascus. One of the attempted explanations is that suddenly he had an epileptic fit. This supposition is purely imaginary since there is not the remotest fragment of evidence pointing in that direction. Another explanation is that he suffered from hallucination. According to the discoveries of modern psychology such an explanation is impossible because one brain state precedes and prepares for the succeeding one. There was nothing in Paul's previous experience which could produce such an hallucination as this. As he journeyed on his way he was certain that he was doing the will of God and felt reasonably sure that he would be successful in His cause. Therefore there was nothing which could possibly produce an hallucination. Another explanation is that he suffered from sunstroke, for which position there is not the slightest bit of evidence. Paul's entire career from his conversion onward is a complete refutation of all such visionary hypothetical theories. On the other hand, his life, labors, and letters are positive proof that he was in full possession of his mental faculties when he met Jesus face to face.

From the day of his conversion onward, that experience was his polar star which guided him across the tempestuous waters of life.

illustrated as follows: If a person, being in full possession of his mental powers, is walking rapidly down the street, evidently with some object in mind, and suddenly turns around, walking just as rapidly in the reverse direction, one would conclude that there was a rational reason for his sudden change. Spiritually speaking, such is what Paul did. He was going in one direction (persecuting the Christians) ; after this experience he turned around and went in the direction from which he came (identifying himself with the Christians and preaching Christ). There was a reason for his turning, which is that he was thoroughly convinced that he had been mistaken, and that Jesus of Nazareth was his true Messiah and Redeemer. Thus one of the intellectual giants of the world of that day and time, being convinced of the Lordship of Jesus of Nazareth, in *full and complete surrender* bowed to Him and accepted Him as his Lord and Saviour, the Messiah of the Tenach.

V. THE NEW TESTAMENT IS THE FINAL WORD IN THE ANALYSIS OF THE HUMAN HEART, IN ETHICS, AND IN SPIRITUAL TEACHING

The Old Testament sets forth great and wonderful spiritual truths, but it is left for the New Testament to analyze man's spiritual condition and needs. To illustrate this point it is well to note that the Old Testament constantly speaks of sin, transgression, and iniquity; but it does not trace these evils to the fountain head as does the New Testament (see Rom. 6, 7), which analyzes the motives that actuate the heart. It reveals man to himself as no other book does. It is a mirror into which man may look and see himself as God sees him. It probes to the very depths of his soul and discovers to him his real self.

In ethics it is the final word. The highest ideal by which man may be guided in his relation to his fellowman is expressed in the Golden Rule.* "All things therefore whatsoever ye would that men should do unto you, even so do ye also unto them: for this is the law and the prophets" (Matt. 7 :12).

In spiritual teaching the New Testament is the acme of per-

---

* Attempts have been made to prove that Jesus was simply quoting from some great sage in making the statement. The attempt is only in vain. It is true that Confucius stated the negative side of the Golden Rule but that is far inferior to the statement of Jesus. Those apocryphal and apocalyptical books where statements which approximate this one appear are later than the statement of Jesus, and are echoes of His statement.

fection. It affirms that man's first duty is to seek God and His kingdom. Man's helpless condition is met by the assistance of the Holy Spirit of God. He has access to a throne of grace to which he may come at all times, obtain forgiveness of sins through the shed blood of Christ and strength and power that will enable him to live a life which will glorify and honor God. Thus the highest possible conception of spiritual life and fellowship with God is set forth. Since such mighty volumes of ethical and spiritual truths pour forth from its pages, one may illustrate the importance of that fact by the following illustration: When Columbus sailed up the Orinoco River, he declared that he had not discovered an island, but a continent; for, he said, such a river can drain only a continent. Since such mighty volumes of spiritual truths flow forth from the New Testament one cannot but exclaim that it came from God.

VI. The Religion of Christ, as Set Forth in the New Testament, Produces the Highest Type of Character

Many great and noble men have lived in the world during the past. Upon an examination of the innermost lives and souls of these great men, it will be discovered that those who have bowed the knee in recognition and worship of Jesus Christ as God manifest in the flesh, Whose shed blood cleanses from all sin, and who have accepted the New Testament as the revelation of God have scaled the highest heights of morality and spirituality. The teachings of the New Testament inspire and inculcate the finer graces and characteristics of the soul; they also produce those heroic qualities which enable men to face the stern realities of life, dealing with every man on the highest principles of righteousness and justice. These statements being true, as can be proved in innumerable instances, the New Testament is evidently not from man but from God.*

VII. The New Testament Has Met and Satisfied the Needs of Millions

God created man with his various faculties and likewise made those things which will satisfy the yearnings of the same. For in-

---

* The fact that the lives of many Christians do not approximate the ideal set forth in the New Testament does not discredit the religion of Christ. The failure is with men and not with Him and His teachings.

stance, He gave men eyes and has created scenes which satisfy this faculty. He gave men the sense of smell and created that which satisfies that sense. The same is true of all of their sense organs.

When He created man He gave him a soul which yearns after God. Millions of souls have sought rest and satisfaction in other things but finally have turned to the New Testament and to the Christ Who produced it and have found satisfaction, peace, and joy for their weary souls. They have lived in the world and have shed forth the fragrance of a holy life and, when the summons came to pass into the Great Beyond, they have met the inevitable hour in the triumph of a living faith, being fully assured that they will meet their God and Saviour Who died for them, together with their saved loved ones on the eternal shore.

From the seven different considerations presented in this chapter it becomes apparent to the truth-seeker that the New Testament is of the warp and woof of the Old Testament. If one accepts the "Ten Commandments," as was stated in Chapter II, he must in order to be logical, accept the entire Torah; if he accepts the Torah he must accept the entire Tenach (O. T.) ; if he accepts the Tenach, he must, to be consistent, accept the New Testament as the authoritative revelation from God.

The sixty-six books constituting the Old and New Testaments are a divine revelation,* i.e., they constitute messages which God gave through His inspired prophets and apostles to man. They are the Word of God in a special and unique sense in which no other book can claim to be, namely, the Spirit of God spoke God's message through them for man's good and salvation (see II Tim. 3:16, 17; II Pet. 1:21).

---

* The young student may be bewildered by the fact that scholarly men often arrive at conclusions concerning the Scripture which are diametrically opposed. The scholarship of each may be unquestioned; the reasoning of each may be flawless, and yet different conclusions are reached. If an engineer survey a certain plot of ground and make his calculations according to his observations, though every step in the process may be flawless, his conclusion is erroneous unless he first locate the monument and from it make his measurements. If the assumptions of a logician, philosopher, or theologian upon which he bases his arguments be incorrect his conclusions likewise will be incorrect.

Any philosophy or theology whose basic principles are antagonistic to revealed religion and miracles and which place the religion of the Bible upon a naturalistic basis is false. Beware of the same!

CHAPTER XII

PREPARE TO MEET THY GOD

(written September, 1961)

WITHOUT doubt the times in which we are living are most ominous. Everyone who is keeping abreast with current events realizes that conditions cannot continue much longer as they are. Practically all the leaders of thought in the free world are frantic lest some sudden turn of events may plunge the world into a holocaust of World War III.

The statesmen and the scientists are convinced that an all-out atomic war would practically blot out our present civilization in a few minutes of time. Our culture and civilization will be all but blotted out, not by man's doings, but by the direct judgments of Almighty God. The writings of Moses and the Prophets and of the Book of Revelation show conclusively that God will send one judgment after another which will wreck and ruin the entire present order. The sequence of events of the day of wrath of Almighty God is set forth in the Book of Revelation, chapters 6, 8 and 9, and 16, under the symbolism of the seal, the trumpet, and the bowl judgments.

The present writer shows in his volume, *Messiah: His Glorious Appearance Imminent,* that the world has already had what Jesus called *the* sign of His Second Coming and of the end of the world (age). Moreover, in the same volume there is a discussion of "The Signs of the Times." An honest and sincere search for truth and facts will convince anyone of the correctness of this interpretation of the prophetic word.

Those who wish to make a further study of the Day of Jehovah (the Great Tribulation) will do well to study Isaiah 2:12-22; 13:1-16; 24:1-23; Jeremiah 30:4-9; Ezekiel 7:1-27; Joel 1:15-2:11; 3:1-17; Zephaniah 1:14-2:3; Zechariah 14:1-11; and Matthew 24:1-31. All these passages mean exactly what they say and should be interpreted in the light of the Golden Rule of Interpretation which is: "When the plain sense of Scripture makes common sense, seek no other sense. Therefore take every word at its primary, ordinary, usual, literal meaning unless the facts of the

153

immediate context studied in the light of related passages and axiomatic and fundamental truths indicate clearly otherwise."

The one who studies the prophetic word must be careful lest he unconsciously begins to play the role of a prophet by making out a timetable of events, both present and future, and assures the people that the Lord is going to carry out his schedule.

In view of the facts thus presented in this Chapter, it behooves everyone to prepare for the immediate ominous crisis and for the life beyond this one. God created man innocent and perfect, endowing him with a free will and the power of choice, as set forth in Genesis, chapters 1, 2, and 3. Satan, the arch enemy of God and man, with his suave words and deceitful connivings, led man to pit his will against God's will. When man thus sinned, his nature became corrupt. Moses, the great law-giver, speaks concerning the fallen nature of man: "These are the words of the covenant which Jehovah commanded Moses to make with the children of Israel in the land of Moab, besides the covenant which he made with them in Horeb.

"2 And Moses called unto all Israel, and said unto them, Ye have seen all that Jehovah did before your eyes in the land of Egypt unto Pharaoh, and unto all his servants, and unto all his land; 3 the great trials which thine eyes saw, the signs, and those great wonders: 4 but Jehovah hath not given you a heart to know, and eyes to see, and ears to hear, unto this day" (Deut. 29: 1-4). Jeremiah, the weeping prophet, speaks of man's fallen sinful nature: "The heart is deceitful above all things, and it is exceedingly corrupt: who can know it?" (Jer. 17:9). King Solomon declares: "Behold, this only have I found: that God made man upright; but they have sought out many inventions" (Eccl. 7:29). The inspired Apostle Paul sounds the same note as Moses and the Prophets: "But if what I would not, that I do, I consent unto the law that it is good. 17 So now it is no more I that do it, but sin which dwelleth in me. 18 For I know that in me, that is, in my flesh, dwelleth no good thing: for to will is present with me, but to do that which is good *is* not" (Rom. 7:16-18). These verses explain man's true nature —having a desire to do good, but being driven by an irresistible force (sin), causing him to do evil.

Is there any hope for man under these conditions? Yes. The

Apostle Paul declares: "Wretched man that I am! who shall deliver me out of the body of this death? 25 I thank God through Jesus Christ our Lord. So then I of myself with the mind, indeed, serve the law of God; but with the flesh the law of sin. 1 There is therefore now no condemnation to them that are in Christ Jesus" (Rom. 7: 24–8: 1).

A Pharisee by the name of Nicodemus, a ruler of the Jews, came to Jesus by night for a personal interview. In the Gospel of John 3: 1-6 is an account of this historic interview: "Now there was a man of the Pharisees, named Nicodemus, a ruler of the Jews: 2 the same came unto him by night, and said to him, Rabbi, we know that thou art a teacher come from God; for no one can do these signs that thou doest, except God be with him. 3 Jesus answered and said unto him, Verily, verily, I say unto thee, Except one be born anew, he cannot see the kingdom of God. 4 Nicodemus saith unto him, How can a man be born when he is old? can he enter a second time into his mother's womb, and be born? 5 Jesus answered, Verily, verily, I say unto thee, Except one be born of water and the Spirit, he cannot enter into the kingdom of God. 6 That which is born of the flesh is flesh; and that which is born of the Spirit is spirit."

In order to be born anew, one must receive the Lord Jesus Christ, the Hebrew Messiah, as the sin-bearer and redeemer of the world. When a person receives Christ into his heart, the miracle of regeneration occurs: "Wherefore if any man is in Christ, *he is* a new creature: the old things are passed away; behold, they are become new" (II Cor. 5: 17). "For by grace have ye been saved through faith; and that not of yourselves, *it is* the gift of God; 9 not of works, that no man should glory. 10 For we are his workmanship, created in Christ Jesus for good works, which God afore prepared that we should walk in them" (Eph. 2: 8-10). Everywhere, the Apostle Paul, in proclaiming Christ, testified "both to Jews and to Greeks repentance toward God, and faith toward our Lord Jesus Christ" (Acts 20: 21).

How can one be born again? The first step is for one to realize that he is a sinner and that he needs a Saviour. The next step is for one to open his heart and invite the Saviour to come in. "Because if thou shalt confess with thy mouth Jesus *as* Lord, and shalt believe in thy heart that God raised him from the dead, thou shalt be saved: 10 for with the heart man believeth unto righteousness; and with the mouth confession is made unto salvation" (Rom. 10:9, 10).

In Acts, chapters 2 and 3, are recorded two gospel sermons preached by the inspired Apostle Peter to Jewish audiences in Jerusalem. As the result of this first sermon, three thousand Jewish people accepted Christ as Lord, Saviour, and Messiah. As the result of the second sermon, the number of disciples increased to five thousand. In Acts, chapter 10, one finds a message, with attending circumstances, preached by the same Apostle to a Gentile audience, all of whom accepted Christ as personal Saviour and were baptized in His name.

All who accept Jesus Christ as Lord and Saviour are exhorted to turn in the opposite direction with respect to their former lives and conduct—right-about-face. The Apostle Peter writes to young believers in Christ, saying: "Putting away therefore all wickedness, and all guile, and hypocrisies, and envies, and all evil speakings, 2 as newborn babes, long for the spiritual milk which is without guile, that ye may grow thereby unto salvation; 3 if ye have tasted that the Lord is gracious: 4 unto whom coming, a living stone, rejected indeed of men, but with God elect, precious, 5 ye also, as living stones, are built up a spiritual house, to be a holy priesthood, to offer up spiritual sacrifices, acceptable to God through Jesus Christ" (I Pet. 2:1-5).

Every believer should grow in grace and the knowledge of the truth: "But grow in the grace and knowledge of our Lord and Saviour Jesus Christ. To him *be* the glory both now and for ever" (II Pet. 3:18). The Apostle Paul urges the young man Timothy to "give diligence to present thyself approved unto God, a workman that needeth not to be ashamed, handling aright the word of truth" (II Tim. 2:15). The Apostle Paul pleads with the Christians in Rome, saying "I beseech you therefore, brethren, by the mercies of God, to present your bodies a living sacrifice, holy, acceptable to God, *which is* your spiritual service. 2 And be not fashioned according to this world: but be ye transformed by the renewing of your mind, that ye may prove what is the good and acceptable and perfect will of God" (Rom. 12:1, 2).

Satan, the arch enemy of God and man, will take advantage of everyone who serves the Lord, especially attacking the young Christian; but he is a conquered foe and must get permission from the Lord before he strikes any of God's people: "There hath no temptation taken you but such as man can bear: but God is faithful, who will not suffer you to be tempted above that ye are able; but will with the temptation make also the way of escape, that ye may be able to endure it" (I Cor. 10:13). James exhorts Christians to "be subject therefore unto God; but resist the devil, and he will flee from you. 8 Draw nigh to God, and he will draw nigh to you. Cleanse your hands, ye sinners; and purify your hearts, ye double-minded. 9 Be afflicted, and mourn, and weep: let your laughter be turned to mourning, and your joy to heaviness. 10 Humble yourselves in the sight of the Lord, and he shall exalt you" (James 4:7-10). God gives victory over self and sin to those who yield their will to Him: "I write unto you, fathers, because ye know him who is from the beginning. I write unto you, young men, because ye have overcome the evil one. I have written unto you, little children, because ye know the Father. 14 I have written unto you, fathers, because ye know him who is from the beginning. I have written unto you, young men, because ye are strong, and the word of God abideth in you, and ye have overcome the evil one. 15 Love not the world, neither the things that are in the world. If any man love the world, the love of the Father is not in him. 16 For all that is in the world, the lust of the flesh and the lust of the eyes and the vain-glory of life, is not of the Father, but is of the world. 17 And the world passeth away, and the lust thereof: but he that doeth the will of God abideth for ever" (I John 2:13-17).

Some think there is a contradiction between Romans 7:7-25 and I John 2:13-17. There is no contradiction between these passages. There is, however, a contradiction between a false interpretation of Romans, chapter 7, and I John 2:13-17. According to this theory, the experience mentioned in Romans, chapter 7, was Paul's own personal experience. The reason for thus interpreting the passage is Paul's use of the personal pronouns—*I, me,* and *my.* Was Paul living in spiritual defeat all the time? No. For in Galatians 2:20, which he wrote at the same time that he wrote the Roman Letter, he claims to be living a victorious life. He would not write to one group that he was living a defeated life and to another group that he was living a victorious life.

Moreover, in Romans 7:9 Paul speaks of himself as though he were alive when the law was given at Sinai: "And I was alive apart from the law once: but when the commandment came, sin revived, and I died; and the commandment, which *was* unto life, this I found *to be* unto death" (Rom. 7:9, 10). The law was given at Sinai approximately fifteen hundred years before Paul was born. He, therefore, was not giving his own personal daily experience; but some insist that he was, because he declares, "For that which I do I know not: for not what I would do, that do I practice; but what I hate, that I do. But if what I would not, that I do, I consent unto the law that it is good" (Rom. 7:15, 16). His making this statement, that he was alive when the law was given, cannot be taken literally; neither can his saying that he lived a defeated life be taken literally, because he plainly declares that he was living in victory. These facts demand an interpretation of his statements in accordance with the facts of the context. In Romans, chapter 7, he was therefore in a figure transferring to himself the universal experience of all men who have never been delivered from the power of sin—through the blood of Christ.

May the writer call attention to the following note of warning by Jeremiah the prophet: "Hear ye, and give ear; be not proud; for Jehovah hath spoken. 16 Give glory to Jehovah your God, before he cause darkness, and before your feet stumble upon the dark mountains, and, while ye look for light, he turn it into the shadow of death, and make it gross darkness. 17 But if ye will not hear it, my soul shall weep in secret for *your* pride; and mine eye shall weep sore, and run down with tears, because Jehovah's flock is taken captive" (Jer. 13:15-17).

Wisdom says to the one who realizes his lost condition and yearns for salvation to lift his heart to God, saying "Lord, be merciful to me, a sinner." He who comes to the Lord in genuine repentance and in real faith will be accepted of Him. For He says ". . . him that cometh to me I will in no wise cast out" (John 6: 37).

"And the Spirit and the bride say, Come. And he that heareth, let him say, Come. And he that is athirst, let him come: he that will, let him take the water of life freely" (Rev. 22:17).

As stated before, everything points in the direction of the possibility of the world crisis occurring in our day, with little or no warning. The world seems ripe for judgment, and the Great Tribulation which will be world-wide will purge the earth of sin, lawlessness, and unrighteousness.

Those who are living at that time will either be translated (the Rapture of the saints) as were Enoch and Elijah or will enter the Great Tribulation and will have to endure untold suffering.

Those who are saved—born again—will be caught up out of the earth in a moment of time. Many of the good moral people and the truth seekers will during the Tribulation turn to the Lord and be saved—but at what a cost of suffering and distress! The only wise thing for a person to do now is to accept Jesus of Nazareth, the God-man and Saviour of the world, and thus make his calling and election sure. "But we would not have you ignorant, brethren, concerning them that fall asleep [physical death]; that ye sorrow not, even as the rest, who have no hope. 14 For if we believe that Jesus died and rose again, even so them also that are fallen asleep in Jesus will God bring with him. 15 For this we say unto you by the word of the Lord, that we that are alive, that are left unto the coming of the Lord, shall in no wise precede them that are fallen asleep. 16 For the Lord himself shall descend from heaven, with a shout, with the voice of the archangel, and with the trump of God: and the dead in Christ shall rise first; 17 then we that are alive, that are left, shall together with them be caught up in the clouds, to meet the Lord in the air: and so shall we ever be with the Lord. 18 Wherefore comfort one another with these words" (I Thess. 4:13-18).

TABLE OF SCRIPTURE TEXTS

OLD TESTAMENT

New Testament

SUBJECT INDEX

A

Abraham, 46
Accuracy of inspired prophets, 21
Age, Golden, 65, 79n
Akiba, Rabbi, 101
Alexander, Dr., 127
Ancient of Days, 60
Angel
  of the Lord, 50; of His Presence, 51
Anointing of the Spirit, 79
Articles of Faith, 39
Atonement, 120, 121, 123, 129
Azazel, 123

B

Balaam, prophecies of, 14n, 65
Balak, 65
Beasts, 61
Believers
  rapture of, 159; secret, 145n
Belshazzar, King of Babylon, 60
Birth, new, 155
Blindness
  judicial punishment, 111; self-imposed, 110; spiritual, 110
Blood, power in the, 121, 124
Burning bush, 46, 51

C

"Canons of credibility," 137
Captivity, Babylonian, 53, 82
Challenge to unbelievers, 21n
Character of God, 119
Charlemagne, 61
Christlieb, Dr. Theodore, 40
Chronometer, universal, 2
Codes of Hammurabi and Moses, 13
Coming
  first and Second blended, 77; Second, 46, 56, 58; sign of Second, 153
Confession, Great, 30, 35, 37-40
Constantine, 61
Constantinople, 61
Contest at Mt. Carmel, Elijah's, 145n
Contradictions to Scripture vanish, 25n
Conversion
  of Israel, 90, 93; of Saul (Paul), 142
Covenant
  Book of the, 11; New, 34

Criticism, Biblical, 11n
Critics
  analysis of, 10n; rationalitistic, 97, 136
Culross, Dr., 123
Curse, 117
Cyrus, 75n, 97

D

Dana, Professor, 13
Daniel, 60
David, 70
Delitzsch, Franz, 86, 99
Dispersion, 54

E

Elijah
  contest at Mt. Carmel, 145n; herald of Second Coming, 47
Empire
  Roman, 61, 62; Russian, 62; World, 62
Enemies of God, 88
Era of Peace, 42

F

Face of the Lord, 52
Fall of man, 117
Future revealed, 153

G

Gamaliel, 141
Genesis, seed plot of Bible, 132
Gibbon, Edward, 22
Glory of God, 53, 54
Grace, 127
Gravity, spiritual, 120

H

Hammurabi, code of, 13n
Hezekiah, 73
Hobbes, Thomas, 22
Holy Spirit, 41

I

Isaiah, unity of Book of, 97
Israel
  lost condition of, 114; not servant of the 53d chapter of Isaiah, 101, 102; penitential confession of, 109, 110

[163]

Satan
  and evil hosts in Old and New Testaments, 131; enemy of God and all good, 118, 157; power limited, 17, 157
Saul, King, 70
Scholarship, 5
Scientists, 12n
Scriptures
  inspiration of, 136; unity of, 132
Seed, spiritual, 124
Second Coming, 46, 56, 58
Septuagint, 87
Sermons, apostolic, 156
"Servant, My"
  meaning of, 100; cut off, 101
Servant of Jehovah
  Messiah, 97, 98; nation of Israel, 97, 98; the faithful remnant, 97, 98
Shekinah Glory, 72
Sheol, 118n
Shepherd of Israel, 57
Shiloh
  meaning of, 132; the Messiah, 81
Sin
  forgiveness of, 151; in the flesh, 119
Son
  of God, 42, 44; of David, 63, 100; of man, 63
Spirits, evil, 17, 43
Stars, innumerable, 16
Syro-Ammonites, 84

T

Tabernacle, 53
Talmud, quotation from, 133
Targum, 82
Teleology, 8
Ten words, 11, 52
Tenach, 9n, 11, 19, 24, 26, 29n, 32, 39, 41, 44n, 49, 80n
Teuton, 61

Theophanies, 63
Theory, "Onion Coat," 12n
Tomb, empty
  witness of, 134, 135
Torah, 9n, 11, 16, 75
Transgressions, 123
Tribulation, sufferings of, 89
Trinity
  in Old and New Testament, 131; of divine personalities, 50
Truth, 24n

U

United States of Nations, 42
Unity
  explanation of, 19; of Book of Isaiah, 97n; of Kingdom, 34; of Scriptures, 132; of Tenach, 19
Urquhart, John, 22

V

Victory in Christ, 157

W

War, fear of nuclear, 152
Warning, solemn to sinners, 158
Way, new and living, 122
Werner, 12n
Wilhelm III, 62
Wilkinson, John, 132
Witnesses
  500 after Resurrection, 136, 138, 139; qualification of, 137
Word of God, certainty of, 133

X

Xerxes, 20

Z

Zion, 55, 59, 60
Zohar, 49